TRADE
secrets

TRADE
secrets

Fix Your Home
Like a Pro!

Reader's
Digest

The Reader's Digest Association, Inc.
New York, NY / Montreal

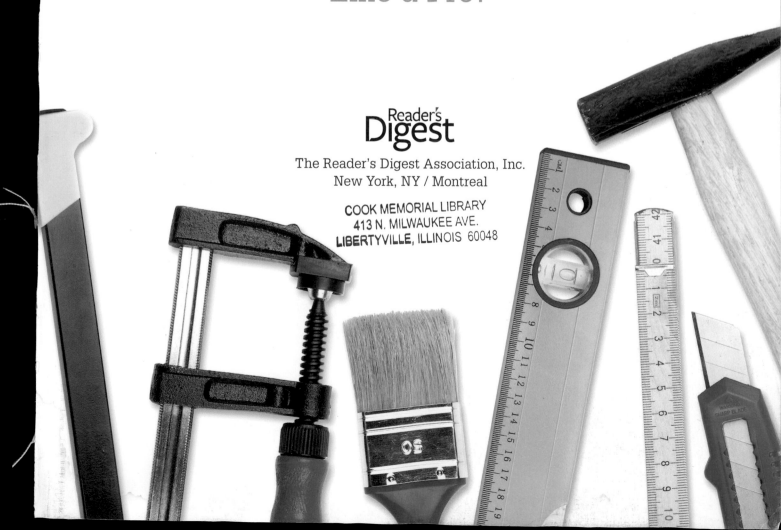

Contents

Appliances and fixtures

Wiring, lighting and plumbing

House exterior

In the garden

Garage and toolshed

Introduction

Have you ever paid a repairman lots of money to do a job you later realized you could have done yourself? If only you'd had a little more confidence and a bit of practical guidance you could have built that shelf, installed that window or fixed that wonky cabinet door, and not only saved some money but boosted your self esteem as well.

Building, repairing and decorating have been part of human DNA since we first built shelter so don't be surprised if you hear a little voice in your head saying, "Go on! You can do it, it can't be that hard," when something needs doing around your home.

And it isn't that hard. Although some more complex jobs are best left to the experts, there are so many day-to-day home repairs, maintenance and improvements that you can master with just a few tricks of the trade.

This is why we created *Trade Secrets*. Many DIY publications are quite technical and complicated, with a high level of assumed knowledge, leaving many would-be-home handy-people floundering in alien terminology and confusing diagrams.

This commonsense guide to everyday home maintenance, repairs and decorating is not that kind of book. It tells you how to go about a task, what to use and how to use it—the way a professional would. You won't need to turn this book upside down with your tongue protruding from the side of your mouth to make sense of the many photos, illustrations and tips.

Trade Secrets fills the gap between "Haven't got a clue" and "Almost a pro" and empowers the enthusiastic amateur to fulfill his or her destiny.

So get off that couch and get to work! There's no job in *Trade Secrets* that you can't do if you apply the easy-to-follow advice and set your mind to it.

Every journey starts with a small step. Make that little voice go away.

The DIY editors of Reader's Digest

Basic tools and techniques

THE ESSENTIAL **TOOLKIT**

A surprisingly small number of tools can cope with a wide range of repair and maintenance jobs around the house. Keep these tools together in a lightweight toolbox or bag, and you will save both time and effort whenever something needs fixing.

1 The toolbox

To start with, choose a light but robust plastic case with a lift-out tray for small tools. Avoid metal toolboxes; they are heavy to carry around and they rust.

2 Screwdrivers

Screws have head recesses of various sizes and types, so screwdriver sets make sense. Those with a master handle that accepts the different bits can save space.

3 Putty knives

Simply a handle with a flexible steel blade, for applying filler. Buy 1 in. (2.5 cm) and 2 in. (5 cm) knives for everyday use. Don't confuse it with a scraper, which has a stiffer blade.

4 Saw

A compact or toolbox saw with fine-point hardened teeth will handle all sorts of household woodwork jobs such as trimming cleats or cutting a shelf to length.

5 Hacksaw

Hacksaws are designed to cut metal, but will also cut through plastic—a curtain rod, for example—and small wood sections. The saw can be inexpensive, but the replaceable blades should be good quality.

6 Hammers and nail punch

You will need a 16 oz. (450 g) claw hammer, which is fine for most DIY jobs, and possibly a smaller 8–12 oz. (225–350 g) model for lighter or finishing work. Also buy a nail punch, used to drive nail heads below the wood surface.

7 Knife

A utility knife with replaceable blades is a DIY essential. There are different blades available: for easy jobs such as paper and plastic sheeting, or for tougher materials such as carpet and linoleum. Choose a knife with a retractable blade—it's safer.

8 Pliers

The serrated jaws of pliers are useful for gripping, twisting and cutting wire, and for straightening bent metal.

9 Cutting pliers

Cutting pliers are designed for pulling out tacks and nails—from floorboards, for example—but can also be put to other tasks, such as removing picture hooks without damaging the wall, or as a ceramic tile cutter.

10 Cable, pipe and stud detector

Look for one that detects electrical cables and plumbing pipes buried in house walls, plus ceiling joists and the wood framing inside a partition wall.

1 Level

A 24-in. (60 cm)-long level will handle inside jobs such as fitting shelves and hanging pictures. Outdoor jobs such as erecting privacy screens, posts and fences may require a longer version.

12 Tape measure

An ideal size is a 16 ft. (5 m) steel tape, which will cope with measuring up a room as well as smaller jobs. Some have both centimeter/meter and inch/foot markings, so if need be, you can use the tape as a conversion device.

13 Drill

A cordless drill/screwdriver, about 12 volts, with rechargeable batteries is a must. It should have forward and reverse, fast and slow speeds, and be comfortable and not too heavy to handle.

14 Drill bits

Look for a set that includes masonry, high-speed steel twist and brad-point bits (for wood), as well as a range of screwdriver bits. Drill bit sets often come with the electric drill.

15 Caulking gun

This inexpensive tool is needed for extruding the contents of the many ready-to-use fillers, sealants and adhesives sold in standard-sized cartridges.

16 Hand staple gun

Choose one that can handle flat staples for jobs such as fastening webbing, fabric or netting, as well as curved staples for speaker and low-voltage cables.

17 Adjustable wrench

Look for an adjustable wrench that opens up to about 1¼ in. (3 cm)—good for plumbing fixtures, and smaller nuts, too. Buy a reputable brand; the jaws on cheap tools may slip or jam.

18 Vice-grip pliers

This versatile tool can be used like a pair of pliers or as a makeshift extra wrench. It has adjustable, lockable jaws that will clamp firmly and hold different-shaped objects.

Tool organization

Here is a handful of clever ideas that will help you save time and money while keeping your enthusiasm high.

When you need to drill into tough materials such as concrete and masonry, use a masonry bit with a carbide tip.

Tool bucket bags

You can buy these bags that hang in a sturdy bucket, or make your own by riveting a couple of canvas toolbelts to the rim of a bucket. Popular alternatives are bucket- or briefcase-shaped tote bags with lots of compartments. ▼

Mobile workbench

Ever wish you had a lightweight, mobile workbench? Here's the answer. Screw a length of MDF to an old ironing board and you'll have a handy workbench that can be moved easily and adjusts to whatever height you need to work comfortably. Remember, lightweight work only.

Color-coded chargers

Strips of colored masking or duct tape take the confusion out of pairing cordless tools with their chargers. No more matching by trial and error.

Handy pants ◄

Don't throw out those old, battered and splattered work pants. Cut off the legs and the front section, leaving just the back pockets and waistband. Load up the back pockets, snap or button it on— pockets facing front—and you've got yourself a useful apron. The side pockets offer more storage.

Drills and drilling

An electric drill, preferably cordless, is often the most-used tool in the box. The following tips will help to get the job done safely and quickly.

Fitting drill bits

Select the right type of drill bit for the job. Open the drill chuck by twisting the knurled ring and fit the end of the drill bit inside it. Tighten the locking ring until you feel it start to slip. The drill bit is now secure. For chucks that need to be tightened with a chuck key, insert the key in one of the holes in the side of the chuck, and gently rotate the key until the chuck is firmly closed.

Straight and steady

To drill a straighter hole and avoid breaking a bit, hold the drill so that the force you exert helps push the bit straight into the wall. Place the palm of your hand in line with the chuck, extending your index finger along the drill body. Pull the trigger with your second finger. ▼

If you have a good eye, check from two angles that the drill is straight

Drill guide

For a perfectly straight hole every time, make a simple drill guide by joining at right angles two square blocks made from ¾ in. (2 cm) thick wood using a wood cleat 1½ in. (4 cm) long and ¾ in. (2 cm) square, as shown. Apply wood glue and fasten with 1 in. wood screws, into countersunk holes. To use, just run the drill bit down the V groove formed at the corner, as shown. You may need "long series" drill bits for small-diameter holes—these are a useful addition to the tool kit in any case. ▼

Depth gauge

Wrap a small strip of masking or duct tape around a drill bit so that the exposed part of the bit is equal to the desired depth of the hole. Alternatively, mark the bit with a grease pencil.

On the level

When drilling into a wall, it's not always easy to tell whether you're holding the drill perfectly horizontal. If your drill has a flat top parallel to the drill bit, try taping a mini level or line level to it and then you'll be able to see exactly when you're straight and level.

Straight bits

A bent bit is likely to break and damage your work. Because bits bend easily (especially the thinner ones), test them for straightness before use and discard any bent ones. To test a bit, roll it slowly with your fingertips on a flat surface. If the bit wobbles, it's bent. Alternatively, place the bit against a straightedge and look for gaps between the two surfaces.

Pointed bits ▶

When drilling wood, use a brad-point bit instead of a common twist bit. The little spur on the tip of a brad-point bit cuts cleanly into the wood and keeps the bit from skating around when you start the hole, or from drifting if the bit hits a knot.

Splinter-free drilling

Drilling a hole completely through wood leaves a rough, splintery edge where it exits. To make a clean hole, look (don't feel) for the point of the bit as it just pierces the back of the work. Pull out the bit, and using the little hole as a centering guide, drill from the back. This method works with spade, auger and brad-point bits.

The hard stuff

When you need to drill into tough materials such as concrete and masonry, use a masonry bit with a carbide tip. When drilling into concrete, start off by making a small hole, then enlarge it. If you have to drill many holes in concrete or masonry, rent or buy a hammer drill to use with the carbide-tip bits. By actually banging the spinning bit into the surface, a hammer drill makes your work much easier.

On the tiles

If you have to drill through the face of a tile, use a sharp glass/tile or masonry drill bit so the glaze doesn't chip. Stop the bit from skating on the glaze by sticking masking tape on the tile where you want to drill; this will give the bit an initial "bite." Make sure the drill isn't set on hammer action, and if it has variable speed control, start slowly.

Oil-drilling rig

Next time you're drilling holes in steel, try this: find a washer with an inner diameter larger than the diameter of the drill bit, firmly tape it to the workpiece and squirt light machine oil into the eye of the washer. This oil pool keeps the bit cool and lubricated as you drill. ▼

Use a new or freshly sharpened drill bit

MONEY SAVER
Sharp point

Your drill bits will stay sharper longer if you spray them with silicone before use. They're also less likely to break after this treatment.

Pilot, clearance and countersunk holes

A pilot hole reduces the possibility of the wood splitting and makes the screw easier to drive. The hole makes room for the screw shaft, but leaves enough material for the threads to bite into. The drill bit should match the diameter of the screw body (not the threads). Hold the screw up to the light and match a drill bit to the lower shank diameter. A clearance hole allows the whole body of the screw to pass through. When it's important to draw one piece of wood tightly to another, drill a clearance hole through the first or top piece. Countersinking allows the screw head to sit just below the workpiece surface for a better finish. ▼

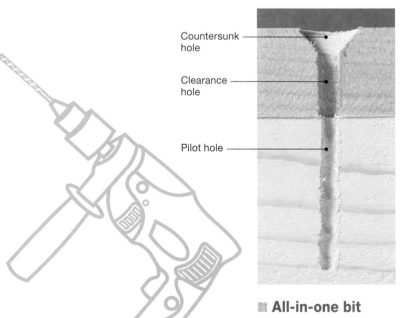

Countersunk hole

Clearance hole

Pilot hole

All-in-one bit

Instead of buying separate bits for drilling the different holes described above, consider buying combination drill bits, available to suit either #6, #8, #10 or #12 gauge depth-adjustable and will drill countersunk, clearance, and pilot holes in one go. ◄

Laser-guided drill ▲

Okay, we exaggerate … but a small flashlight taped to a drill can make it much easier to use in dimly lit places, such as under the sink.

Replace the brushes

Always have the brushes in your power tools replaced before they wear out. Continuing to work your drill or saw with badly worn brushes—indicated by excessive sparking at the armature—will do major (and expensive) damage to your valuable equipment.

Quick-draw drill holder

Here's how to make a neat storage holder for your drill. Cut a 12 in. (30 cm) piece of 4 in. (10 cm) diameter plastic pipe. Cut a notch in the rim about 2 in. (5 cm) wide. Now mount your drill holder vertically or horizontally with wood screws. ▼

Make a drill holster for your stepladder

To keep your drill handy when you're working up high, mount a holster on the side of your stepladder with sheet metal screws or pop rivets. To save the cost of the holster, use a length of 4 in. (10 cm) diameter PVC pipe. The holster will save trips up and down the ladder.

In the bag

Cut down on the mess when drilling through drywall by taping an open garbage bag below the area in which you'll be drilling. As you drill, the debris will fall straight into the bag, not all over the floor.

Contact breaker

When drilling a tough surface that you don't want to damage, such as a car body, simply push a rubber washer onto the drill bit. If you accidentally strike the surface with the drill chuck, the impact will be cushioned by the rubber—better safe than sorry.

Longer-lasting drill bits

Overheating will weaken and blunt drill bits, so if the going gets tough, don't try to force it. It's the debris stuck on the bit and in the hole that usually causes the problem, so remove the bit from the hole from time to time to clean it out. Dip masonry bits in water to clean, lubricate and keep cool.

Quick Fix

ANOTHER BIT

Broken your last $5/64$ in. (2 mm) drill bit and don't have time to get to the hardware store? Snip a nail head off with a wire cutter. The chiseled nail tip drills clean holes fast.

When drilling a thick or tough material, remove the bit from the hole from time to time to clean out any debris.

The right (angled) connections

Driving screws at an angle (toe-screwing) is a common technique for securing right-angle connections. You'll need a clearance/pilot hole, so first drill a shallow hole to give you a starting point, then drill the angled pilot hole. A combination bit is very handy here.

straight starter hole

1 Drill shallow starter hole
Estimate the entry point using the screw length as a guide. Drill a shallow hole straight into the wood at this point to start you off.

Take care not to push the joint out of alignment

angled pilot hole

2 Finish at an angle
As soon as the drill bit engages the wood, tilt the drill to the desired angle and drill the pilot hole. Now drive the screw in to complete the job.

Screwdrivers and screws

The traditional slot-head screw has diversified into many styles. Screw-driving is easier—you just need more screwdrivers! Or do you?

Don't use a worn bit

If you're applying reasonable pressure on the drill but the bit is still skipping in the screw head, it's time to replace the bit. The trick is to have spare bits on hand so you can replace them at the first sign of wear.

worn-out Phillips bit

Magnetic attraction

Magnetize your screwdriver by stroking a bar magnet along the shaft (in one direction only!) a few times. Now you won't lose those little screws you're trying to get into tricky, hard-to-reach spots. To demagnetize it, just run the magnet along the shaft in both directions.

Wax it

Lubricating a screw with some beeswax will make your job much easier. Don't be tempted to use soap, oil or grease as lubricants—they could stain the wood.

Powder power

Dip the tip of a screwdriver in some scouring powder before attacking a screw. The powder gives the tool increased holding power in a slippery screw slot.

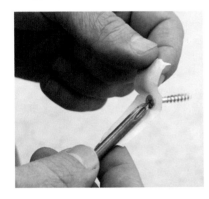

Sticky screw gripper

To get a screw started in a hard-to-reach place, just poke the screw through a piece of masking tape with the sticky side of the tape toward the head. Place the screwdriver in the slot, then fold the tape up onto the screwdriver. When the screw is well started, you can pull the screwdriver loose and remove the tape.

Photo opportunity

Before you disassemble something with more than two or three interconnected parts, take a photo of the assembly with a digital camera. That way you'll have an instant reference when it comes to putting it back together.

CHOOSING THE BEST SCREW

To use the various screws, you'll need a set of screwdrivers that fit the different head shapes. To save space, buy a set that has one driver handle with a range of different interchangeable heads.

★ Slot head
Have a limited range and are difficult to use with a power driver.

★ Phillips head
Have a simple cross and are used widely. The coarse-threaded variety works well with particleboard and other wood joinery.

★ Star
Torx, Hex, Star and other specialty bits have unique shapes that grip the screwdriver tip more securely than a slot or Phillips head screw. It's usually best to buy them when you need them.

★ Robertson (square head)
Mostly found in stainless-steel decking screws. Also now in coated screws for treated pine, ideal for outdoor projects. Choose a screw pack that includes a bit.

Screwing wood to wood

"If you don't have an awl, a nail will do"

① Make the clearance hole

Mark where you want the screw hole in the piece of wood you are fixing. Fit a twist drill bit slightly larger than the screw shank in your drill, and drill a clearance hole right through the wood. Place scrap wood beneath the workpiece so you do not drill into your workbench.

② Countersink and mark

Exchange the twist drill bit for a countersink bit and drill the countersink for the screwhead. Hold the piece of wood you are fixing in position over the piece you are fixing it to. Push an awl through the clearance hole to mark the screw position on the piece below.

③ Fasten tight

Drill a pilot hole the same diameter as the screw shank, to half the depth of the wood. Reposition the two pieces of wood and insert the screw through the clearance hole in the top piece. Tighten it fully until the screw head is fully recessed in the countersunk hole.

Screwing metal to wood

"Screws with raised countersunk heads look most attractive"

① Mark the position

Decide where you are going to place the fixture. Hold the fixture in position and mark each screw position on the wood in pencil. Use a level if necessary.

② Drill the pilots

Drill a pilot hole the same diameter as the screw shank at each mark, to half the thickness of the wood. If you find it difficult to gauge the depth, use a guide on the drill bit— a strip of masking tape, for example.

③ Fix the fixture

Replace the fixture over the holes and drive in the screws. If there is more than one, tighten them fully only when you are sure the fixture is straight and level.

Hammers and nails

A hammer is usually the first tool we learn to use—remember those childhood toys? But did we learn correctly? Read on …

▦ Using a claw hammer ▶

Hold the hammer near the end of the handle and make sure that it strikes the nail head squarely. Hold the upper part of the nail between your thumb and forefinger. Don't hold it at the base. This way, if you miss the nail your fingers will be knocked out of the way rather than crushed. Start it with a few gentle taps, then release the nail and drive it in with harder blows. For large nails, keep your wrist stiff and swing hammer and forearm from the elbow. On rough work, hammer the nail head in flush. When you require a neater finish, leave the nail head proud and drive it below the surface with a nail punch.

▦ Angled nailing

Where possible, drive nails in at a slight angle for a more secure fastening. If you are double nailing, drive each nail in at a different angle.

▦ Extracting a long nail

This is easier if you rest the hammerhead on a block of wood. The wood provides the necessary leverage to withdraw the nail.

▦ Single-handed

Only one hand free? Grasp the hammerhead in your fist as shown, and hold the nail firmly between your fingers and against the side, or cheek, of the hammer. To start the nail, rap the nail point against the work. ▼

When driving large nails, keep your wrist stiff and swing hammer and forearm from the elbow.

▦ Removing a bent nail ◀

If you bend a nail as you drive it in, don't try to straighten it; remove it. Place a piece of card or thin wood on the surface beside the nail to support the hammer and protect the work, fit the claw under the nail head and pull the handle toward you to draw out the nail. Keep the handle close to vertical so you don't widen the nail hole. Need more leverage? Read on!

▦ Instant mallet

You need a mallet and yours is missing. Try this: slip a rubber doorstop or chair-leg tip over the head of your hammer. It's a good stand-in and is easily removed.

Fixing loose heads

A loose hammer or axe head is easily fixed, especially if its wedge has worked loose. First tape a plastic bag around the handle just below the head. Fill the hole with epoxy resin, replace the wedge and allow the glue to dry. Remove the bag, and you'll find the movement has gone and the handle is firmly attached once again.

Drink bottle nail pouch ▲

Make a nail holder from a plastic drink bottle. Cut the top off an empty bottle, leaving a container 3½ in. (8.5 cm) tall. File off any sharp edges or cover with tape. Cut two 1½ in. (4 cm) vertical slits 1 in. (2.5 cm) apart in the center of one side. Slide the end of your belt through the slots.

Light but strong

Use corrugated metal fasteners to secure butt joints in light wood frameworks. They make a stronger joint than nails, with less risk of splitting the wood. ▼

Fingertip saver ▶

When you're driving small brads or nails into awkward spots, push the nail into a thin strip of cardboard to hold it in position while nailing and to shield the wood from an errant hammer blow.

Hand cushions

A simple bicycling glove is a good defense against blisters and cramps when using a hammer or screwdriver for any length of time. The fingerless style allows complete mobility while the padded palm cushions your hand.

Prevent a split

When nailing near the end-grain, try this to prevent the wood from

splitting. Hold the nail upside down on the spot, hammer the pointy end two or three times, and you have a dulled point plus a countersink hole for the nail head. To be extra sure, drill a pilot hole first.

CHOOSING THE RIGHT **HAMMER**

Most types of hammers come in a variety of head weights and handle lengths. Handles made of hardwood, tubular steel (with a rubber grip) or fiberglass absorb shock and are comfortable to hold. The face of a hammer should be smooth and have a slightly beveled edge.

★ **Claw hammers**
The basic everyday household hammer is a 16 oz. (450 g) curved-claw hammer. For rough construction work, choose a 22 oz. (680 g) straight-claw hammer, sometimes called a ripping hammer; for finished carpentry, use a light 12 oz. (350 g) hammer.

★ **Pein hammers**
Instead of a claw, these hammers have a second striking surface, called a pein. The rounded ball pein is used to shape soft metal. The cabinetmaker's hammer has a long, thin cross pein to start a panel pin, as well as a flat face. A bricklayer's hammer has a flat end as well as a long chisel-like face to score bricks.

★ **Mallets and sledgehammers**
To strike woodworking chisels and assemble wooden parts, use a carpenter's mallet. Assemble other projects and pound out dents in metal with a rubber mallet. Long-handled heavy sledgehammers are used for demolition work. The short-handled sledge can be used with stone-cutting chisels and to drive stakes.

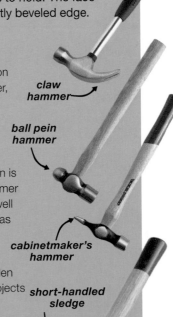

claw hammer

ball pein hammer

cabinetmaker's hammer

short-handled sledge

Staplers and staples

For lighter work, either permanent or temporary, staplers are worth considering as a convenient alternative to hammers and nails.

▦ Using a staple gun

If the staple gun accepts staples of different lengths, select the correct size for the job in hand. Load the magazine and test the gun by firing a staple into some scrap material. Position the material to be fixed. Place the staple gun over the fixing position and squeeze the trigger to fire the staple. Repeat the process to make further fixings, reloading the magazine as it runs out.

▦ Temporary stapling

Some fastening jobs, such as stapling plastic sheets over a window, are meant to be temporary and you will need to remove the staples later. Here's a way to make staple removal hassle-free. Slip a heavy-duty rubber band around the staple gun as shown. The rubber band acts as a spacer, leaving the staples sticking up slightly so that they are easy to remove with a staple remover. This method also keeps the staples from cutting through very thin materials. ◄

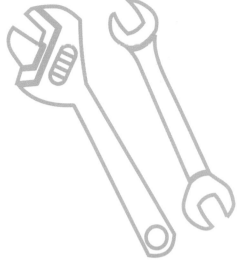

> Keep the head of the tacker STRAIGHT and LEVEL as you strike

▦ Hammer tacker ▲

This handy tool is great for attaching vapor barriers, insulation and building wrap. A hammer tacker is useful for any job that does not require great accuracy of placement. The tacker also makes it easier to work overhead and is kinder to arm muscles and hands than a regular stapler. To set a staple, just strike the tacker against the workpiece. If you do a lot of stapling, a power stapler is a worthwhile investment.

▦ Fixing phone wire

A quick, neat way to run phone and stereo wire is to staple it in place with a special wiring tacker. This tool shoots staples that bridge the wire without damaging it. Wire tackers shoot various-sized staples, so measure the wire you are running to determine which tacker to buy. You can also buy a multi-purpose stapler that will fire curved staples for cabling as well as different straight staples.

COMMON **STAPLES**

★ Size	★ Use
0.25 in. (6 mm) leg	Light upholstering, cornices and blinds.
0.30 in. (8 mm) leg	Heavy upholstering, curtains, foil insulation.
0.40 in. (10 mm) leg	Light insulation, weather-stripping, roofing papers, wire mesh.
0.50 in. (13 mm) leg	Carpet underlay, canvas, felt stripping.
0.60 in. (15 mm) leg	Insulation board, thin hardboard or MDF.

Wrenches and pliers

Wrenches are good for working on nuts and bolts and pliers are not—follow that advice and your hardware will last longer.

▦ Tips for using an adjustable wrench

To work on a nut, open the jaws of the wrench and slip it into place. Tighten the moveable jaw so the wrench grips opposite flats on the nut securely. Work out which way to turn the nut. A nut is screwed on in a clockwise direction, so your wrench must move in the same direction to tighten the nut, and counterclockwise to loosen it. Use reasonable force to turn the wrench as required.

▦ A third hand ▲

Locking pliers act as a third hand that can grip small objects while you assemble, solder or clamp them. You can convert a pair of ordinary pliers into a mini-vice by slipping a rubber band over the handles. The rubber band will keep the pliers' jaws closed while you work.

▦ Getting leverage

Place a short length of pipe over the handle of an adjustable wrench to provide more length and leverage on a stubborn job.

▦ Bridging the gap ▲

Say you need to remove a nut with an open-ended wrench that's too large for it. Simply insert an appropriate-sized coin or washer between the wrench and the nut. The coin or washer (you'll have to experiment to determine which best fills the gap) will serve as a wedge, making it possible to turn the nut.

▦ Saving your skin

When loosening a very tight nut or bolt, push the wrench with your open palm rather than grasping it with your hand. If the nut suddenly loosens or breaks, or the tool slips off, it means you won't smash or scrape your knuckles.

▦ Remote nut starter

Need to get a nut started in a tight space where your fingers won't fit? Try this: stick a piece of masking tape on the back of a wrench that fits the nut, then place the nut in the tape—it'll hold the nut during that tricky first turn.

▦ Put an end to loose nuts

Dab some clear nail polish to the bolt before tightening the nut and it will hold fast for good.

Place a short length of pipe over the handle of a wrench to provide more leverage on a stubborn job.

Cutting and shaping tools

A successful DIY project depends on accurate cuts to the building materials. Get off to a good start with sharp tools and a clean workspace.

> Keep your fingertips well clear of the blade

Apply a coat of paste wax to a handsaw blade to protect the metal teeth and ease them through wood.

▦ Using a utility knife ▲

When using a utility knife, place a cutting board or a piece of scrap hardboard beneath whatever you are cutting. Hold the knife securely and draw it along the straightedge in one continuous movement. Make two or three passes rather than trying to cut the material in one go; the harder you have to press, the more risk there is that the blade will slip off the line. Always cut against the side of the straightedge next to the waste side.

▦ Snap-off blades

If you do a lot of light-duty cutting, invest in a retractable blade knife with long blades, pre-scored to snap off and give you a new sharp cutting point. Use the snap-off tool attached to the knife and wear protective glasses.

▦ Using a handsaw ◄

Whatever you are cutting must be held securely. To cut a piece of wood to length, hold it securely against a bench block, or clamp onto your workbench.

Place the thumb of your free hand next to the cutting line to guide the saw blade so it will cut just on the waste side of this line, and draw it toward you at about 45° to start the cut. Once the saw teeth begin to bite, move your free hand away and start to cut with light but firm forward strokes. Start to flatten out the angle of the saw. Complete the cut with gentle strokes, holding the saw almost level with the wood surface, to avoid splitting the underside of the wood.

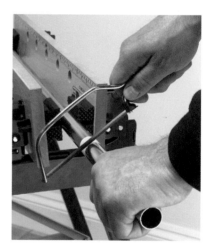

▦ Using a hacksaw ▲

Fit the blade with the points of the teeth facing away from the handle, so it will cut on the forward stroke. Secure the workpiece in the jaws of your workbench, especially when cutting thin metal sections. Start the cut on the waste side of the marked line, using masking tape as a cutting guide. Draw the blade toward you two or three times to start, slowly so that the blade doesn't jump out of the cut. Complete with a few gentle forward strokes.

Keeping your (hacksaw) teeth clean

If you are cutting soft metals with a hacksaw, the saw's teeth will soon clog. You can avoid this problem by using a blade with bigger teeth, slowing down your strokes (so the metal doesn't melt) and pushing down more gently on the saw.

How to hold a handsaw

Instead of gripping the handle with all four fingers around it, extend your index finger and place it against the handle as though you were pointing along the saw blade. You'll have better control and cut a straighter, truer line.

Teeth guard

To keep saw teeth out of harm's way, slide the plastic spines used to bind documents and reports over the blades of your handsaws.

How dull

How can you tell if a saw is dull before you use it? Check the teeth closely to see if the points are rounded and the cutting edges show wear. (Use a magnifying glass to inspect fine-tooth saws.) If the saw appears dull, take it to an expert for resharpening. ▼

Dull blade

New or resharpened blade

The right blade

Two kinds of circular saw blades will see you through just about any job. The first should be a general-purpose combination blade with 20 to 24 teeth; the other should be a fine cutting blade with about 40 teeth (best for crosscutting). Both blades should be carbide-tipped.

Wax works ▶

Want your saw to glide as it cuts? Rub a block of paraffin wax on the underside of the saw's baseplate. If you first heat the surface slightly with a hair dryer, the wax will coat the area more completely.

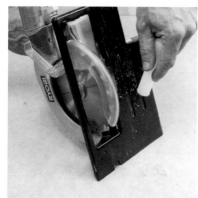

Don't gum it up

Sawing resinous softwoods such as pine clog saw teeth with a gummy build-up that soon makes the saw seem dull. To remove the resin, apply oven cleaner. To keep the sticky stuff from adhering in the first place, spray silicone on the teeth. Or try polishing them often with hard paste wax or running an old candle across them.

Cutting metal

If you plan to cut metal, use a special metal-cutting blade—and brace yourself for a shower of sparks. Wear hearing protectors and goggles or a full-face mask and work far away—say 50 ft. (15 m)—from sawdust, flammable liquids and anything else that is likely to catch fire. Don't try to saw metal unless your saw has a metal blade guard; a plastic guard will melt.

Permanent marker

The cuts you make with a circular saw will be more accurate if you highlight the cutting line mark on the front of the saw's baseplate. Do it with paint or a felt-tip marker.

Cord drape

To keep the saw cord out of your way, drape it like a cape across your shoulders. It will move with you and be less likely to snag on something.

Cutting-edge tip

Most circular saw blades become blunt due to a build-up of resin and fine sawdust. To get that edge back, soak the blade for two hours in a 50:50 mixture of kerosene and turpentine and then give it a light scrub. This treatment also keeps the rust away.

Easy glider

To make a plane glide across a surface, rub the sole-plate with paste wax or a piece of candle. Buff well to spread a thin, even coating. Warming the sole with a hair dryer first will make the job easier.

Tray organizer

Nothing dulls chisel blades faster than contact with other tools. Either store them individually in a kitchen utensil tray, or if you must store them together, wrap them in cotton cloth or bubble wrap. Professional carpenters use a "chisel roll" of canvas or leather.

Guard duty

Another way to keep chisels away from other tools is to protect the ends with plastic chisel covers. You can make your own chisel protectors out of slit tennis balls or hollowed-out pieces of cork. Always rest a chisel with the bevel down to prevent wear to the cutting edge.

Plane rest

To protect the cutting edge of a plane when it is not in use, set it down on its side or rest it on a block of Styrofoam. To store the plane, secure a block of Styrofoam to the tool with a couple of sturdy rubber bands.

One-way stroke

Files cut only on the push stroke, never on the return. To avoid dulling the teeth, lift the tool off the work at the end of each push stroke.

Card sharp

If your file glides over the work without cutting the surface, you need to clean the file teeth. There is a special brush for this task called a file card. To use the card, run the wire bristles over the file, parallel to the grooves of the file teeth.

Keep your chisel blades sharp with protectors made out of slit tennis balls or hollowed-out pieces of cork.

GET INTO **SHAPING**

★ **A single-cut** file has parallel rows of ridged teeth that smooth and sharpen metal.

★ **A double-cut** file has a second, crossing set of parallel ridges; it removes metal and wood excess rapidly.

★ **A rasp** has individual teeth rather than ridges and gives a rough cut on wood and soft metals; the bigger the teeth, the coarser the finish.

★ You can use a **bastard** file for a coarse finish, a **second-cut** file for a medium to coarse finish, and a **smooth** file for a smooth, fine finish.

★ Most jobs require an all-purpose flat file. But if you are enlarging a round or contoured shape, use a round or half-round file. If you're working on rectangular holes or corners, use a square file, and for acute internal angles, a triangular file is best.

Marking and measuring

Accurate measuring and marking are essential in any DIY job, so invest in a quality tape measure and follow these simple tips.

Eyes right

Always read off and mark measurements with your eye vertically above the tape if it is horizontal, or level with the tape if it is vertical. If you do not do this, a visual error called parallax occurs and the mark you make will be inaccurate. Always measure and mark twice as a double check to help eliminate this risk.

Ensuring accuracy ▲

Set a wooden or folding rule on edge when you're using it to mark measurements on a workpiece. Then the graduations on the face can be transferred straight onto the workpiece. If you lay the rule flat, the absence of any edge markings makes it difficult to mark the dimensions accurately.

Using a level

To check a horizontal, rest the level on the surface being checked and view the vial in the long edge from directly above or beside the level. Adjust the surface until the bubble is precisely centered between the marks on the vial. To check a vertical, hold the level against the surface and view the vial at the end with the eye at the same level. Adjust the position of the surface until the bubble is centered in the vial.

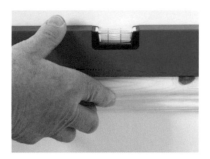

Level check ▲

Place the level on a relatively level surface. Shim up the low end until you get a level reading. Make sure to stand perpendicular to the vial when looking at it. Once you get a level reading, turn the level around 180°. If the vial still shows level, you're getting accurate readings. Check the vial that gives you a plumb reading by placing the level against a door frame. Tape paper shims to the jamb until it's plumb, then flip the level upside down and check for plumb again.

Anti-skid level

Levels tend to slip when you're trying to mark a line on a wall. Make it an anti-skid level by slipping several rubber bands (or one fat one) over each end. ▼

Quick Fix

MARBLE CHECKS THE LEVEL

If you don't have a level, you can still check your work. Place a marble at the midpoint of the work and at various positions along the work surface. If it doesn't immediately roll off in any direction, your work is level.

▓ Pick the right pencil

Select your pencil with care when you're marking measurements on wood. One with a hard lead (marked #1 or higher) will score the wood surface surprisingly deeply, leaving a mark that has to be sanded or even planed off. Use a #2 pencil instead. You'll have to sharpen it more often, but the marks it leaves can be removed easily with a soft eraser. A proper carpenter's pencil is the best buy; its flat sides mean it won't roll off the bench, as a round one will. Sharpen it regularly with your utility knife.

▓ Setting square corners ▲

No need to employ a form-worker to prepare a site for a paved patio or a concrete slab for a new shed. You can set exact square corners by using the 3–4–5 triangle set out method. Make a mark 3 ft. (90 cm) from the corner on one side and 4 ft. (120 cm) from the same corner on the other side. Measure between the two marks. The angle is exactly 90° when the distance equals 5 ft. (150 cm). If the distance is greater or less than 5 ft. (150 cm), move one side to correct the angle.

▓ Pencil it in

Mark ½ in. (1 cm) increments on a carpenter's pencil so that you can make rough measurements quickly. It's more accurate than estimating, yet faster than pulling out a tape measure or ruler.

▓ Make a measuring stick

Next time you have a heap of repeated measuring to do, such as marking out pickets for a fence, mark the measurements on a stick or spare picket. Then just lay the stick on the bottom rail and transfer the measurements. It's a lot easier than trying to use a tape measure on a windy day.

▓ Save time measuring

If you are cutting several pieces to the same size, cut the first to the required measurement using your tape measure or ruler and then use the first cut piece as your measuring stick to cut all the others.

▓ Equal marks

To mark equal segments, angle a ruler across the work. Place the zero-point of the ruler on one edge of the work, and adjust the angle so that a measurement divisible by the number of segments needed lies at the other end of the work. For example, divide the work into 7 segments, measure 5¼ in. (14 cm); mark every ¾ in. (2 cm). ▼

▓ Walk this way

Another smart way to mark equal segments is with dividers or a pair of compasses. Set the points at the desired width of the segments; then walk the dividers along a straightedge by swinging one point in front of the other.

▓ Test for a flat surface ▲

Any true straightedge can be used to check that a surface is flat. Place a level, a metal rule or the sole of a hand plane—with the blade retracted—across the wood and rotate it. Any light visible beneath the edge is a sign that the surface is bowed (raised in the center) or cupped (low in the center).

▓ Made to measure

If you're trying to measure where a tape is hard to read, run two thin pieces of wood up to the measuring points, clamp them together (or just mark the overlap) and remove, then measure with your tape. Easy! ▼

Adhesives and sealants

Most adhesives and sealants are quite specific in their usage, so it's important to read the fine print. Here are a few helpful hints.

Timing the job

The best time to seal a joint outdoors is during the spring or autumn. That's when the width of the joint is halfway between its seasonal extremes.

Mess-free filling

Avoid the most common caulking mistake: cutting the nozzle too far back from the tip. It makes the hole in the nozzle too large and allows too much caulk to gush out. Professionals match the hole size to the size of the gap they're filling. But a hole that's smaller than the gap gives you more control: you can move quickly where the gap is narrow and slow down to feed more caulk into larger gaps.

Cut the nozzle carefully

Cut the nozzle very near the tip at a 45° angle. For most jobs, the hole you create should be no more than ⅛ in. (3 mm) across. Remember, you can always make a second or third slice to enlarge the hole, but you can't make it smaller.

Avoiding bead bumps

For a smooth bead, start at one end and finish at the other—no pit stops in between, not even at corners, if you can help it. Stopping and starting causes a bumpy bead.

Keep it slow and steady

For a pleasing, even finish, you want the caulk to flow out of the nozzle at an even rate, so pull the trigger slowly and steadily. When the trigger reaches the end of its stroke, release it fast and begin pulling again instantly. The pressure in the tube will keep the flow going during the split-second interruption.

Reach out to seal

A plastic drinking straw makes a handy extension tube for sealing hard-to-reach places. Secure your extender with duct tape. Leave it on when you've finished and tape up the end. Remove when ready to use it again and you'll have a fresh start.

Push or pull?

Even experts disagree about whether it's best to pull or push a caulking gun as you fill a crack. Actually both methods work well, as long as you force the sealant well into the crack. To pull, cut the sealant tube spout at a 45° angle, then hold the gun at a 60° angle as you pull it along the crack. To push, cut a double angle on the spout and hold the gun at a 45° angle as you push it along the crack. ▶

Don't touch

Don't smooth sealant with your finger. Some sealants contain harmful chemicals, and some are hard to remove from your skin. Get an inexpensive plastic smoothing tool, or use a plastic spoon, a craft stick, a piece of potato cut to shape, or even an ice block for solvent-based sealants. Any of these will do a tidier job than a finger.

Seal for later

Like most of us, you probably shove a screw into the nozzle after you've used a small quantity from a new tube of sealant—and found it dried out when you wanted it months later. Try pushing a blob of putty into the nozzle instead of the screw. It keeps the sealant fresh for longer.

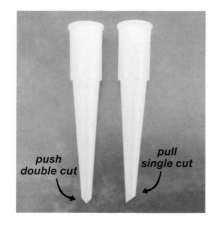

push double cut

pull single cut

MAKING A **PERFECT SEAL**

Cartridge sealants come in several varieties; make the right selection for the job at hand.

★ **Door and window** sealants are used outdoors to fill gaps between trim and the surrounding siding material. Most can be painted over and some sanded.

★ **Silicone** sealants are used in bathrooms and kitchens to seal the joint between the edges of faucets, sinks, countertops and walls.

★ **Roof and gutter** sealant is either butyl or polyurethane specially formulated for repairing gutters, downpipes, roofs and flashings.

★ **Painter's caulk** is a paintable gap-filler used indoors around doors, windows and ceilings, and along baseboards.

SECRETS from the EXPERTS

A **broken hacksaw blade** spreads adhesive quickly over a large, flat area. The teeth let the adhesive flow easily and keep it to a smooth, even overall depth.

As any model-maker knows, toothpicks are perfect for applying glue in tight areas with precise control.

Which wood adhesive?

There's more than one way to glue two pieces of wood together. Ordinary white wood glue, which becomes clear as it dries, is perfectly all right for most indoor jobs, but for outside jobs try a polyurethane adhesive. It's weather resistant and stronger than the standard stuff, making it good for boatbuilding and outdoor furniture in very exposed conditions. It is more expensive than the wood glue adhesives and is solvent based, so wear gloves and a mask when using it. If any spills, be sure to wipe it up immediately. Also don't overlook construction adhesive, which is ideally suited for use on rough exterior joints.

Dry run

Here's a good way to tell when adhesive has dried. At the same time as you apply adhesive to your work, glue together two scrap pieces of the same material as the work. Test the scraps to determine when the work is dry. If the label on the adhesive specifies a drying time, you can jot it down on the wood as a reference.

Epoxy mix-up ▲

Many epoxy adhesives require you to mix resin and hardener in equal parts for a strong bond. An easy way to gauge the proportions is to squeeze out the resin and hardener in parallel lines of equal width and length.

Make it hot

When applying hot adhesive to a large area like a flat roof, you may find that the adhesive is cooling and hardening too fast. To slow it down, try warming the work with a heat gun. Or put the work out in the sun on a hot day.

Sure-shot injector

A simple plastic syringe, found in hobby shops or in woodworking stores or catalogs, is ideal for injecting adhesive into narrow places, such as in a hole made to reach a loose tenon. After filling the syringe barrel, insert the plunger and hold it upward while you depress it. This will expel air bubbles and prevent the adhesive from drying.

Keeping wood glue fresh

How do you keep a large container of wood glue adhesive fresh? Take the cap off, squeeze the sides of the container together until the wood glue comes to the top, then ask someone to replace the cap. With a minimum of air in the container, the adhesive will stay fresher for longer.

CLAMP DOS AND DON'TS

Here are some pointers to keep in mind when you're clamping.

★ Don't rely on clamps to pull together a poorly fitting joint. Adhesive and pressure may hold things together for a while, but in the long run the joint will fail. Make sure the pieces fit properly.

★ Before applying adhesive, test-fit the parts. Pre-adjust the clamps so they're ready to apply pressure with just a few twists.

★ Never force a clamp or use a wrench to tighten it. If the clamp isn't strong enough, use a bigger one or add another clamp next to it.

★ Too much clamping pressure can squeeze all the adhesive out of the joint and compress the wood. Too little pressure can result in a line of adhesive that is too thick and therefore weak. If a ridge of adhesive appears between clamped parts, stop applying pressure.

★ Leave the clamps on for the recommended length of time.

Working safely

Safe work practice must be your priority. Choose quality safety gear that's comfortable to wear and get into the habit of all having tools and equipment on hand before you start.

Eye protectors

Don't rely on eyeglasses to guard your eyes. Wear special protective safety glasses with side shields, or safety goggles, which can be worn over your normal glasses. For full-face protection, wear a face shield.

Ear protectors

Earmuffs are easier to take off and put on than earplugs and are harder to misplace. But both protect equally well if their noise-reduction rating is the same.

Respiratory protectors

Choose a respirator that filters toxic dust and fumes. For ordinary dust, use disposable dust masks. Don't buy a mask that doesn't have a rating guide on it.

Watch out for asbestos

Never cut anything that might contain asbestos, such as old pipe insulation and roof sheeting. If in doubt, don't cut it! Cutting asbestos can spread dangerous fibers over a huge area.

Go ahead and blow it

Sawdust is the enemy of all power-tool motors. It accumulates inside the motor, around the motor housing and in the motor vents.

Disposing of hazardous waste

Products containing solvents or other ingredients that carry warning labels (such as "flammable" and "corrosive") are likely to be classified as hazardous waste. Before you buy such a product, try to find a safer (water-based) substitute. If none is available, buy only as much as you can use. If you are unsure of how to dispose of a material, contact your local waste disposal center, environmental protection agency or health department. Never pour it down the drain.

Vacuum sawdust from the housing and from the vents every month or so. Alternatively, blow it out with compressed air, using either an air compressor or canned air, available at photography supply stores. (Be sure to wear eye protection.) If you fail to keep the vents open and the housing free of sawdust, your tools will probably overheat.

Create a draft

About 10 minutes before you begin drilling, sanding or cutting wood, position a fan so that it's blowing out of an open window, turn it on, and open a door or window on the opposite side. This will create a gentle breeze before you generate sawdust, helping to keep the airborne dust from settling.

Unplug for safety

Always unplug a power tool when you're adjusting or cleaning it, and when you're not using it. To keep a young child from plugging in a power tool, insert a key ring through the hole in a plug prong. If there isn't a hole already, drill one yourself.

No more fog-ups

To keep safety goggles fog-free, squeeze a little dishwashing liquid on the inside of the lenses, and spread it into a thin, even coating with your finger.

POWER TOOLS:
AVOIDING ACCIDENTS

Whenever you use a power tool, make safety your main concern. The following are general power tool safety rules:

Read, understand and follow the directions in the owner's manual. Use a tool only for the jobs for which it was designed. Don't force a tool or otherwise cause its motor to overheat.

Analyze the job environment. Never operate a tool in a damp, wet, or fume-filled atmosphere. Keep your workspace well lit, well ventilated and free of unnecessary clutter.

Dress safely. Don't wear jewelry or loose clothing. Keep long hair tied back. Wear the appropriate safety equipment.

Evaluate your mood. If you are not feeling well, ill or taking a medication that could affect your alertness, postpone the job. An alcohol-free worksite is also mandatory.

Concentrate on the job. Don't talk to anyone while you work, and keep children and pets away. Focus on what you are doing at the moment, not on the next step.

Take your time. Hurrying and taking short cuts are major causes of workshop accidents.

Maintain your balance. Wear non-slip footwear, and make sure your footing is secure. Grip a tool firmly. Don't reach too far with a tool or work with it held over your head; stand on a sturdy stepladder instead.

Think before you act. Know the consequences of every move you make. This will slow you down at first, but after a while knowing what's safe—and what's not—will become second nature to you.

Tool care

Rusty, damaged or blunt tools slow down the job and give second-rate results. A small investment in tool care will repay you many times over.

Discourage rust
Keep some charcoal or a couple of pieces of chalk in your toolbox. They will absorb moisture and so discourage rust.

The good oil
Wipe your saw blades with a little light oil or WD-40 before you put them away after use—no more rust! Good tools are expensive to buy; paying a little extra attention to their care will keep them in great working order for years to come.

Saw safety
Protect the edge of your handsaw with a piece of old garden hose or PVC pipe cut to the length of the saw and slit along its length. Slide the pipe over the edge of your saw (starting at the back) to help it keep its keen edge—and make it safe from inquisitive little hands.

Maintain an edge
Dull tools are both dangerous and inefficient. Save time and money by learning how to sharpen the blades of chisels, planes, knives and shears. However, let a professional sharpen tools that have complex or contoured cutting edges, such as router and drill bits, handsaws and circular saw blades. Similarly, leave the sharpening of carbide-tipped surfaces to the professionals.

Substitute bench-grinder
You can use a belt sander, fitted with a worn 120-grit aluminum oxide belt, to rough-grind a tool. Have a helper hold the sander on its side on a mat of foam carpet padding. Put on safety goggles. Hold the tool against the belt, pointing it in the direction of the belt's movement so that the tool does not snag on the belt. ▼

Be sure to match the SHARPENING angle to the BEVEL angle

Sharpening a knife ▲
Sharpen a dull knife on a coarse stone first; then finish on a fine stone. Use lubrication, and move the blade to the right as you pivot and pull it. Repeat on the other side of the blade, pushing it away as you pivot. Stroke alternate faces the same number of times. Keep the angle and pressure consistent.

Even strokes ▲
Use a honing rod for long-bladed knives. Holding the rod motionless, begin with the heel of the blade near the rod handle. Move the length of the blade along the rod in an arcing motion. Stroke each side equally. Keep the blade angle and the pressure constant.

Hard to lose
To stop your tools getting "lost" when you lend them to friends, simply spray the handles with paint. It's amazing how quickly they'll turn up when painted a bright color.

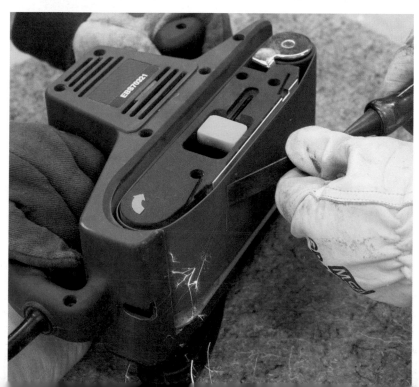

Doors and windows

Fix a door that won't close

If a door refuses to shut or keeps swinging open, first diagnose and fix the problem, then spray the hinges regularly with oil-based lubricant.

Keep latches in trim

Help avoid latch problems by lubricating them every six months. Use an oil-based lubricant such as WD-40. Fix the plastic straw in the nozzle to focus spray around the bolt, then wipe off the excess with a rag. Graphite powder is another effective latch lubricant. However, never mix lubricants—it's a sure way to gunk up a latch assembly.

Pinpoint the problem ▲

Check if the latch and the strike hole are out of alignment by smearing lipstick on the latch edge and sticking masking tape to the strike plate. Open and close the door. If there is a gap between the smudge and the hole, measure it. If there is no gap, check if the latch is going far enough into the strike hole, or if it is sticking due to paint build-up.

Unstick a latch

If there is a build-up of old paint, use a utility knife to break the seal around the latch and scrape paint off its surface. If the latch in an old mortise-type lock case that continues to stick, repair the lock case. See "Overhaul an older-style lock case," page 42–3.

TRADE TALK

Cross section

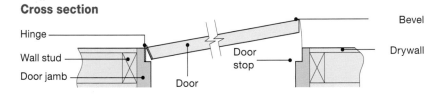

- Hinge
- Wall stud
- Door jamb
- Door
- Door stop
- Bevel
- Drywall

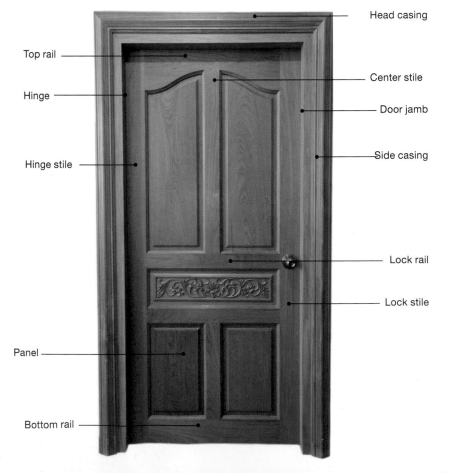

- Top rail
- Hinge
- Hinge stile
- Panel
- Bottom rail
- Head casing
- Center stile
- Door jamb
- Side casing
- Lock rail
- Lock stile

▓ Tighten the hinges

If the latch is too high or low for the strike hole, make sure all the hinge screws are tight. If that doesn't work, remove a screw on the jamb side of the hinge. Then drive in a 3 in. (7.5 cm) screw: this will grab the wall framing and draw in the whole door jamb slightly. To raise the latch, do this at the top hinge. To lower the latch, do it at the bottom hinge.

▓ Enlarge the latch hole ▲

If the latch is missing the strike hole by 1/8 in. (3 mm) or less, enlarge the hole. Use a simple metal grinding bit suitable for use in a drill, or a half-round file matched to the curve of the hole.

▓ Double up

If the latch on an old interior door no longer extends far enough out of the latch hole to keep the door from swinging open, install a second plate over the first. If you can't find a matching strike plate, shim out the old one with cardboard or laminate.

▓ Move the strike plate

If the latch isn't going into the strike hole far enough or is missing the hole by more than 1/8 in. (3 mm), move the strike plate up or down, in or out as required. Use a sharp chisel to enlarge the mortise. Then hold the strike plate in place and drill new holes for the screws. Install the strike plate and fill the gap in the remaining mortise with wood filler. ▶

Mark the new strike plate and mortise position before you start chiseling

Fix a door that sticks

If a door keeps sticking, you may be able to sand or plane it into shape but first, try tightening the screws and if necessary, adjust the mortises by shimming or deepening them.

A sticking door is usually caused by repainting, slight movement of the house or moisture absorbed by the wood.

▦ Check the clearance ▲
An interior door should have ⅛ in. (3 mm) clearance, the thickness of an average coin, all around, and about ½ in. (1 cm) at the base, depending on the floor covering.

▦ Plane or sand
Use chalk or pencil to mark the spot on the floor, jamb or frames where the door is rubbing. Close the door, reopen it, then look for smeared marks. Finally, plane or sand them away.

▦ How to shim a mortise
To shim a mortise (that is, make it shallower), remove the hinge and place a shim of cardboard, about the thickness of two playing cards, behind it in the notch. Refasten the hinge and test the door. If necessary, add a second or third shim to square the door in the opening and stop the binding.

▦ How to deepen a mortise
Remove the hinge and score the perimeter of the mortise with a utility knife. Holding a wood chisel with the beveled edge facing the mortise, work from the center of the recess toward the perimeter, cleaning out the mortise to the required depth. If you cut the mortise too deep, shim it with cardboard. Refasten the hinge and test the door. If necessary, deepen the mortise a fraction more until the binding stops.

▦ Make a door stand
Square a line across a 24 in. (60 cm) long 2 x 4 in. (5 x 10 cm) piece of scrap. Mark a second line at a 10° angle with a 2¼ in. (6 cm) space between. Square the lines down the sides to half the depth and cut with a handsaw. Break out the waste using a hammer and chisel, then sand the notch. To make a wedge, cut a 10 in. (25 cm) long scrap at a 10° angle, then sand. Stand the door in the notch and tap in the wedge. ▼

Two door stands are more stable than one

CORRECTING
A BINDING DOOR

Many sticking and rubbing problems are caused by faulty mortises. First, determine the location of the rub. This will tell you which mortise is at fault and how to solve the problem.

If the door binds on the top side, shim the top hinge or deepen the mortise of the lower hinge.

If the door binds on the bottom side, shim the lower hinge or deepen the mortise of the top hinge.

If the door rubs at the top on the latch side, deepen the mortise of the corresponding hinge.

If the door rubs along the length of the latch side, deepen all the hinge mortises or plane the edge.

If the door binds in the latch area, deepen the strike plate mortise.

If the door binds on the hinge side just before it closes, insert shims under each of the hinge leaves.

BEFORE YOU BEGIN

Check if the hinge pins are fixed or loose. Most exterior and security doors have fixed pin hinges, while most internal doors have loose pin hinges. You can tell a loose pin if it moves when you tap it with a pin punch or a nail.

Dismount a door

1 **Wedge and scrape**
Wedge the door open with shims. This will hold the door steady and take the weight off the hinges. Scrape off any paint or corrosion that may be binding the hinge pins to the hinge knuckles.

Start with the LOWEST hinge and work up

2 **Take it off the hinges**
Loose pin hinges: tap the hinge pin out with a pin punch or a 4 in. (10 cm) nail and a hammer until about ½ in. (1 cm) of the pin is exposed. Pull the pin out by hand. If it won't budge, knock it free with a screwdriver and a hammer. Fixed pin hinges: unscrew the hinges from the jamb, leaving them attached to the door. Lift the door down carefully.

SECRETS
from the EXPERTS

To **accurately mark screw holes,** insert a Phillips head screwdriver into each hole and push or tap it into the wood. The crosshairs impressed into the wood indicate the exact center.

▓ Scribe a door ▶
Before planing the edge of the door, you need to scribe the cutting line. Run masking tape down the edge of the stile on the hinge side. Set a pencil tip and compass point ⅛ in. (3 mm) apart, then run the point along the stile. If you don't have a compass, use a carpenter's pencil trimmed to the right width. The tape makes the line visible.

▓ Plane the edge
Use a belt sander, hand plane or electric planer to sand the stile down to the pencil line. A hand plane will give you the most control. If you are using a belt sander, begin with an 80-grit sanding belt. When you are a hair away from the line, change to a 100-grit belt and sand to the line. Use a 120-grit belt to finish off.

▓ Prevent splintering
When planing or sanding the top or bottom edges of a door, always work from an edge or end toward the center. Going in the other direction will chip the wood when the tool passes over the outer edge, resulting in damage that will be difficult to disguise.

Follow the grain

Always plane or sand along the grain of the wood. If you encounter resistance and see any raised wood fibers or chipping, you are working in the wrong direction.

Hold that door

You don't have to take a door off its hinges to plane or sand the top, latch and hinge sides. To stop the door swinging as you work on it, tap in a pair of wedges beneath the door. If you are planing the latch side and there's a chance the plane will strike the lock or latch, remove it.

Sawing the bottom ▲

When using a saw to square the bottom of a door, use a straight edge to draw a cut line, then score the line with a utility knife to prevent the wood from splintering. Clamp a board along the line to guide the saw, placing wood scraps beneath each clamp to protect the door. If you're using a circular saw with a fine carbide-tipped blade, place the most prominent side of the door down when cutting. If using a handsaw, place the prominent side up.

Sealing the edges

Always seal the top and bottom edges of a door prior to fitting. This keeps moisture out and prevents the wood from swelling.

A professional angle

For a really professional result, try planing or sanding the long edges of a door at a slight angle. This is called "beveling." (See diagram on page 34.) When a door is beveled at the hinge side, the hinge is still slightly open when the door is closed, greatly reducing stress on the door and door frame. When the door is backed off at the latch side, the door will not bind or stick because the leading edge remains clear of the door frame.

Fitting doorstops

Always fit doorstops to prevent impact damage to walls or to the door. Avoid fitting doorstops on bathroom floors, as the fastener and fastening process may pierce the waterproof membrane beneath the tiles. In bathrooms, fit doorstops to the door or wall if possible. A variety of doorstops is available for different applications.

Painting the bottom edge

A strip of carpet is useful for painting or sealing the bottom edge of a door if you want to avoid taking it off its hinges. Apply some paint or sealant to the pile side of the strip of carpet, slide it under the door and rub it back and forth to coat the bare wood. ▼

Protect the floor with newspaper or a piece of cardboard

Quick Fix

LOOSE SCREWS

Over time, the weight and daily use of the door can combine to pull the screws out of the jamb. Give the old screws something to grip. Simply push a matchstick into the hole, and snap it off flush. No glue is needed—the screws will wedge the matchstick tight.

BEFORE YOU BEGIN

Misaligned rollers on a screen door can cause the door to stick or bind. Eventually this will over-stress the corner joints and, unless you take action, you may have to buy a new door.

Fix a screen door that sticks

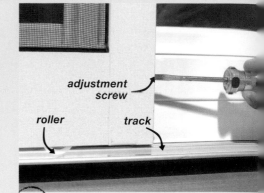

adjustment screw

roller   *track*

① Check for damage

Lift the door out and clean the track. Check the rollers, and replace any damaged ones. Replace the door and locate two adjustment screws near the bottom, one at each end. Then turn the screws counterclockwise so the door rests on the track.

② Even the gap

Raise one roller until it lifts the door about ¼ in. (5 mm) off the track, then slowly raise the other roller until the gap between the door and the bottom of the track is even. Make sure there's also a gap between the top of the screen and the upper track.

Hinges

Always keep hinges in good order to avoid squeaking, latching and sticking problems.

▤ Silence a squeaky hinge

To silence a squeaky hinge, lubricate the hinge with an oil-based lubricant such as WD-40. If the hinge has a pin, raise the pin slightly and drip oil onto the shaft above the upper barrel. Swing the door back and forth a few times to distribute the lubricant along the pin.

▤ Avoid an oily mess

Alternatively, use petroleum jelly, as it works its way into the hinge, adheres well and won't run off. If the hinge has a fixed pin, a few puffs of graphite powder will work as well as light oil.

▤ Not all screws are equal

Heavier doors, and any doors attached to softer wood, require longer hinge screws to make them secure, so check that the screws on all your doors are the right length for the job.

▤ Smothered in paint

If hinge screws are covered in thick paint, use the point of an awl to scrape out the screw slot. Once the slot is clear, place the tip of the screwdriver in the slot and tap the screwdriver handle with a hammer. This initial impact will help to release the grip of the screw.

Don't mark the frame: place SCRAP WOOD beneath the jaws

▤ Repair a split frame ▲

A frame can split along the line of the hinge screws if the door it encloses blows open violently. Fix the split by squeezing woodworking adhesive into it, then forcing it shut with a G-clamp. Alternatively, drive screws through the face of the frame and through the split, countersinking the heads so that they can be concealed with filler.

Locks and keys

Keep your locks and lock cases well maintained by cleaning and lubricating them every six months. If you do have problems, here are some quick fixes.

Basic maintenance

Apply powdered graphite to locks every six months. Alternatively, rub very soft graphite pencil along both sides of the key, insert the key in the lock and work the bolt back and forth to help the graphite penetrate the lock.

Lubricate a lock

Another effective lubricant is petroleum-based lubricant spray. Fix the plastic straw in the nozzle to focus spray into the keyhole and around the bolt. Spray liberally to saturate the assembly, then wipe off the excess with a rag. Never mix petroleum-based lubricant with graphite powder in the same lock. This can gum up the lock, requiring disassembly and cleaning.

Broken key in the lock

If a key breaks in a lock, try to extract it with a pair of long-nose pliers or a fine, stiff wire bent at the end. Alternatively, insert the blade of a coping saw into the lock, then pull the key out very carefully and slowly. Don't tug at the key shank or you may damage the lock. ▼

Frozen out?

In very cold weather, moisture inside a lock may freeze and jam the pins. Before inserting the key, put on some gloves and heat the key's teeth with a match or lighter. Spraying de-icer into the lock may also help.

Straighten a bent key

To straighten a bent key, put it on a solid flat metal surface such as an overturned iron skillet and hammer it lightly.

No more fumbling

Drill a second hole near the edge of your house key so it will hang on your keyring at an angle from the others. Result? No more fumbling in the dark for your house key. ▶

A lock is only as strong as the frame to which it is fitted.

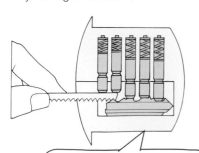

Keep the blade PARALLEL to the top of the keyhole

To keep brass hardware shiny bright, apply a furniture wax as soon as it's installed and reapply regularly.

Knobs and latches

Few items in the house receive as much wear and tear as doorknobs and latch assemblies. Luckily, the inevitable defects are easy to fix.

Tighten an old doorknob

Older doorknobs can be tightened by simply adjusting the spindle. Loosen the setscrews holding the knobs, and center the spindle so it extends equally on both sides of the door. Then reposition the knobs so they fit snugly against the door but do not bind. ▼

Setscrew service

When tightening the setscrews to firm up a loose, older-style doorknob, remember to match the size of the tip of the screwdriver to the size of the setscrew. Setscrews tend to be set into the shaft of the doorknob and if the tip of the screwdriver extends beyond the edges of the setscrew, you may not be able to tighten it as firmly as you need to.

Seaside wax and shine

Bright brass hardware doesn't survive well on external doors in coastal areas where the salty sea air can undermine the protective lacquer finish. To keep brass hardware shiny bright, apply a furniture wax as soon as it's installed and reapply regularly.

Refresh lost lacquer

Most bright brass door hardware is covered with a protective lacquer finish. Over time the lacquer can be weakened by chemical cleaning agents, extreme temperatures, exposure to ultraviolet light and everyday handling. The first sign that the coating is compromised and the brass is starting to tarnish is the appearance of small, dark spots. If you want to maintain a bright brass finish, remove all the remaining lacquer using a very fine grade of steel wool, then recoat.

What you will need

- Utility knife
- Screwdriver

BEFORE YOU BEGIN
Older lock cases are increasingly rare, so keeping them in good working order is always well worth the effort.

▨ Clean a lock case ▲

Working in a well-ventilated area, and wearing rubber gloves to protect your hands, wash a stiff lock case in a shallow tub of mineral spirits or turpentine. Set the lock case on newspaper to dry for an hour or so. Finally, apply light machine oil through the holes scattered over the surface of the case cover plates.

▨ Fix a rattling doorknob

First, tighten the screws on the escutcheon (the piece of metal or porcelain that frames the knob). To access the baseplate, remove the knob by activating the button, tab or wire clip that acts as a release. Twist and pull the escutcheon off the shank. Tighten the mounting plate screws to stop the knob assembly from rattling. ▼

escutcheon

Overhaul an older-style lock case

① Unstick the latch

Paint build-up is a common cause of a sticking latch. With a utility knife, break the paint seal around the latch and scrape paint off its surface. If the latch continues to stick, remove the lock case for repair or replacement (Step 2).

② Remove the lock case

Unscrew one of the doorknobs and pull it off its shaft. Then withdraw the shaft from the door by pulling on the other knob. Scrape away any paint blocking the screw slots at the top and bottom of the lock case edge plate. Remove the screws and carefully pry out the case.

SKETCH or PHOTOGRAPH the interior layout before you work on it

③ Open and repair

With the lock case on a flat surface, unscrew the cover plate and remove it. Spray the works with a silicone lubricant. If either the latch spring or the deadbolt tension strip is damaged, replace it. Check the action on both the latch and the bolt. If either will not budge, enlarge the openings in the lock case with a file.

Draftproof a door

What you will need

- Tape measure and utility knife
- Nail-on vinyl or rubber ½ in. (1.2 cm) diameter tubing
- Nails (usually included, if not use ¾ in./1.8 cm nails)
- Hammer
- Door seal or sweep and screws for installing
- Hacksaw
- Screwdriver and awl

1 Cut strips

Make sure the door jamb is clean. Measure the head and hinge sides of the door jamb at the inside stop. Cut lengths of tubing to fit. Starting on the hinge side, nail strip to jamb with tubular part flush against stop.

2 Nail strips

Nail the strip to the stop along the top and latch sides, with the tubular part extending slightly over the edge so that it just touches the door when it is closed. Next, install the seal on the inside door bottom.

3 Install seal

Cut the seal to length if needed, using a hacksaw on the metal and a utility knife on the vinyl gasket. With the door closed, position the seal so it touches the floor. Mark screw holes with an awl and install.

Make a door safe and sound

A few simple jobs can make a big difference to both your comfort and security.

Repair a hole

Repair a hole in a hollow door by removing any splinters and filling it with expanding foam. Leave the foam to cure overnight, trim away excess and coat with drywall filler. When the filler has dried, sand and paint. ▼

Fill the cavity no more than TWO-THIRDS FULL to allow for expansion

Silence a banging door

Two or three ¼ in. (5 mm) dabs of clear silicone sealant applied to the edges of a door will create an almost invisible cushion. Otherwise, dot the door jamb with a few self-adhesive felt pads or use a doorstop.

Identify visitors

If your peephole doesn't always show you who's there, install a wide-angled viewer. If your door is fire rated, choose a viewer that won't affect the rating (if you live in an apartment building, check with your landlord).

Windows

Windows should always open and close smoothly, stop drafts and never leak.

Apply sealant

Try using sealant to draftproof window sashes, fixed frames and the glass in skylights. Sealant will also reduce dust, dirt and noise, keep out rain and insects, and help your heating and air conditioning to work more efficiently, thus saving you money.

Check for leaks

Dampen the back of your hand and move it all around a door or window. Your skin will feel cooler when your hand is near a leak. If no breeze is blowing, enlist a helper to stand outside and aim a hair dryer at the window seams.

Seal a warp

You can make your own draft excluder. Simply seal the bottom of a badly warped double-hung window by opening the lower sash and applying a ribbon of sealant to the sill. Lay some plastic wrap over the sealant, gently lower the window and lock it. When the sealant sets, raise the window and carefully remove the plastic wrap. You'll be left with a perfect draft excluder.

Remove old paint ▶

Old sash windows, especially in cases where the sash cords were broken long ago, are almost always painted firmly shut. The ideal tool for freeing them is a pizza cutter, which won't damage the wood. Run the blade backward and forward a few times between the sash and the frame to break the seal.

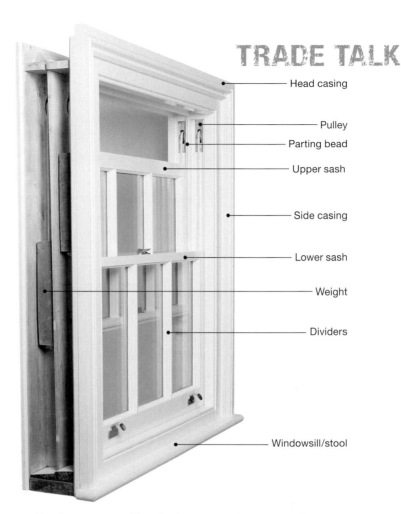

- Head casing
- Pulley
- Parting bead
- Upper sash
- Side casing
- Lower sash
- Weight
- Dividers
- Windowsill/stool

Seal empty pulley holes

If drafts are getting in through the pulley holes after you have removed old sash-weights, pour vermiculite or loose-fill cellulose through the pulley hole at the top of the jamb. Then fill the top of the pocket with unfaced fiberglass batt insulation.

You'll need a utility knife to reach the corners

Draftproofing your windows will reduce dust, dirt and noise, as well as keeping your heating and air conditioning bills to a minimum.

Sticking sash

A window may stick for any number of reasons, including warped or swollen wood or accumulated dirt or paint. Before undertaking major repairs, try lubricating the channels with a little soap, candle wax or silicone spray.

Burglar-proof window

Cut a dowel or board to fit flat in the interior window track. This will stop a sliding window from opening, even if the lock is forced.

Bolt up older windows

For added security on older windows, install a key-lockable bolt. In most cases, the lockable mechanism is positioned so that the pin runs through the sash and into the windowsill. When windows are locked, keep a key in the room so a window can be opened in an emergency.

What you will need

- Hammer
- Chisel
- Electric drill and ¼ in. (5 mm) bit
- Wood hardener
- Rag or disposable brush
- Rubber gloves
- Exterior wood filler
- Putty knife
- Sandpaper
- Primer
- Paint
- Paintbrush

Filling in a rotted windowsill

Dry the wood FASTER with frequent short blasts from a hot air gun

1 **Remove rotted wood**
Cut rotted wood from the sill with a hammer and chisel. Let the sill dry, covering it if it rains. After a few weeks, drill a honeycomb pattern of ¼ in. (5 mm) holes into the damaged area, holding the drill at an angle.

2 **Apply wood hardener**
Saturate the damaged area by applying wood hardener with a rag or paint brush. Protect your hands with rubber gloves. Let the wood hardener dry thoroughly.

3 **Fill and finish**
Apply exterior wood filler to the damaged area with a putty knife. Smooth the filler so it's level with the sill. Let it dry, then sand, prime and paint.

▦ Cranky crank
A sluggish casement window might be caused by a dirty crank mechanism. Apply a silicone spray or light oil to the crank works for ease of operation. ▼

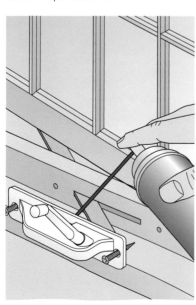

▦ Nice and smooth
If your sliding aluminum windows no longer slide easily, it's probably because you haven't cleaned out the track or lubricated the rollers with a dry silicone spray for a couple of years. Try this: sometimes there's a non-weight-bearing set of rollers at the top of each window. Swap this with the dry or damaged bottom set, add a little lubricant, and you should be back in business!

▦ Remove a sliding window
To remove a sliding aluminum window for a thorough clean, first slide the window to a partly open position. Then grip the sash on both sides before lifting or pushing upward into the top frame channel, at the same time pulling the bottom of the sash out toward you. The sash should easily slip out and down.

SECRETS from the EXPERTS
Wash windows on **cloudy days** for a dazzling shine. Bright sunlight dries out window cleaner too rapidly, causing streaks.

▦ Replacing a sill
Cutting out and replacing a wood windowsill, or even a section of one, should not be a difficult job. Simply take a section of the original sill to a home center, where they will use the profile as a guide in helping you select a matching replacement. If you have an unusual window, you may need to have the replacement sill specially cut and shaped.

Glass

With a little knowledge you can fix household glass problems easily.

Use elbow grease

Minor scratches on glass can be removed successfully by rubbing hard with jeweler's rouge or toothpaste. It's cheaper than buying new glass!

Glass for a new window

If installing a new window, the thickness of the glass will depend on how large the pane is and where it is to be used. If there is a chance that people may walk into the glass by mistake—in a picture window, for example—then you may have to buy safety glass. Small windows need a relatively thin float glass. Larger windows need thicker glass, and windows in bathrooms, at floor level or next to door openings may require laminated or tempered glass. Check your local building code to ensure the correct thickness.

Cracks and holes

Seal cracked glass temporarily, or plug up a small hole in an instant, by brushing the breach with clear shellac or nail polish.

Soften putty ▶

Remove stubborn window putty with a hair dryer. Wave the dryer back and forth along a 4 in. (10 cm) length of putty, being careful not to scorch the frame or overheat the glass. Once the putty softens, slide a putty knife underneath it and pry up and away from the frame.

If glass breaks

If glass breaks, take a shard to the store to buy a replacement pane. If it's old glass, make sure the replacement conforms with local building standards.

What you will need

- Duct tape
- Hammer and stiff putty knife or chisel
- Needle-nosed pliers
- Paint primer or other sealer
- Tape measure
- Glazing putty
- Replacement glass
- Glazing points or push points
- Screwdriver (if required)
- Exterior paint and brush

Replace a broken window pane

Tape over CRACKED GLASS to prevent it from falling apart during removal

1 Remove old glass
Wearing gloves, goggles and a long-sleeved shirt, use a hammer and putty knife or chisel to remove the old putty. Use pliers to pull out the nails or glazing points or sprigs —thin metal wedges that hold the glass in the frame. Finally, carefully remove the glass.

2 Scrape, prime and seal
Scrape out the old putty from the rabbets and paint any unfinished wood with primer or sealer, such as linseed oil. Order new glass: use the old glass as a pattern, or carefully measure the opening and deduct ⅛ in. (3 mm) from both the width and the height.

▦ Beveling for beginners ▶

Creating a perfect bevel on glazing putty is second nature for a professional glass installer. Here's a simple way to get the same result. Simply place the end of the putty knife against the glass, and draw the bevel across the putty.

▦ Wear rubber gloves

Wear rubber gloves when handling new glass. They provide a sure grip and won't leave fingerprints on the pane, as well as protecting you from getting nicks.

▦ Shatter-resistant film

To make existing glass safer without having to replace it, cover it with virtually invisible shatter-resistant film. This can usually be applied to the smooth side of frosted or patterned glass.

Be safe when handling glass

Carry large pieces of glass vertically. They can break under their own weight when carried horizontally.

Wear eye protection, leather gloves, thick leather shoes and a long-sleeved shirt when you're working with glass.

To dispose of broken glass, wrap it thickly in newspaper and put it in your garbage, clearly labeled "broken glass."

SAFETY FIRST

③ Putty glass into place

Using a clean, straight-edged putty knife, apply putty to the channel all around the opening. The putty should not be visible from indoors. Position the new glass and press it firmly against the putty so that it forms an even layer under the edges of the glass.

④ Install glazing points

To set the glass securely, press glazing points into the frame and against the glass with a screwdriver or stiff putty knife. Use at least two per side, spacing them every 4 to 6 in. (10–15 cm). When you have finished, use a putty knife to scrape off any excess putty.

Keep the **PUTTY KNIFE MOIST** with turpentine. That way it won't stick.

⑤ Putty the edges

Apply putty over the edges of the glass with a putty knife. Holding the knife at an angle, draw it across the putty, pressing firmly and working out from the corners. See "Beveling for beginners," above. Let it cure for a couple of weeks before painting.

Screens

Repairing holes and tears in fiberglass and metal screens is much more economical than replacing the whole screen.

▦ Patch a fiberglass screen

Patch tiny holes in fiberglass mesh with a few drops of Super Glue. Larger holes are easily fixed using an inexpensive self-adhesive screen patch kit. Cut two identical patches that will overlap the hole by about ¾ in. (2 cm). Remove the screen and center the hole and the underside patch on a wood block. Press the upperside patch for a few moments and you're done. ▼

Fiberglass screen is not as durable as metal, but it's less expensive and easier to handle.

▦ Patch a metal screen ▲

Seal tiny holes in a metal screen with a few drops of waterproof glue. To repair a larger hole, measure it and cut a patch from the same material, allowing an overlap of 1¼ in. (3 cm). Unweave each edge of the patch for about ½ in. (1 cm), then bend the wires at right angles to the patch. Push the patch into the hole and bend the strands against the screen. Sew the patch in place with nylon thread and seal with a few coats of clear nail polish.

▦ Screen saver

Lean dirty screens against a wall and dampen them with fine spray from a hose. Gently scrub both sides with a scrubbing brush or sponge dipped in hot, soapy water. Hose down, then leave to dry.

SAFE AND SMART **SCREENS**

★ Larger holes

If a tear or hole in a screen is less than 4 in. (10 cm) away from the edge of the frame, it's better to replace the screen than to patch it.

★ Match the metal

If you are replacing metal screens, make sure you choose screens made of the same metal as the frames (unless the frames are made of wood).

★ Wood frames

If your screens have wood frames with mitered corners, reinforce the corners by screwing a metal brace to the back of each corner.

★ Screen clean

The best (and easiest) way to keep screens clean is to run a vacuum over them from time to time. If the mesh needs more thorough cleaning, use warm, soapy water and a soft brush.

What you will need

- Screen rolling tool
- Screen material (metal or fiberglass mesh)
- Spline
- Utility knife
- Small clamps (optional)

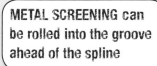

METAL SCREENING can be rolled into the groove ahead of the spline

Replace a screen

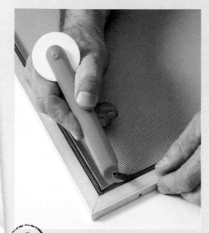

1 Remove the old screen

Using the hook at the end of the screen rolling tool, ease out the old spline holding the screen in place and discard it, as spline material gets hard and brittle and should not be reused. Remove and discard the old screen.

2 Clamp the mesh

Lay the new screen over the frame, allowing an overlap of ¾ to 1 in. (2–2.5 cm). If you haven't replaced a screen before, you'll find it a lot easier if you clamp the new material to one short side of the frame.

3 Spline the new screen

Begin installing the new spline at a corner on the side opposite to the clamps. Use the screen rolling tool to push the spline and screen material into the groove around the edge of the frame.

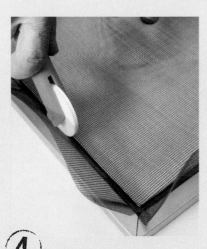

4 Work the corners

Continue around the frame. If wrinkles or bulges appear in the mesh, remove the spline and try again. Small wrinkles should vanish as you near the starting point. As you near each corner, cut screening at a 90° angle to corner.

5 Trim excess mesh

Using a utility knife with a sharp new blade, trim off any excess screening material. A dull blade will pull the material, rather than cut it. Cut with the blade on top of the spline and pointed toward the outside of the frame.

KNOW **YOUR BLINDS**

On their own or teamed with curtains, blinds can provide both shade and privacy. They come in a variety of styles to suit a range of decors (and budgets).

Roller blind

A roller blind is a smooth, stiffened panel of fabric that winds around a roller fixed at the top of the window. Some are spring-loaded so that a simple tug to the bottom edge of the panel will trigger the blind to retract. Others have manually operated sidewinder mechanisms. Older blinds may have pulley cords, but modern blinds tend to be fitted with chain-operated controls.

Roman blind

When lowered, a Roman blind lies flat against the window; when raised—by means of cords and loops attached to the back of the blind—it folds into neat horizontal pleats. A wooden batten along the lower edge of the blind holds it straight, while smaller battens may also be inserted across each pleat to define the folds.

Venetian blind

A Venetian blind is made up of horizontal slats of wood, plastic or aluminum. When the blind is raised, the slats stack neatly on top of one another. When it's lowered, the slats can be angled to control the penetration of light. If choosing blinds for a bathroom, consider using a wide-bladed, PVC Venetian that will be guaranteed to last in damp conditions.

Roll-up blind

Roll-up blinds may be made from woven grass, PVC, bamboo, split cane, thin wood slats or wooden reeds. Roll-up blinds are raised and lowered by means of a pulley cord. These blinds typically allow a degree of filtered light through.

Vertical louver blind

Vertical blinds are made from slats that move in sync when operated. Usually, a chain control is used to alter the angle of the slats, while a cord is used to draw all the slats to one side. They're particularly useful for wide windows and patio doors. For a new take on vertical blinds, look to panel glide blinds. These are composed of broad panels that retract one behind the other, to expose some or all of the glass.

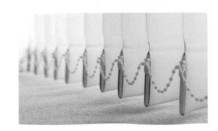

Blinds

Blinds help control the amount of light and heat that gets into a room. To get the best out of them, be sure the components are in good working order.

Put on the gloves

Dust blinds by putting on some cotton gloves and wiping the slats with your fingers. It's faster and more effective than vacuuming or using a duster. Dampen the gloves slightly to remove thick dust from dirtier slats. ▼

Restore the magic

If the blind's rotating plastic wand doesn't do its job, take the blind down and inspect and lubricate the screw assembly inside the headbox. Also check that the tape or string that holds the slats is still attached to the horizontal tilt tube.

Revive old blinds

Instead of discarding worn blinds, give them a face-lift. Choose a fabric to complement your decor, and cut it to fit the blind. Apply a thin coat of rubber cement or spray-on adhesive to the blind; then attach the fabric. Carefully smooth the fabric to eliminate air bubbles that could cause the blind to wrinkle when it's rolled up.

Double up

Consider installing dual roller blinds on a double wall-bracket. A blind made from mesh or a translucent fabric will give light with privacy during the day, while a second blind made from a heavier fabric can be drawn for privacy at night or to protect against bright sunlight.

Get that straight

When raising or lowering a Venetian blind, always have the slats in a horizontal position. It reduces the risk of tears or tangles to the cords and tapes that make the blind move.

Take out the slack

If a spring-loaded roller blind won't roll up with a snap, take it down, roll it up by hand to halfway, then rehang and test the tension. If it's still slack, take it back down, roll it up a little more and try again.

Relax and unwind

To restore a spring-loaded roller blind that has wound itself up too tightly, take it down, unroll it by hand to halfway, then rehang and test.

Keep wood blinds in damp areas free of mold by applying a fresh coat of linseed oil once a year.

Make a good match

When ordering new blinds, ask your supplier to match the color of the brackets to the color of the window casings rather than the color of the blind fabric. This approach ensures that the brackets will blend in unobtrusively with the surrounding wall.

Take a bath

Clean vertical blinds in the bath. Pull the blind to one side and then, holding the blades together in a bunch, unhook from the hangers. Lay stacked blades in a bathtub half-filled with cool, soapy water. Leave to soak for about 45 minutes, then drain the dirty water and refill the bath with clear rinsing water. Lift the blades out of the water and rehang to dry. Some old towels laid across the windowsill will catch drips.

Soak away mold

To remove mold from a bamboo blind, soak it for a few minutes in a solution of one part bleach to two parts water, then put it under a shower or hose to rinse. Hang the blind out to dry in a sunny spot.

Triple your chances

Measuring the width of a blind that's going to be mounted inside an old window frame can be a challenge. The best strategy is to measure the width at the top, middle and bottom of the frame and then use the narrowest measurement.

Allow for overlap

Blinds that are fixed to the surface of the window frame should be sized so that they overlap the window at the bottom and on both sides. For most windows, an overlap of 2 in. (5 cm) all around will be sufficient.

What you will need

• Venetian blind (correct width)
• Screws
• Screwdriver
• Knife or scissors

BEFORE YOU BEGIN
Consider whether or not you might add curtains in the future before deciding how to mount your blind. If the blind is mounted on the surface of the frame, you'll need to use a rod with extended brackets.

Installing a Venetian blind

1 Attach the brackets
Decide whether you want to mount the blind on the surface of the window frame or inside the frame. If you're mounting the blind inside the window frame, you can choose to attach the brackets to the side jambs or to the underside of the head jamb. Attach the brackets with screws.

headbox

2 Hang the blind
Insert the headbox into the brackets. Some models have hinged fronts that you'll need to swing open first. If your blind comes with tie-down clips and attachments for the bottom rail to prevent it from swinging and banging against the window in the breeze, then you'll need to fit these now.

TRADE TALK

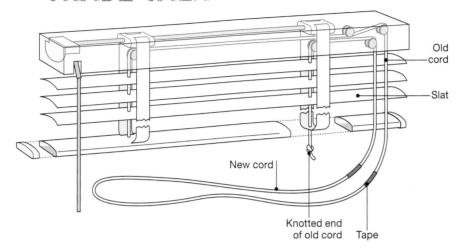

Old cord

Slat

New cord

Knotted end of old cord

Tape

▦ String it together ▲

You can replace the cord that lifts the blades of a Venetian blind up and down without even taking the blind off the wall. The trick is to use the old cord to pull the new one into place. First, remove the buckle on the cord, then clip the cord about 1 in. (2.5 cm) above the loop. Tape the ends of the new cord to the cut ends, then open the bottom of the blind and pull on the knotted ends of the old cord to draw the attached new pieces through.

(3) Trim to size

Open the blind to its full length, then remove the plugs or clips of the bottom rail to reveal the knotted ends of the pull cord. Untie the knots and remove the bottom rail. Now slide off any unwanted slats.

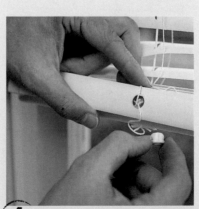

(4) Tidy up

Once you have the desired length for your blind, thread the bottom rail back on to the cord and knot the cord to secure. Trim the cord and replace any plugs or clips that were removed. Put the leftover slats into storage—they may be useful for repairs at a later date.

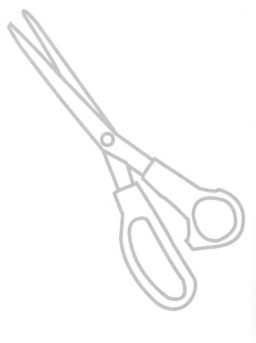

A string and pulley mechanism applies extra pressure to curtain tracks, so it's important brackets are firmly fixed.

Hanging curtains

A well-chosen, well-maintained curtain can hide an unpleasant view, give you shade and privacy, and improve the look of your room.

Weigh your options
Make sure your tracks can carry the load of your curtain. First weigh yourself, then get back on the scales with the curtains in your arms. The difference between the two weights is the weight of the curtains. Refer to the load rating printed on the packaging to select the most appropriate track.

Doing the job solo
Having an extra set of hands available when you're installing curtain rods is a help—but it's not essential. If you're working solo, use masking tape to hold the brackets in place. That will leave both your hands free for marking, drilling and screwing tasks.

Get a good grip
For a firm hold when screwing curtain track brackets to masonry, you'll need to pre-drill holes and insert wall plugs first. If you're attaching them to a wooden frame, screws alone will do. ▼

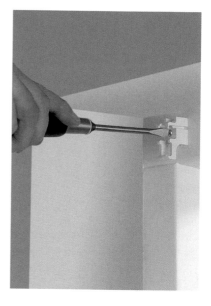

Choose your screws ▲
When attaching brackets to a metal or PVC frame, either use self-tapping screws or pre-drill and plug the holes, then attach with 1½ in. #8 screws. Some frames that appear to be made of metal or PVC are really hybrid frames, with a wood core. If it's a hybrid frame, standard screws are all you need for a firm hold. To test, drill a small hole in an inconspicuous spot: if you see sawdust, it's a hybrid frame.

Trimming the track
Wait until you've installed all the brackets, then measure the space to determine the length of track you'll need. Use a junior hacksaw to cut through the track, then lightly sand the cut ends with fine grit sandpaper. If you don't, the rough surfaces may snag the curtain fabric.

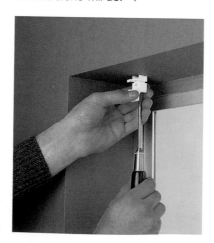

THE PROS AND CONS OF
POLES AND TRACKS

Though they serve the same purpose, curtain poles and curtain tracks couldn't be more different in style. Where poles are conspicuous and often decorative, tracks are designed to be all but invisible.

 ## Curtain poles

POLES FOR PROMINENCE

Commonly made of wood, metal or plastic, curtain poles are usually exposed to view and are often seen as decorative features in their own right, complementing a curtain. Ornamental end-stops, called finials, stop the curtain from sliding off the poles.

SHORT AND SIMPLE

Poles are most effective across a short distance such as a recess, a single window or a short, straight run of windows. Longer poles require more supporting brackets which can interfere with the running of the curtain.

HANG THEM HIGH

There is almost always a gap between the pole and the top edge of the curtain, and this gap can be an entry point for unwanted light. For that reason, poles must be set at a significant height above the window.

MANAGING ODD SHAPES

If you're fitting a curtain into a bay window, you can either use a metal curtain pole bent to the appropriate shape or ask your supplier to put together a combination of poles and angled connector joints to achieve the required shape.

MATCH THE WEIGHT

For lightweight curtains or curtains running across short distances, slim poles measuring less than 1 in. (2.5 cm) in diameter are appropriate. Heavyweight curtains and curtains running across longer distances should be hung on thicker poles.

 ## Curtain tracks

TRACKS FOR DISCRETION

Designed to blend against the wall or be concealed behind a curtain, cornice or valance, curtain tracks are meant to be discreet. They're commonly available in PVC and metal.

BENDING AROUND CORNERS

Most PVC and metal tracks can be bent to shape for installation in bay windows and other unusual window arrangements. Remember that curtains will run more smoothly over gentle bends than abrupt ones.

CHECK THE LOAD

The track must be strong enough to hold the weight of the curtain fabric. Refer to the load rating printed on the packaging of the curtain track, or ask your supplier for advice.

CORDED OR UNCORDED

Corded tracks are opened and closed by means of a cord attached to pulleys and gliders. They are particularly useful for curtains on very tall windows or for those made of heavyweight fabric, both of which can drag or jam when pulled by hand. They're also ideal when the curtain is made from a delicate fabric. The curtains on uncorded tracks are very simply pulled back by hand.

SLIDE TO FIT

Expandable tracks are a good product if you're planning to do your own installation work. As the name suggests, expandable tracks have moving parts that slide to make the track longer or shorter to match the size you require.

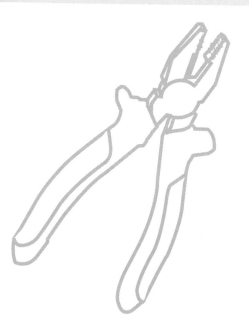

What you will need

- Long wood or metal ruler
- Hacksaw
- Pencil
- Level
- Drill with wood or masonry bit
- Wall plugs
- Screws
- Screwdriver
- Track or pole

BEFORE YOU BEGIN

When choosing a curtain pole or track, you need to take into account the size and shape of the window and the weight of the curtain.

Putting up poles and tracks

1 Measure and cut

Measure the width of the window then add your desired overlap on each side (6 to 18 in./15–45 cm on either side is common). If possible, buy a pole or track that matches the size you need. Otherwise, buy something slightly larger and cut to size with a hacksaw.

2 Determine the height

Hold the first end bracket (or its fixing plate) at the desired height above the window. For poles, it's standard to mount brackets 3 in. (7.5 cm) above the top edge of the window. For tracks, the standard distance is 1 in. (2.5 cm) above the window. Use a pencil to mark the positions of the screw holes.

▤ Rule out tab tops

Ready-made tab top curtains can't pass over pole brackets. If you want to be able to draw your curtains to either side, you'll only be able to use the two end brackets plus a single central bracket. Poles over 6½ ft. (2 m) need more than three brackets, so if you have a wide area to cover, don't choose tab top curtains.

▤ Fixing to concrete

If there is a concrete lintel above the window opening, putting up a curtain track can be a complicated matter. One solution is to mount a wooden batten onto the lintel, and attach the track to that. Drill holes in the lintel, insert wall anchors, then screw the batten into place. Now attach the brackets for the curtain track to the batten.

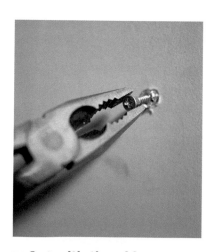

▤ Out with the old ▲

Before reinstalling an existing curtain track, check the condition of the old wall anchors. If you find frayed or split wall plugs, insert a screw just far enough to engage in the plug, then tug at the screw head with pliers: the screw should come away with the plug attached.

> The supplied screws may not be long enough—replace them if necessary

③ Position the brackets

Now do the same for a bracket at the opposite end of the window, using a level to check that it's level with the first bracket. For a pole longer than 5 ft. (1.5 m), mark the position of an extra central bracket. For a track, mark further bracket positions at 6 in. (15 cm) intervals along the wall.

④ Fix them in place

Using a power drill fitted with a masonry bit, drill a hole at each of the screw hole marks you've made. Insert a wall plug into each hole, then screw on all the bracket-fixing plates and brackets.

⑤ Hang it up

Fix a finial or end stop to one end of the pole or track. Feed on the rings or runners (there will be one for each curtain hook) then attach the other finial or end stop. Fit the pole or track onto the brackets, centering it over the window. If necessary, secure the pole or track to the brackets using the fixings provided.

▨ Disappearing acts

New curtain poles usually come with screws to match the color of the brackets. If the product you're installing doesn't come with matching screws, or if you're reusing old, mismatched components, there are a few tricks you can use to achieve that seamless look. On white brackets, dab the silver screw heads with correction fluid. On black brackets, use a black permanent marker.

▨ Make your own brackets

The brackets supporting a curtain pole above a window can be a decorative feature, but if the pole is fitted inside the window, the supporting brackets will go unseen. To save money, you can make your own end brackets with nothing more than a few pieces of wood,

a coping saw and some screws. Make the simple shaped cut-outs (as shown below) using a coping saw, then screw the brackets into place and slot in the pole. A small removeable metal plate screwed in place across the top of one bracket will prevent the rod from being accidentally dislodged. ▼

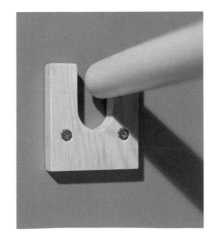

For a perfect length on new curtains, hang them in place, pin the fabric to the desired length, then take down and hem.

Walls, floors, ceilings and stairs

setting plaster or other impurities get into the next mix. A drill with a stirrer attachment will make the job much easier, but be sure that the stirrer is submerged before starting the drill.

▓ Use it or lose it
When working with any type of plaster, pace yourself by mixing only as much as you think you can apply in 20 minutes or less. It's always better to throw out plaster once it begins to set than to reconstitute it with more water. Reconstituted plaster will have a lumpy finish.

▓ Think of the shrink
Plaster commonly shrinks as it dries. The shrinkage in a shallow patch often goes unnoticed, but in a deep patch it can show up as a significant crack. To avoid the problem, patch deep holes and cracks in several shallow layers. Wait for each layer of plaster to dry thoroughly, then score the surface before adding more plaster on top.

▓ Staple a crater
Prepare a large, shallow wall crater for plaster by driving staples part way into the surface being covered. The staples act as anchor points for holding the filling compound in place until it makes a secure bond. Make sure the level of the staples is slightly below the surrounding wall surface. ▼

Wall repairs

You'll be surprised by what you can do yourself to fix cracks and dents in plaster walls using just a few simple tricks.

▓ Is this crack serious?
If a crack is large, recessed and uneven in width then you could be looking at a structural problem. Get professional help to remedy what might be wrong with the house's structure before attempting to fix the crack. On the other hand, a small crack that affects only the surface of the wall or the plaster material itself is probably superficial and can be easily repaired with filler.

▓ Keep it clean
The container in which you mix plaster, any implements used to mix it and the water itself must be absolutely clean. Wash and rinse between mixes, so that no lumps of

What you will need

- Drop cloths
- Dust mask, eye protection and work gloves
- Scraper
- Clean paintbrush
- Spray bottle with water
- Bonding agent
- Plaster
- Putty knife
- Taping knife
- Sanding block and medium-grit sandpaper

Repairing cracks in plaster

1 **Clean out the crack**
To repair a plaster crack, first move furniture out of the area and put down drop sheets. Wearing a dust mask, some form of eye protection and work gloves, rake out any loose material with a suitable scraper. Then dust out the inside of the crack with a clean paintbrush.

2 **Dampen, bond and patch**
Use a spray bottle to lightly dampen the wall with water. Wait a few minutes until the plaster absorbs the water, then apply a bonding agent to bond the new plaster to the wall. Leave to dry for 45 minutes. Mix the plaster according to the instructions on the package and fill the hole.

Repair holes in plaster

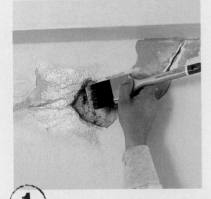

1 **Clean the damage**
To repair a hole, first remove any loose or crumbling plaster with a scraper. Dust out the inside of the hole, then use a spray bottle to lightly dampen the wall with water. Wait a few minutes until the plaster absorbs the water. Next, apply a bonding agent and leave to dry for at least 45 minutes.

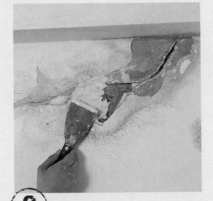

2 **Fill the hole**
Mix up some plaster according to the directions on the package. Using a putty knife, fill the hole from the center out, to a depth just below the wall surface. Before the plaster sets, score the surface with a putty knife to produce a crosshatch pattern. This will give the next layer of plaster something to hold onto. Let the plaster dry.

> Use a knife that's WIDER than the area under repair

3 **Finish the job**
Apply a second coat of plaster using a taping knife. Look closely to make sure the surface is level and that there are no indentations caused by air bubbles. When the patch is dry, sand lightly with a sanding block covered with medium-grit sandpaper.

Repairing damaged drywall

Drill HOLES AT THE CORNERS so you can get the blade in

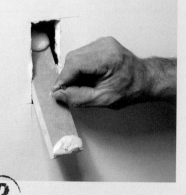

1 Make the backing
Use a narrow-bladed saw to trim the hole to a square. Saw a piece of drywall or MDF into the same shape, allowing a 1 in. (2.5 cm) overlap at top and bottom. Drill a wood screw into the drywall leaving sufficient length to form a handle.

2 Insert the backing piece
Apply adhesive to the front of the backing piece at the top and bottom edges, then guide it through the hole. Pull the piece into position against the back of the hole. Once you are sure the backing piece is stuck firmly, remove the screw.

Repairing larger holes

1 Square up the damage
Use a narrow-bladed saw to cut out a section of drywall that reaches to the edges of the studs on either side of the hole. Mark your cutting lines with a pencil and a level, and use a square to make sure corners are 90°.

2 Prepare the studs
Cut some pieces of scrap wood so that they measure longer than the height of the newly-cut opening. Fasten these battens to the inside of the studs with drywall screws. Measure and cut a drywall patch with a utility knife and straightedge. If possible, use the removed piece of drywall as a template.

3 Patch and finish

Using a putty knife, start filling the hole with setting compound. A shallow hole can be filled in one go, but a deeper hole should be filled in layers to allow for shrinkage. When the setting compound is completely dry, sand the patch so that it's flush with the surrounding drywall, then repaint.

3 Patch the hole

Position the new piece in the opening. Using drywall screws, fasten the patch to the wood battens. Apply a coat of setting compound over all seams. Apply drywall joint tape over the seams and cover with more compound. When the first coat dries apply a second that extends 6 in. (15 cm) beyond the first coat. Sand to finish.

▓ Putty knife too narrow?

If you don't already own a putty knife that is wider than the hole you're filling with plaster, consider buying a cheap plastic one to see you through the job. Alternatively, do the patching with the narrow putty knife then draw the edge of a metal ruler across the patch to make a clean finish.

▓ Match your patch

An old plaster wall or ceiling often has a distinctive texture that needs to be matched when it is patched. While the plaster patch is still damp, use a comb, sponge or stiff brush to replicate the texture. Practice your texturing technique on a piece of scrap board first.

▓ Keep it clean

For a smooth finish, clean your putty knife frequently by running it over a scrap of wood to scrape off excess compound. This prevents dried bits of plaster from getting into the fresh compound and marring the final coat.

▓ Deal with dents

If the surface of your drywall is dented but not broken, simply cover the dent with a coat of sandable setting compound and allow to set hard. Apply a finishing coat, allow to dry and sand smooth with 120-grit sandpaper.

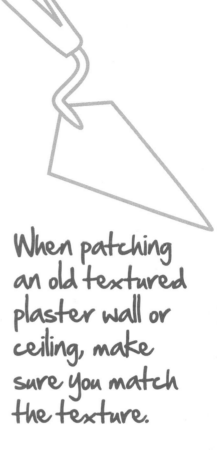

When patching an old textured plaster wall or ceiling, make sure you match the texture.

SECRETS from the EXPERTS

A **chef's hand whisk** is the best tool for mixing up plaster. Once it's at the right consistency, stop whisking, otherwise the plaster may start to dry.

Repairing damaged corners

What you will need

- Wood cleat (1 x 3 in./2.5 x 7.5 cm, and longer than the height of the area to be patched)
- Saw
- Masonry nails
- Hammer
- Cold chisel
- Paintbrush
- Ruler and level
- One-coat plaster
- Plaster trowel

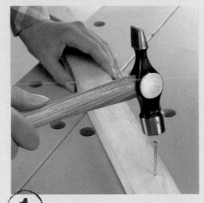

1 Make a straightedge

A homemade wood straightedge is the key to repairing damage to a corner. Cut a wood cleat so that it measures slightly longer than the height of the area to be patched, then drive in two masonry nails. Position these so they line up with the mortar between bricks, or so they will fix into the firm plaster well beyond the damaged area.

It's VITAL to keep the edges perfectly vertical

2 Fix it in place

With a cold chisel, chip back crumbling plaster to a firm surface, then brush away debris from the damaged area. Using a ruler and level to ensure a perfectly plumb position, hold the wood straightedge vertically against the damaged corner. Nail the cleat gently to the wall, leaving the nail heads protruding.

3 Patch one wall at a time

Patch the exposed wall, extending the plaster to meet the edge of the cleat. When the plaster has dried, remove the nails and gently pull away the batten. Next, nail the cleat to the other wall and plaster the remaining damaged area in the same way.

▓ Protect corners

If an external corner is prone to damage, think about reinforcing it with expanded metal angle beading before replastering. The beading is made from galvanized steel, stainless steel or PVC mesh and can be cut to the required size with tinsnips and a hacksaw. Use stainless steel or PVC beading in external walls. Penetrating rainwater can corrode galvanized steel and result in stains down the length of the corner. ▼

▓ Flatten bubbled wallpaper

To flatten a wallpaper bubble, you need to get wallpaper seam adhesive under the wallpaper. The best tool for this is a glue injector. Inject adhesive into the middle of the bubble. Using a wallpaper roller or straightedge, spread the adhesive out to the edges of the bubble, then drive any excess adhesive back toward, and out of, the needle hole. Wipe away the excess with a damp sponge. ▼

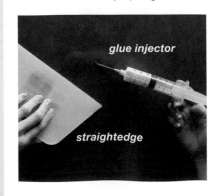

glue injector

straightedge

WATER DAMAGE—
WHAT'S THE PROBLEM?

Water damage in a house can be due to a number of causes, such as rain getting through the walls or roof, moisture being absorbed from the ground, condensation settling on cold surfaces or a mixture of these. Make sure you determine the cause of the dampness before you try to cure it, otherwise you could be using the wrong remedy altogether.

Water seepage

If you have damp patches, bubbling paint, crumbling plaster or powdery deposits on wall surfaces close to the floor, seepage is probably the culprit. Seepage usually occurs in masonry walls because of the failure or absence of a vapor barrier, although poor subfloor ventilation and bad site drainage can also be contributors.

WHAT'S THE REMEDY?

- Improve the drainage of the site. Make sure the surrounding ground slopes away from the building.
- Check that there's enough room under the floor for moisture to evaporate from the soil below and pass out through subfloor wall vents.
- Install a damp-proof course. This job is best left to the professionals.

Water patches

Water patches on walls are generally the result of outside water getting into the brickwork through gaps and cracks. If the patches are clustered around windows and doors, then it's likely that rain is getting in through gaps around the frames. If the water is below the opening, it may be because there is no drip groove below a projecting sill. Any other patches of damp are most likely caused by faults in the brickwork, including cracked pointing.

WHAT'S THE REMEDY?

- Keep external walls, including the pointing and the paint, in good condition.
- Seal the gaps around window and door frames.
- Clear out or cut drip grooves below windowsills.

Condensation

If you're not sure of the cause of a water patch on a wall, try the foil test. Dry the wall surface with a fan heater, then tape some kitchen foil tightly over the affected area. If the surface of the foil is wet after 24 hours, you have condensation. Condensation occurs when moisture-laden air builds up inside the house. Poor ventilation and over-efficient draftproofing are often to blame.

WHAT'S THE REMEDY?

- Install ventilation fans in kitchen, laundry room and bathroom so that moist air is expelled outside the house before it causes problems inside.
- If a room is windowless, install one to allow air to circulate freely.

Leaks

Faults in the roof structure, including damaged or missing shingles, poor flashing and broken or cracked gutters and downpipes, can be the cause of water damage in the house. They're usually easy to spot, being located either around the ceiling or on sections of wall that line up with the external pipes. Water patches may also be the result of leaks in pipes embedded in the wall or from poorly sealed bathrooms.

WHAT'S THE REMEDY?

- Repair a faulty roof. For advice on tracing roof leaks, see page 266.
- Deal with leaky pipes. For advice on tracing and fixing leaky pipes, see page 231.

WALL FASTENERS

Fastening things to walls is the key part of many everyday DIY jobs, from hanging shelves and curtain tracks to putting up a mirror or hanging a display cabinet. It is an easy job as long as you use the right fasteners and the correct technique. Done wrongly, the fasteners will fail, with potentially serious consequences.

Assessing the job

The first step is to discover what sort of wall is involved, because this dictates how you fasten an item to it.

- Masonry walls sound solid when tapped. Many exterior walls and internal ground-floor walls are of this type.
- Wood-framed walls and ceilings sound hollow, whether they are drywall or lath and plaster.
- Stucco walls are made from wood, stucco brick or concrete block with a surfacing of cement on their face. They are cold and somewhat rough to the touch.

Wood-frame walls and ceilings

You can make attachments to wood walls and ceilings in one of two ways.

- Locate the wall studs or the ceiling joists, and screw through the wall covering into solid wood. To do this, you need to use an electronic stud detector, or make some test drillings through the drywall or plaster.
- If the stud or joist positions do not coincide with where you want to make your attachments, drill a hole in the wall and insert a cavity-fixing device that will expand and grip the inner face of the wall. The device must be strong enough to support the load on the fastener.

Masonry walls

For fasteners in solid masonry, you have to drill a hole in the wall and insert a hollow plastic anchor that will grip a screw when one is driven into it.

- To make a secure fastener, the plug and screw must penetrate the masonry to a minimum depth of 1 in. (2.5 cm).
- On a stucco wall you need to make an allowance for the thickness of the stucco.
- For heavy-duty attachments the screw should penetrate up to 1½ in. (40 mm), so use a 2 or 2½ in. (50 or 63 mm) screw.

Pin picture hanger

 These hangers come in various sizes, with holes for as many as four pins. Choose a hanger based on the weight of the picture or mirror to be hung. Heavier items will require two hangers spaced about 10 in. (25 cm) apart.

To mount, simply place the hanger against the desired spot on the wall with the pins in position and gently tap them into the drywall. To remove, pull the pins upward with a slow twisting motion, using pliers.

Removable adhesive hook

Removable adhesive hooks come in a variety of sizes. Because they don't leave a mark when removed, they are great if you are likely to reposition anchor points or are renting.

Hard wall hook

 These fixtures are ideal for hanging lightweight items in masonry or drywall. They come with four pins already inserted and just need to be lined up and tapped into place.

Plastic toggle

These anchors are suitable for light to medium loads (up to 18 lb./8 kg) on drywall. They form a strong corrosion-free anchor point, opening out and gripping the drywall firmly.

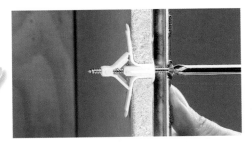

Drill a hole the same diameter as anchor. Squeeze the wings together and insert into hole. Tap in flush. When a screw is inserted and tightened the wings fully open and clamp the back of the board.

Metal toggle

When plastic anchors aren't up to the task consider a metal toggle. These smart, self-drilling fasteners are slightly trickier to install but will hold up to 45 lb. (20 kg).

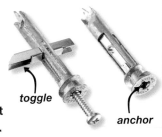

toggle

anchor

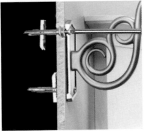

Install using a drill with a Phillips head bit, slowing as the thread engages in the drywall. Secure the screw by winding it into the anchor. As it tightens the metal toggle pops out and is drawn to the back of the drywall.

Wing bolt toggle

Wing bolt toggles are the strongest type of fixing you can use in drywall (45 lb./20 kg and over). The metal arms spread the load over a large area of the drywall.

Attach the toggle to the screw, fold up its wings and push them through the hole. Check that the wings have opened by pulling on the screw, then tighten it fully. If the fastener needs to be removed later, the wings will fall into the wall cavity.

Hollow-wall anchor

These fasteners can hold loads up to 33 lb. (15 kg) in drywall. They have four wings that grip the inner board face as the screw is tightened. Conveniently, the screw can be removed without affecting the anchor.

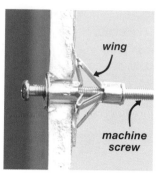

Drill a hole the same diameter as the anchor. Insert the anchor and tighten the machine screw. This will collapse the sleeve against the inside wall. Use the head of the machine screw as a hanging point or use it to secure an object such as a shelf bracket.

Screw-in anchor

Screw-in metal or plastic anchors are ideal for fixing fairly light (up to 22 lb./10 kg) decorative items and small shelves and directly to drywall. These anchors have coarse threads that bite into the core of the board.

Install the anchor using a drill with a driver bit, slowing down as the large thread engages with the wall. Secure the screw leaving enough space behind the screw head to form a hanging point.

Plastic anchor

Use plastic anchors for light loads on plaster or masonry. They come in a range of lengths and gauges. As a general rule, the heavier the item you are fixing, the larger and deeper the anchor.

Measure the length of the anchor you intend to use, and wrap a piece of tape round the drill bit to act as a depth mark. Position it at a distance of 1/4 in. (5 mm) plus the anchor length from the tip of the bit.

Drill until the tape reaches the wall surface. Insert the plastic anchor to check that it will fit. Pass the screw through whatever you are fastener and then drive it into the anchor.

Plastic nail sleeve

Use frame fasteners for heavy-duty jobs such as attaching a new door or window frame to masonry. The plain sleeve of the fastener passes through the side of the frame and into the wall behind it.

Drill a hole through the wood frame and masonry using drill bits of the same size. Countersink the frame to suit the head of the fastener. Push the fastener in fully, then tighten the screw to expand the fastener and secure the frame.

Wood trims

Casings, baseboards and other pieces of decorative wood trim are the details that can lift a room from the mundane to the magnificent.

▥ Pull nails without dents

With a little care you can remove a nail from a piece of wood trim without leaving a dent. First grab the nail head with locking pliers, then slide a piece of plastic laminate between the jaws of the pliers and the wood surface below before gradually easing the nail out of the wood. The locking pliers put a super-strong grip on the nail head, and the laminate protects the wood from the metal jaws. ▼

▥ Fix loose woodwork

Nails don't draw pieces together like screws do, and it's not unusual to see nail-fixed wood trim hanging loose. Often the best way to tackle these trouble spots is to tighten them up with a trim screw. Since these have a thin shank and a tiny head, you can easily hide them with putty.

▥ Spare the hammerblow

When nailing any wood that will remain exposed, such as base-boards, casings and picture rails, never hammer the nail in all the way.

Leave the last ⅛ in. (3 mm) exposed and finish nailing with a nail punch to avoid marking the wood. If the wood is to be painted then the dent can be filled, but dents on stained wood can be very unsightly.

▥ Repair split trim

When attaching trim, always pre-drill holes for your nails. If you don't, the wood is very likely to split, especially if the nail has gone in too close to one of the ends. If the split occurs, leave the nail in place while you get some wood glue into the gap (a corner of the sandpaper can help you get the glue into the groove). Gently ease the nail out and fit a spring clamp across the trim, then wipe away excess glue with a damp cloth. Leave to dry, preferably overnight. ▼

Wipe away any excess glue with a damp cloth

spring clamp

It's always a smart move to paint or stain trim before installing it.

Quick Fix

MAKING A PICTURE RAIL PICTURE PERFECT

When installing a picture rail, use the ceiling line as a guide, rather than the floor. Floors are often uneven and if you take your measurements from the floor up you may set your picture rail at a slope. Instead take your measurements down from the cornice or ceiling.

Very light or very dark tiles will show up every speck and smear. Solid midrange colors provide the best camouflage.

Tiled surfaces

Learn how to look after tiled walls and how to make a few simple repairs, and they will serve you well for years to come.

Planning for the future

Buy extra tiles when you start a project, and carefully wrap them to guard against breakage. Mark the package with the brand, color name, date, source and the room where the tiles are installed. Also set aside some grout of the same type and color, and store it in a tightly sealed container near the tiles. The tiles and grout will be invaluable for the inevitable future repairs.

Stop drill bits skating ▲

Attach fixings to tiled walls by drilling into the grout lines wherever possible. If you have to drill through the face of the tile, use a sharp glass/tile bit or masonry drill bit so the glaze doesn't chip. Stop the bit

What you will need

- Grout saw or hacksaw blade
- Drill and masonry bit
- Hammer and cold chisel
- Putty knife
- Dustpan and broom
- Replacement tile
- Tile adhesive and notched trowel
- Plastic tile spacers
- Rubber mallet and level
- Grout
- Sponge squeegee
- Large sponge
- Penetrating grout sealer

Replacing a ceramic tile

Work the grout saw with a back and forth action

1 Clear out the grout

Use a grout saw to remove the old grout from around the damaged tile. Use two blades for floor joints and a single blade (or broken hacksaw blade) on wall joints. Take care not to damage the surface of the surrounding tiles.

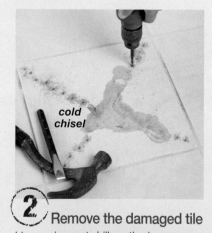

cold chisel

2 Remove the damaged tile

Use an impact drill on the hammer setting and a masonry bit to drill through the tile (but no further) in an X shape. Use a cold chisel to remove the tile from the center. Scrape the underlay with a putty knife. Sweep up all the tile pieces, making sure not to touch any sharp shards with your bare hands.

from skating on the glaze by sticking masking tape on the tile where you want to drill—this will give the bit an initial "bite." Start slowly if your drill has variable speed control.

Test for tile-friendly walls

You can tile directly over a surface painted with an oil-based paint, but not over one painted with an acrylic-based paint. Test the surface by dabbing some denatured alcohol onto a rag and rubbing a small area of the wall. If the color comes off, it's an acrylic-based paint and cannot be tiled over. If it doesn't come off, then it's an oil-based paint and you're free to proceed, though you'll need to rough up the surface by sanding it lightly before you begin laying the tiles.

KEEP TILED SURFACES LOOKING GOOD

★ Clean between the tiles

A toothbrush is the ideal tool for cleaning grout. Dirt and grease can be scrubbed away with a solution of liquid detergent in warm water or a non-abrasive cream cleaner. Don't use abrasive cleaners on tiled surfaces—they may dull the glaze and "pit" the grout.

★ Regrout for a fresh start

To regrout a large area, begin by scraping out the old grout. Start at the top of the wall, taking care not to chip the edges of the tiles as you go. Use a small, stiff-bristled brush or a vacuum cleaner with a narrow nozzle attachment to remove all the debris from joints before regrouting.

★ Scrape off messy grout

Dried-on grout can be removed from tiles with a glass scraper. If you squeeze a little dishwashing soap along the edge of the blade, it will glide over the tile without scratching the glaze.

★ Whiten tired grout

Revive discolored grout by painting it with a proprietary grout whitener, applied with an artist's brush. But be warned—it's a tedious job.

★ Keep tiles sparkling

A solution of liquid household ammonia in hot water will revive tiled surfaces discolored by dirt and grease. Rinse the tiles with clean water then dry them off with a chamois leather.

③ Apply the adhesive

Test fit a tile to ensure that the area has been completely cleared. For floor tiles, apply the adhesive to the floor using a notched trowel. If you are replacing a single wall tile, it is better to spread adhesive on the back of the tile.

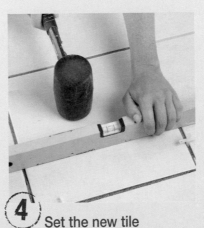

④ Set the new tile

Place the tile and apply even pressure with a slight twisting motion. Use tile spacers to ensure even gaps. Check that the new tile is level. A rubber mallet will help if it is at a slight angle or is sitting slightly proud of the bordering tiles.

⑤ Grout the joint

Let the adhesive set for 12 hours. Blend matching grout and use a sponge squeegee to spread it over the repaired area, forcing it into the joints. Leave the grout to set slightly, then use a damp sponge to remove the excess. Wait at least 24 hours before touching the new work. Seal the grout after a few weeks.

Floors

The best floors not only look good—they're also free of squeaks, gaps and other flaws.

▓ Silence the squeaks

Those exasperating floor squeaks can be caused by a number of things, some more easily fixed than others. To stop a squeak caused by the movement of the flooring against a joist, simply tap a small wood shim or wedge between the joist and the floorboard in the vicinity of the squeak. Don't force it in too far or you'll cause more problems than you solve. Dabbing a little construction adhesive on the shim before installation will help it stay in place. ▼

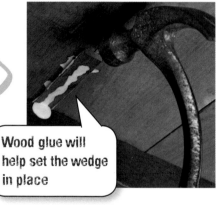

Wood glue will help set the wedge in place

▓ Stop the rub

The best fix for a squeaky floor is to eliminate the most common culprit: the rubbing of wood against wood. If that's not possible, try lubricating the squeak. Any number of lubricants have been known to work, including talcum powder, chalk dust, furniture wax, lubricant spray, graphite and liquid soap. Sometimes linseed oil or teak oil dribbled into the cracks between floorboards will expand the wood enough to tighten the flooring.

What you will need

- Electric drill
- Wood chisels
- Claw hammer
- Circular saw
- Prybar
- Nails
- Nail punch

BEFORE YOU BEGIN

Take a piece of the old flooring to a recycling yard or wood supplier and select replacement boards with a similar color and grain. Identify the finish: you'll need to use the same product for a seamless repair.

▓ Brace noisy boards

Some squeaks are caused when neighboring floorboards rub together. One way to stop that is to screw a wood cleat to the underside of the boards. Use a 2 x 2 in. (5 x 5 cm) cleat and coat it with construction adhesive before screwing it. ▼

Be sure not to drive screws right through the floor

Remove and replace a floorboard

This is called a "PLUNGE CUT." Take extra care!

1 Cut the new joints

It's preferable to replace an entire board, but if that's not possible take out a section long enough to cross three joists. Draw a line for each cut, then drill a series of overlapping holes just inside the line at either end. Complete the cut using a sharp chisel to trim the full edge of the butt joint.

2 Chisel out the old board

Use a circular saw to make two parallel cuts 1¼ in. (3 cm) from each side. Use care when performing this operation: lower the blade slowly and don't position any body part in front of or behind the blade. Lift out the center, use a hammer to remove nails, then use a prybar to extract the tongue and groove parts.

3 Ease in the new board

The trick to fitting the new board is to chisel off the lower lip on the board's groove side. With the lower lip gone, it's a simple matter of easing the tongue of the new board into the groove of the neighboring board, then tapping the board into place and nailing it.

▓ Block out the squeaks

Wood blocking is sometimes used between floor joists to help them withstand heavy loads without twisting. Over the years that blocking can work loose, resulting in annoying squeaks. The solution is simple: just get into the subfloor space and reattach the blocking.

▓ Bend back a bowed board

Before you go to the effort of replacing a warped floorboard, try this solution. Strip the finish from the offending board and cover it with a damp cloth for a couple of days. If the moisture temporarily solves the problem, secure the board to the joists with countersunk wood screws before it dries and springs back.

▓ Wedge the gap

You can fill a wide gap between boards with a long, thin length of square-edge molding. Plane the molding to a slight wedge shape, then apply a little adhesive to the sides before tapping it into the gap. After the adhesive has set, plane the molding down to floor level. ▶

Stain the wedge if it doesn't match the boards

Talcum powder or chalk dust can temporarily silence a squeaking floor.

Always keep the machine moving while the belt is in contact with the floor.

Sanding floors

All you need to restore a wood floor is rented equipment. Go at a slow and steady pace, and you'll be rewarded with a flawless finish.

▓ Respect an old floor

To avoid damaging an old floor, check the depth of the boards before sanding. Pull up a threshold from a doorway to reveal the edges of the existing boards and see how much wood remains above the tongue of the hardwood strip. If it's less than ⅛ in. (3 mm), sanding will cause cracks.

▓ Remove the old finish ▲

You'll need a coarse grade of sandpaper to remove old finish; a 40-grit sandpaper is standard. Start with a belt sander. Get as close as possible to the edges of the room, then finish off with an edge sander. Don't be surprised if you have to repeat the process several times.

▓ Sand to a smooth surface

You'll need an 80-grit sanding belt to sand the surface of a newly-laid wood floor, or an existing floor that's already been sanded to remove the old top surface. Get as close as possible to the edges of the room, then use an edge sander to finish. Finally, swap over to an even finer 100-grit sanding belt and repeat the process. ▼

Use a 100-grit sanding screen for the buff stage

▦ Buff the floor ▲

Go over the floor using a buffer with a 100-grit sanding screen. For areas the buffer can't reach, sand by hand using a handheld orbital sander with 100-grit paper. Scrape away any finish the sander misses with a carbide scraper.

▦ Spare the belts

Carpet tacks, staples and projecting floorboard nails will shred the expensive sanding sheets a floor sander uses. Before you start sanding, inspect the floorboards carefully. Pull out any tacks you find, and punch nail heads well below the surface of the boards. ▼

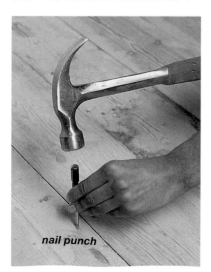

nail punch

▦ Dust busting

Sanding floorboards creates a great deal of fine dust, despite the collection bag on the machine, so take down curtains and remove lampshades, pictures and other fixtures before you start. Tape plastic sheeting over heating and air-conditioning vents. Plastic sheets pinned over door frames will help to keep the rest of the house dust free.

▦ Conceal old nail holes

Before the final stage of machine sanding, top up all the old nail holes with a suitably colored wood filler. Wait for the filler to dry and then carry on sanding the boards.

▦ Gouge-free sanding

Don't let a belt sander come to a halt while resting on the surface of the floor; if you do, it's likely to gouge the boards. Instead, tilt the belt sander at the beginning and end of each line of sanding, gently lowering it as you push it across the floor. It's a good idea to practice the technique using a very fine grade of sandpaper before you start.

▦ Mark your progress

During each sanding and buffing stage, carry a pencil in your back pocket and circle around the areas that need more concentrated work. Deal with them before the next full round of sanding.

▦ When the dust settles

Once the dust caused by sanding has settled, and immediately before varnishing the floor, clean the entire room with a vacuum cleaner. Then get rid of any remaining dust by wiping the floor with a lint-free cloth dipped in mineral spirits.

▦ Coping with tight spaces

In small rooms where a drum sander is unwieldy to maneuver, the edging sander may be the only machine you need. If you are thinking of doing an entire floor that way, consider renting kneepads because you'll be working on your knees all the time. ▼

No noise, no dust—no worries!

Wear safety glasses, dust mask and earplugs when operating sanders.

Empty the dust bag frequently. If the dust you're collecting gets hot, it can catch fire spontaneously.

Look after your hands. Wear heavy work gloves and take frequent breaks—don't wait until your hands start tingling.

SAFETY FIRST

Varnishing floors

A well-applied topcoat of clear finish will protect your wood floorboards and keep them looking beautiful for years to come.

TYPES OF **FLOOR VARNISH**

★ **Solvent-based polyurethane**
These varnishes produce a durable topcoat, but are slow-drying, have to be cleaned up with mineral spirits and are likely to yellow with age.

★ **Water-based polyurethane**
These are easy to work with, as they're quick-drying and clean up in water. They are also less likely to discolor.

★ **Catalyzed lacquers**
These are formulated with a chemical catalyst that makes them extremely quick-drying. They're more often used by professionals than homeowners.

★ **Oil finish**
Oils penetrate wood for a natural matte finish. Buy ready-made or mix your own using 1 part of linseed oil to 8 parts mineral spirits.

SECRETS from the EXPERTS
Don't leave **windows open** in the room you have just varnished, or you may find your work peppered with a layer of dust and insects.

▦ Keep a tight focus

It pays to be methodical when applying the floor finish. Concentrate on two or three boards at a time. Work with the grain and pass the applicator pad smoothly from one end of the boards to the other. Keep spreading the finish until you get to the other end of the room.

What you will need

- Screwdriver
- Pliers
- New threshold
- Metal snips or hacksaw
- Nails or glue
- Knee kicker
- Stiff putty knife
- Rubber mallet

BEFORE YOU BEGIN

This repair is much easier if you remove the door first. You can do it with the door in place, but it'll take a little longer and you'll risk scratching the door.

Reattach loose carpet

Don't scratch the hard flooring— work from the carpeted side

(1) Bend back the lip
If carpet has pulled away from a metal threshold, act quickly to fix the problem before the carpet edge begins to fray. Using a screwdriver, pry up the lip of the threshold. Then use pliers to ease the carpet away from the teeth inside the threshold. Take care not to snag the carpet as you work.

(2) Take out the strip
Pull the nails and discard the old threshold. Measure the opening and cut a new threshold to match. If the carpet edge is in good shape, you can place the new threshold exactly where the old one was. If the edge is badly frayed, you'll need to trim off the damage. Then nail the new threshold further in to compensate for the width you trimmed off.

Use wool pads

They cost a bit more, but lambs wool pads are the best applicators for floor finish. They tend to produce fewer air bubbles, giving you a better chance at a flawless finish.

Think ahead

Don't get caught in the corner. Plan your escape route before you begin applying the finish—start at the far side of the room and work back toward a doorway.

Keep moving

Work quickly so that the finish on the floorboard you've just coated is still wet when you're applying finish to the board beside it. If wet finish overlaps a section of floor that's already dry, streaks will show on the finished floor.

(3) Ease in the carpet

Starting at one side, nudge the carpet toward the new threshold with a rented knee kicker and force the carpet into the threshold's teeth with a stiff putty knife. To finish the job, drive down the lip of the threshold, tapping gradually with a rubber mallet back and forth along its entire length. On the final pass, pound hard to fix the carpet in place.

Carpet care

Soft, carpeted floors make rooms warm, comfortable and quiet—but they need some attention from you in return.

Buff the burn

You can sometimes remove a light burn or scorch mark in carpet simply by rubbing the affected area with plain steel wool. The light buffing will lift away any of the scorched fibers.

DIY carpet cleaning

Many supermarkets and rental companies rent equipment for cleaning carpets. These are efficient and easy to use. Reserve the carpet cleaner in advance. Most companies rent the machines by the day, so if you get the cleaner first thing in the morning, you can clean all your carpets for the price of a day's rental. Read the instructions carefully. Before filling the unit make sure the switches are off and the hoses on the back are connected.

Abolish carpet shock

Keep your carpet static-free with a mixture of 1 part fabric softener and 5 parts water. Lightly spray the solution on the carpet and let it dry undisturbed overnight. The effect should last for several weeks.

Restore dented carpet

Depressions made by heavy furniture can spoil the look of a carpet. To lift them, lay a wet, wrung-out towel over the "dent" and press with a hot iron for about a minute. The steam will release the crushed fibers and make them pliable again. Remove the iron, lift the towel and hand fluff the area to remove the depression. ▼

Don't let the iron touch the carpet—it might burn

What you will need

- Phillips head screwdriver
- Carpet knife or utility knife
- Carpet offcut
- One-sided carpet tape
- Scissors
- Carpet tractor or fork

Patch damaged carpet

BEFORE YOU BEGIN

If you don't have an offcut, steal a patch of carpet from inside a closet.

> This repair works best with "plush" carpets with no pattern

① Mark the cuts

First, use a Phillips head screwdriver to mark out a squared-up section of carpet around the damaged area, parting the carpet fibers as you go. These partings will let you make cuts in the carpet backing without tearing the fibers.

② Remove the damage

Ease a carpet knife or utility knife into the parting and cut through the carpet backing. Make the cuts as straight as you can and avoid cutting through to the pad below. Use the cutout as a template to prepare a replacement patch.

③ Test-fit the tape

Use carpet tape to hold the new patch in place. Cut pieces of tape and, without removing the backing, arrange them so that they will sit partly under the new plug and partly under the surrounding carpet without overlapping.

④ Plug the hole

Peel off the tape's backing, pull back the carpet and ease the tape into position. Set the new plug tightly against one side of the hole, then lower the other edges into place. For a seamless finish, mesh fibers together with a carpet tractor or fork.

▦ Rescue wet carpet

Once carpet becomes wet, you must dry the carpet and replace the soggy carpet pad immediately. Grab the corner nearest the wet patch with a pair of pliers and pull the carpet off the tack strip until you can fold back the wet section. Remove the wet pad, then roll back the carpet so you can fan-dry it flat for a few days. When the carpet is dry, glue or staple new pad to the floor. Reattach the carpet to the tack strip using a rented knee kicker. ▼

▦ Fix snagged carpet

To fix a running snag in a loop-pile carpet, count the curls in the pulled yarn and cut it so that you have the right amount to refill the run. You'll notice little spots of the original adhesive still clinging to the yarn (called "scabs"). Squeeze a bead of carpet glue into the run. Then use a nail punch to press each scab into the carpet backing, pushing until the reset loop is at the right height. ▼

> Keep the glue contained with masking tape

RIP UP THE CARPET—
FIX UP THE FLOOR

Installing new carpet isn't a job for the average home handyperson: it's a time-consuming task that requires a lot of specialist tools, and if you do make a mistake you could end up ruining an expensive piece of carpet. However, you can help your professional carpet layer, and save money too, by pulling up the old carpet yourself.

Ready the room

If you strip the room yourself instead of paying your carpet layer to do it, you could make a big saving.

- First, pull up the carpet, cutting it into strips with a carpet knife as you go to make it easier to handle. Take care not to damage the floorboards underneath. Next, rip up the pad—it's a thin, easily torn material and shouldn't cause you much trouble. Finally, get down on your hands and knees and work your way around the room, using needlenosed pliers or a sturdy screwdriver to pry out all the old nails and staples.

Replace the rot

If there's rot in the wood floor, it will have to be removed before the new carpet is laid. You can save a lot of money by doing this yourself.

- Rotten subflooring is common near exterior doors, especially patio doors. Mark out a section around the rot, sizing it so that it runs along the joists on either side of the affected area. The new patch will have to rest on those joists. Set the depth of the circular saw to match the depth of the floor and cut out the section. Remove the rotten section of floor and set the new patch in place, attaching it to the joists with screws. (For detailed instructions, refer to pages 74–5.) To prevent additional damage, stop the water source.

Silence the squeaks

With the wood floor exposed, you'll be able to do some quick repairs.

- The simplest way to get rid of squeaks is to fasten the floorboards to the floor joists with screws (see page 74). Existing nails or screws will tell you where the joists lie. Walk around the room and mark the squeaky spots, then go back and drive screws into the joists nearest each squeak.

Stop the smell

If there have been pets in the house, it's possible that pet urine stains have seeped through the carpet and the pad to the floor below.

- To stop the stench, wet the area with a mixture of equal parts bleach and water. After five minutes, wipe up the bleach and let the floor dry completely. Once dry, seal the stained area with a stain-blocking primer.

Hide the cables

Keep phone lines, speaker wire and coaxial cables out of the way by installing them before the new carpet goes in.

- Run them alongside the inside of the tack strip, securing with insulated staples. Make sure the plastic sheathing of the cabling isn't punctured. Run the cabling around the perimeter of the room, but not across doorways or other pathways where foot traffic will damage it. Don't use this technique to hide extension cords or electrical wiring.

Vinyl flooring

If you're looking for an affordable floor covering, it's hard to ignore vinyl sheet and tiles. And best of all, it's something you can install yourself.

Think thin

If you've never installed sheet vinyl before, choose one of the thinner products—they're easier to handle than the bulkier ones and usually less expensive. If you prefer a thicker, higher-quality vinyl, consider hiring a professional to install it.

Make a clean start

Before laying new vinyl, make sure the existing floor is free from dirt, polish, paint spills and bits of plaster. Any imperfections remaining on the floor can cause the vinyl to deteriorate from the underside.

Relax and unroll

Sheet vinyl comes in rolls, but it needs to be flattened out before it's installed. Unroll the vinyl and let it straighten out before you begin. If you have space, do it inside, or spread it on the front lawn or driveway and let the warm sunlight soften the material.

Get settled

After the vinyl flooring has relaxed, roll it out in the room where it will be installed and let it sit for at least an hour. This will give the vinyl time to adjust to the room's temperature.

Hammertime

To secure a loose vinyl tile, apply adhesive beneath the edges, then drive small nails into each corner and midway along each seam. Conceal the nail by filling the depressions with sealant in a matching color.

Replace a vinyl tile

Soften the damaged tile and its adhesive by warming it. You can do this with a hair dryer, or by laying down a towel and applying heat with an iron. Starting at a corner, use a stiff-bladed scraper to pry up the tile. Scrape off any remaining adhesive, then use a notched applicator to apply a fresh coat. Warm the new tile, then set it in place. Tap with a mallet and wood block to secure and wipe off excess adhesive with a damp cloth. Cover the tile with a board and heavy weight and leave to cure for 24 hours. ▶

Replacing a section

Use a straightedge and a sharp utility knife to cut out the damaged section. Cut down the center of any simulated grout lines. Use the section as a pattern to cut the replacement piece from leftover scrap or from behind the refrigerator. Test-fit the patch, apply adhesive, set the patch, roll flat and seal the seams.

What you will need

- Utility knife
- Scrap of vinyl flooring
- Adhesive tape
- Straightedge
- Stiff-bladed scraper
- V-notch trowel
- Flooring adhesive
- Rolling pin and damp cloth**
- Heavy weight

BEFORE YOU BEGIN
If you don't have an original offcut, buy a matching piece or steal a patch from inside the pantry or under an appliance.

Soften stubborn adhesive with mineral spirits

Patch vinyl flooring

Heat the damaged layer with a hair dryer if it's difficult to lift

Use a stiff-bladed scraper

1 Cover and cut
Cut out an oversized patch and place over the damaged area. Align the pattern, tape it in place, then use a utility knife and straightedge to cut through both the patch and the flooring beneath.

2 Scrape and paste
Remove the top (new) piece of vinyl and set it aside. Peel up the damaged flooring. Scrape any remains of the old adhesive from the underlayment with a stiff-bladed scraper. Use a small V-notch trowel to apply adhesive to the floor.

3 In with the new
Position the patch and press, starting at the center and working toward the edges. Roll firmly with a rolling pin, wipe away excess adhesive with a damp cloth and leave to dry under a heavy weight for 24 hours.

Ceilings

Working above your head can be a pain in the neck, but it's worth the effort for a perfect ceiling.

▦ Repair from above
If you have to cut into a drywall ceiling, do it from the attic if possible. You'll keep the dust out of your face, but more importantly, you'll eliminate the risk of cutting through unseen wires. Place a box on the floor below to collect the debris.

▦ Get a handle on it
If you must cut into a drywall ceiling from below, start by switching off the power at the circuit breaker. Next, twist a corkscrew into the center of the waste area. This becomes a handle. You can use a narrow-bladed saw to make your cuts, but for smooth, easy-to-patch edges, cut with a utility knife.

▦ Patch a ceiling hole
Holes in the ceiling are unsightly and a potential hazard. To patch a medium-sized hole, first cut out a squared-up section around the damage, then cut out a replacement patch that's just slightly smaller than the section you've removed. Attach a wood cleat to the back of the patch so that it extends beyond the edges for about 3 in. (7.5 cm) on either side. Tilt and drop the patch into position and screw the cleat to the ceiling. Finish the joints with tape and joint compound. For a large hole, trim back the squared-up section to the center of the ceiling joists on either side and secure the patch to the joists. ▶

▦ Repairs around ceiling roses and light fixtures
Turn off the electrical circuit as a precaution when dealing with light fixtures. Repairs to the edge of a ceiling rose generally do not carry any risk of electric shock. For small, difficult-to-reach holes and breaks in the plaster, use a small amount of expanding foam filler. Squirt some filler into the space. Allow it to harden and then cut away the excess with a sharp knife.

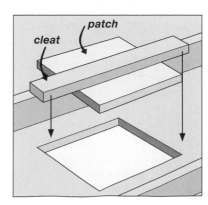

patch

cleat

BEFORE YOU BEGIN

Decide if you want to use adhesive or nails—or both—to snugly position your crown molding. If you choose nails, using a nail gun greatly facilitates the job.

Install crown molding

> Always begin at an internal corner

1 Make the cuts

Place a full length of molding in the miter box so that the ceiling edge sits in the bottom of the box and the wall edge sits on the far wall of the box. Cut the first length of molding at a 45° angle to fit on the left-hand wall of an internal corner. The molding for the right-hand wall will be cut at a 45° angle in the opposite direction.

2 Paste in place

Use a taping knife to apply the adhesive along all the edges of the molding, then firmly press the molding into the wall and ceiling junction. Remove excess adhesive with your taping knife. Fill any gaps and smooth over with a wet brush or sponge. After you've installed all the moldings, go back and give all the mitered joints a second coat of adhesive.

It helps to have someone stand on the step while you drive a screw from the tread into the riser.

Stairs

Take some simple steps toward a sturdy staircase.

▓ Make strong connections

Staircases are complex structures. Do what you can to make the connections between individual elements as strong as possible. A pair of nails, placed 1 in. (2.5 cm) apart and angled toward each other, will make a stronger hold than a single nail. For an even tighter grip, drill pilot holes slightly smaller than the nails you're going to use. Fill the nail or screw holes with wood putty, then sand lightly.

▓ Wedge from below

To silence squeaky stair treads, try getting underneath the staircase and tapping wood wedges into the joints until they are just snug. You may want to coat the wedges with wood glue. ▼

Bracket the racket

You can also quieten a creaky stair tread with L-shaped metal shelf brackets. Install two brackets, positioning them underneath the tread and behind the riser. Space them so that they are each about a third of the way in from the stringers.

Fasten loose balusters

As a house settles, handrails and balusters that once sat firm can become loose. Tighten them by drilling a hole at an angle through each baluster and up into the handrail and using a screw to lock them into place.

Wedge the gap

A very loose baluster can be tightened with a small wood wedge or shim. Using a block and a mallet, tap the shim into the gap between the baluster and the rail. ▼

Renew stair carpet

Carpets wear most heavily along the nosings of the treads. Instead of replacing a worn carpet, simply take it up, and slide it along the length of the stairway so the bare spots are less conspicuous. A good carpet installation will include the extra length.

Renewing a newel post ▲

To tighten up a loose newel post, attach small angle brackets on either side of the base, and screw in to the sides of the staircase. If you want to make the repair less conspicuous, chisel out a ⅛ in. (3 mm) recess for each bracket. Once the brackets are attached, cover them with wood filler, then sand and finish with paint or stain as necessary.

TRADE TALK

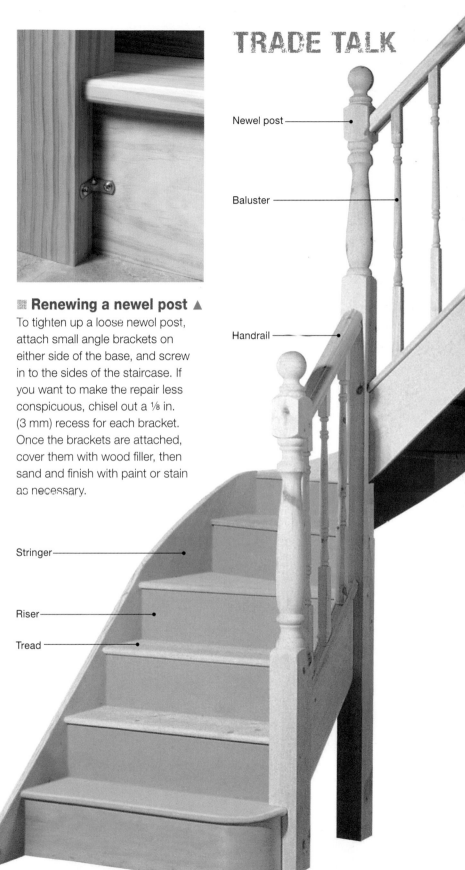

Newel post

Baluster

Handrail

Stringer

Riser

Tread

Around the home

Kitchen

A good kitchen is well equipped and safe, as well as a great place to be—and designed so that it is easy to keep that way.

▣ Ensure countertop edges are child friendly ◄

Toddlers emerging from under tables and benches often bump their heads as they stand up. Cushion the underside corners with glued-on erasers, or the entire edge with strips of foam. Hold erasers or foam in place with a C-clamp until the adhesive dries.

▣ Design for easy use

When deciding on the layout of your kitchen, try to position the main food preparation area, the stove and the refrigerator in a triangle, spaced equally apart. This "working triangle" formation makes your kitchen easy and efficient to use.

▣ Scraps to soil

Composting kitchen scraps provides you with excellent organic material for your garden. Select a compost container with a tight-fitting lid (a coffee can is ideal) and get into the habit of emptying your container into the compost pile each day.

When using a utility knife, make sure you use the appropriate blade for the material you are cutting.

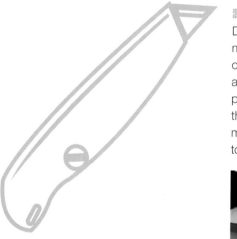

▣ Make a patch

Don't put up with a burn or other major blemish in a plastic-laminate countertop. Cut away the damaged area and create a marble or wood patch to insert in its place. Secure the patch with mitered strips of molding and remove it from time to time for cleaning. ▼

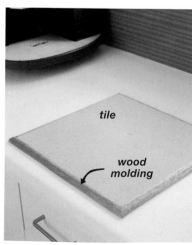

tile

wood molding

What you will need

- Utility knife
- Contact adhesive
- New laminate
- Craft sticks
- Roller

BEFORE YOU BEGIN
Save on new laminate by applying fresh adhesive to the existing laminate as soon as you notice peeling or bubbling.

Repair peeling or bubbling laminate

If needed, soften the adhesive with a hairdryer or iron on low heat

1 Pull back laminate

Pull back the peeling laminate gently and gradually, slicing the adhesive with a utility knife as you go. If you pull too hard or too quickly, the laminate may snap. To reach an area where there is bubbling, start pulling back the laminate at the nearest edge or joint.

2 Apply new adhesive

Clean off the old adhesive with the utility knife. Apply new adhesive to the underside of the laminate and the corresponding area of the countertop. Keep the surfaces separated with a craft stick until they are ready to stick together. Check adhesive instructions for guidance.

3 Join the surfaces

Press the surfaces together firmly, working carefully from the center out to the edge and covering every part. Use your fingertips first, then the heel of your hand or the side of your fist. Remove any air bubbles by applying a clean dry roller firmly, especially along edges and joints.

BEFORE YOU BEGIN

Most kitchen drawers slide in and out on plastic or metal runners with built-in rollers. You can replace runners that are rough or sticky or have broken rollers.

Keep kitchen drawers on track

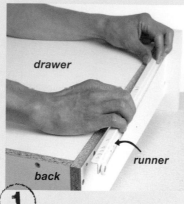

drawer

runner

back

(1) Measure the runners

Remove the drawer from the cabinet, remove the existing runners with a screwdriver and measure the length to buy new ones. If the existing runners are shorter than the drawer, buy new ones that reach the full length.

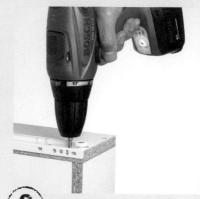

(2) Attach the runners

Install the runners on the sides of the drawer at the base. Make sure they are butted against the front with the rollers at the rear, then secure with the screws provided. If the existing holes don't align, drill pilot holes through the runners.

If the screws that come with the new handles are too long, cut them to the required length.

▓ A carousel saves space

Conventional drawers are not always the best storage solution, depending on the layout of your kitchen. If there are two base units fitted around a corner, it may be better to install 180° or 270° revolving shelves, known as lazy Susans or carousels. The shelves or wire trays glide around a central pivot, allowing you to reach whatever is stored in them without having to ransack dark corners.

▓ Install new door handles

Update kitchen cabinets with new door handles. Slimline pull handles look good and don't come loose as readily as knobs. To install, drill an extra hole in line with the existing one. If the machine screws that come with the new handles are too long, measure the door's thickness plus ⅛ in. (3 mm), clamp the screw in a vice, and cut it to the required length using a hacksaw. ▼

Don't over-tighten the screws

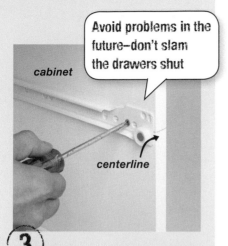

cabinet

Avoid problems in the future–don't slam the drawers shut

centerline

(3) Position cabinet runners

Align cabinet runners with drawer runners, marking the centerline with a pencil. Set them back so the drawer closes flush, with the rollers at the front. Secure with screws provided. If the existing holes don't align, drill pilot holes through the runners.

Light the way

In a tall, deep cupboard, a door-operated switch is the ultimate convenience. The light comes on automatically when the door is opened. Best of all, when your hands are full, the closing door hits the button and automatically switches off the light.

Installing and adjusting cabinet doors

When fitting cabinet doors, avoid future problems in alignment by ensuring the top and base are level and leaving a small gap between the door and the end panel. If the cabinet is under a counter, leave a ⅛ in. (3 mm) gap between the top of the door and the countertop. Consider installing concealed cabinet hinges—these allow you to realign the door more easily than is possible with other hinges.

TRADE TALK

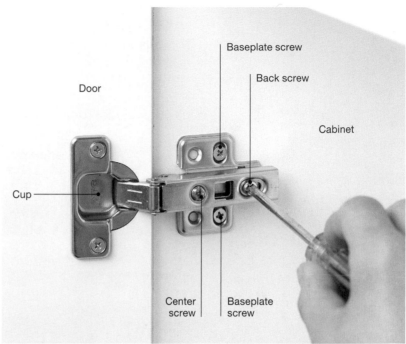

Door

Cup

Baseplate screw

Back screw

Cabinet

Center screw

Baseplate screw

Easy-adjust hinges

Concealed cabinet or "cup" hinges look complex, but they're actually the simplest hinges around. Although designs vary, most allow for three-directional adjustment just by turning screws. Baseplate screws let you move the entire door up or down. The back screw lets you move the hinged edge of the door closer to or further from the cabinet. The center screw lets you move the door sideways to adjust the spacing between a pair of doors.

SECRETS
from the EXPERTS

There is often a **button behind the back screw** to release the hinge from the baseplate.

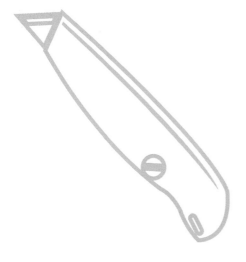

What you will need

- Iron-on melamine edging
- Iron
- Small roller
- Fine square-edged file
- Medium-grit sandpaper

BEFORE YOU BEGIN

The edges of shelves and doors can become chipped and torn as time goes by. Make them fresh and neat again in just a few minutes using iron-on melamine edging.

Repairing edges with melamine

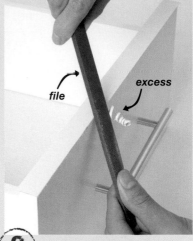

Set the iron to HIGH with the steam off

paper

strip

1 **Apply the new strip**
Cut melamine to length allowing ½ in. (1 cm) extra at each end. Make sure that the underlying surface is clean and smooth, then press the melamine into place. Cover with parchment. Iron the strip in a short forward-and-back motion.

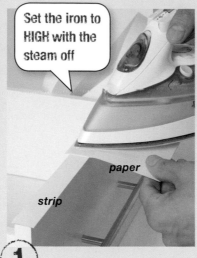

file

excess

2 **Trim the edges**
Use a small roller to apply pressure to the edging until the adhesive cools and sets. Use a fine square-edged file held at 20° to trim the excess, working downward. Smooth the edges lightly with medium-grit sandpaper.

▨ Grab a bag ▶
The next best thing to not using plastic bags is to reuse them. To make a dispenser, cut the cap and bottom off a 2 or 3 liter plastic soft drink bottle. The top hole should be about 3 in. (7.5 cm) in diameter. Using small screws and washers, mount the bottle on the back of a cabinet or cupboard door with the 3 in. (7.5 cm) opening at the bottom. Stuff the bags into the bottle and pull them out as needed.

▨ An even shine
When applying wax or finish to wood, cork or similar flooring, give the entire surface one coat and then add a second coat to high-traffic areas. Both areas will wear evenly, avoiding the need for the application of interim touch-ups.

▨ Just add vinegar
Soap residue can dull a floor no matter how vigorously you mop. Add a little vinegar to the rinse water to neutralize lingering suds and leave your floor sparkling clean.

No more scrapes ▶

Glue felt to the bottom of kitchen chair legs to protect a tile, wood or vinyl floor from scrapes and nicks. You can buy self-adhesive felt pads from hardware stores.

Loosen a lid

Loosen a tight lid by running very hot water over it for a minute or so (for safety, wrap glass jars in cloth first). For extra grip, wear rubber gloves or wrap a wide rubber band tightly around the lid.

Cellar in a cupboard

Take out shelving from an existing cupboard (pick one that's well away from any heat source or cooking appliance). Install in its place two pieces of plywood, each slotted halfway through and assembled diagonally to form an X. This maximizes storage space, allowing you to stack bottles horizontally in each quarter of the cupboard.

Bags and boxes

Recycle paper bags and cardboard boxes promptly or risk stocking your shelves with cockroaches as well as groceries. Cockroaches thrive on paper and glue, and the bags and boxes will become infested with eggs and even live insects if left for too long, especially in dark places like pantries.

Catch a cockroach

An empty jam jar filled with a little beer, a few banana slices and a couple of drops of anise extract makes an effective cockroach trap. Wrap masking tape around the jar to help the cockroaches climb up, and smear petroleum jelly around the inside of the rim to keep them from climbing out.

Catch a mouse

Mice are wary of human scent. So before setting a mousetrap, wash it with hot soapy water, rinse and allow to dry. Wear rubber gloves when laying the bait. ▼

PEANUT BUTTER makes the best bait

A jam jar filled with a little beer, some banana slices and anise extract makes an effective cockroach trap.

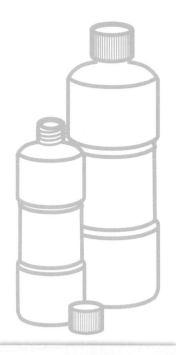

Bathroom

Water in its natural state is free and wild. Taming it for showers and baths is bound to cause problems like leaks, stains and crumbling grout.

▦ Chips and nicks

Disguise flaws on a bath tub by cleaning the area with denatured alcohol and covering with thin coats of epoxy touch-up paint. Don't scrub the affected area for at least a week.

▦ Rusty porcelain

Rust stains on porcelain often come clean with a paste made from cream of tartar (available in most supermarkets and also found in some baking powders) and hydrogen peroxide. Scrub the paste on gently with an old toothbrush. Let the paste dry, and then rinse. Repeat if necessary.

▦ Rusty steel

If a chipped steel bathtub has developed rust spots, coat the affected parts with a rust inhibitor and fill in the chips with fine car body filler. Smooth the repair with very fine wet-and-dry sandpaper (used wet) before disguising it with enamel paint.

▦ Stained enamel

Remove stains from the enamel surface of a cast-iron or steel bathtub with a paste made from baking soda mixed with lemon juice. Cover the stain with the paste and let it sit for five minutes. Scrub gently with a sponge, then rinse clean. Use an enamel paint touch-up kit to conceal minor scratches.

▦ Polish it up

Treat an old metal bathtub that's lost its shine with car body restorer. Then put a shine on the surface with a high-glaze liquid car body polish. A lambs wool polishing bonnet fitted to an electric drill does the best job.

▦ Replace old sealant

To replace silicone sealant, cut away the bulk of the existing strip with a sharp utility knife and then use special silicone sealant remover to take off the last traces. Wipe the cleaned surface with a cloth soaked in denatured alcohol before you apply new sealant.

▦ Get rid of scale

An effective way to remove lime scale from toilet bowls is by using a paste of citric acid powder (available from supermarkets, pharmacies or health food stores) and water. Push and dam some of the water around the bend with a mop. Brush the paste onto the ring of lime scale. Leave overnight before rinsing. Repeat as necessary. The paste also works well on scale beneath the rim of the bowl.

SECRETS from the EXPERTS

Fill the bath with water before sealing the joints between the bath sides and walls with silicone. This allows the bath to **settle into the position** it will be in while in use, so the sealant will be less likely to pull away from the wall.

TROUBLESHOOT **BATHROOM LEAKS**

Most bathroom leaks can be traced to the shower area and are commonly caused by pipe leaks inside the wall. Other causes may include a failure or break in the waterproof membrane in the floor, or poor sealing behind the decorative cover flanges on wall faucets. Keep your shower area in good condition and minimize the need for repairs by scheduling an overhaul every so often that includes:

★ Removing all the faucet handles and covers

★ Thoroughly cleaning all surfaces

★ Applying a paintable surface sealant to tiles

★ Applying a flexible sealant to all perimeter corners (both vertical and horizontal)

★ Sealing faucet spindles to the wall before replacing the handles

What you will need

- Grout knife or Dremel tool
- Tile cleaner
- Rubber gloves
- Grout
- Rubber float or squeegee
- Sponge
- Toothbrush
- Clean dry cloth
- Grout sealer
- Applicator with sponge tip (optional)
- Clean rag

Regrouting bathroom tiles

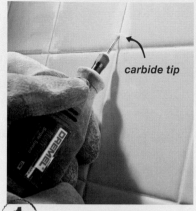

carbide tip

1 Remove old grout

To keep the dust under control, shut the bathroom door, cover the air vents and turn on the exhaust fan. Cut into the old grout with a grout knife or Dremel tool (pictured). The Dremel tool quickly cuts a smooth, deep joint. Hold it nearly flat against the tile, then draw it downward while applying light pressure to the bit.

2 Clean the tiles

Wash the tiles with a tile cleaner. An acid-based tile cleaner will remove soap scum, mineral deposits and grout residue. Wear rubber gloves to protect your hands.

Consider SPRAY-ON SEALER if you have small tiles and lots of grout

rubber float

3 Apply new grout

Mix new grout to the consistency of toothpaste. Pack the joints. Sweep a rubber float or squeegee diagonally across the grout lines to fill the large areas. Use a dab of grout on your gloved finger to fill in the hard-to-reach areas. Allow the grout to set but not harden before wiping off the excess with a damp sponge.

4 Neaten and leave

Run the end of a toothbrush along the grout lines. This packs the grout and straightens the line for a neater look. Wipe over the grout a second time. Leave overnight and wipe off any remaining film with a clean, dry cloth. Allow the grout to cure for two more days.

5 Seal and wipe

Finish with a sealer to stop water and dirt from penetrating and staining the grout. An applicator with a sponge tip speeds up the job. Wipe the edges of the tile with a clean rag as you work so that the sealer doesn't dry on the tile and dull the glaze.

What you will need

- Tube of silicone sealant and caulking gun or a combined silicone tube/dispenser
- Water sprayer filled with sudsy water (use detergent)
- Craft stick
- Piece of old towel
- Utility knife

BEFORE YOU BEGIN
Clean the area thoroughly and leave to dry.

Applying silicone sealant

(1) Apply silicone
Attach nozzle to cartridge and cut off the tip to release a silicone bead just over ⅛ in. (3 mm) in diameter. Fit cartridge to gun (unless using a combined tube and dispenser) and apply silicone in a continuous bead in 3 ft. (1 m) lengths to start.

(2) Spray silicone
Lightly spray the bead with sudsy water, taking care not to wet any surfaces to which silicone is yet to be applied. Start at the bottom and work upward if you are working on a vertical corner.

Shelving

When it comes to storage solutions, the humble shelf is unsurpassed. Make sure any shelves you install are securely fixed and strong.

▦ Floor saver
Installing a wall-length floor-to-ceiling bookcase? You may have to strengthen the floor first. The average floor is strong enough for general domestic loads, but a fully filled bookcase may weigh too much. If in doubt, talk to an architect, carpenter or engineer before proceeding.

▦ Be firm
Make a flimsy shelf firmer by gluing and screwing a reinforcement strip under the front edge. Bear in mind, however, that the strip will restrict the height of items you can store on the shelf below slightly. ◄

▦ Adequate support
To prevent shelving from sagging, a good rule of thumb is to space the supports every 31 in. (80 cm) along the length of a ¾ in. (2 cm)-thick shelf. The heavier the load, the closer the supports should be.

▦ Use the right screws
Shelving of all types will collapse and may cause injury if it is not fixed firmly to the wall. For masonry walls, use screws that penetrate at least 2 in. (5 cm). Drive them into the wall through plastic wall plugs matched to the screw size. On wood-framed walls, use screws with 1½ in. (4 cm) penetration, or

Silicone with a MOLD INHIBITOR is best for bathrooms

3 Trace and cure
Trace the bead with the curved edge of the craft stick held at almost a right angle to the surface. Wipe silicone off the stick onto a piece of towel. Leave to cure for 72 hours.

19⅔ in (50 cm) if the shelf is likely to carry heavy items.

▓ Vertical tracks
Make sure the tracks of adjustable shelving systems are vertical by hanging each one loosely from its topmost screw hole. Then hold a plumbline—more accurate for verticals than a level—alongside it. When the track is vertical, mark the other screw positions through the holes in the track. Swing the track aside while you drill and anchor if needed. Reposition the track and drive in the screws.

▓ Making alcove shelves
The alcove beside a chimney surround is an ideal site for shelves on which to store decorative objects or books. However, few alcoves are square or have perfectly flat walls, so square-cut shelves

supported by cleats fixed to the side walls will leave gaps. To achieve an exact fit, you will need just two sheets of cardboard. Butt the edge of one sheet against the back wall of the alcove and place the other piece on top so that it butts against the side wall. Tape the sheets together and mark the angle on one end of the shelving wood. Repeat the whole process for the other corner. Your shelves will fit perfectly. ▼

2 in. (5 cm) if the shelves are likely to carry a heavy load such as books. Make sure the screws drive directly into the studs.

▓ Load test
Before fixing a shelf in place, check whether it will bow under the weight that you intend to put on it. Rest the shelf on bricks set at the proposed support spacing, load it up and lay a straightedge along the top surface. If the shelf bows, move the supports closer together or increase the thickness of the shelf material.

▓ Sturdy glass
Glass shelves should be made from tempered glass at least ¼ in. (5 mm) thick and set on brackets spaced no more than 15¾ in. (40 cm) apart. If the thickness of the glass is increased to ⅓ in (9 mm), the spacing can increase to 27½ in. (70 cm); but keep the spacing at

COMPARING **SHELVING MATERIALS**
Shelving products have their pros and cons. Use this chart to select the best material for the job.

★ Type	★ Advantages	★ Disadvantages
Hardwood	Fairly easy to work. Accepts most finishes. Attractive.	Expensive.
Softwood (pine)	Easy to work; accepts paint well. Attractive with clear finish.	Boards may be warped. Pick flat, straight ones with few knots.
Plywood	Strong and durable. Wide range of attractive veneers available.	Raw edges need to be finished. Can be expensive.
MDF	Easy to work; accepts paint. Finer and stronger than chipboard.	Must be painted or varnished. Rarely available ready-cut. Dusty.
Particle-board (veneered)	Wide range of veneers available.	Will bow under heavy loads. Raw edges need finishing. Rarely available ready cut.
Particle-board (melamine coated)	Cheap to buy (comes in ready-cut lengths suitable for shelving). Can be used as-is.	Can get dirty easily. Will bow under heavy loads.

Care of indoor plants

Plants bring life and color into the home and require little in the way of maintenance. Follow these simple tips and your plants should thrive.

▓ Position plants carefully
Look for the best place in the house for each plant, and don't be afraid to try different locations until you find the best spot.

▓ Re-create a forest floor
If a room seems too dark to sustain a healthy plant, don't be fooled. Some indoor plants originate in tropical and subtropical regions, particularly in equatorial forests, and they thrive in dim environments and filtered light. The ideal spot is in front of a large window facing east or west, filtered if necessary through a thin curtain.

▓ Sun-lovers face south
If you have a plant that thrives on lots of sun, place it on a windowsill facing south or southeast. Check soil moisture levels regularly and inspect the leaves to check that they are not being burned. At the slightest sign of withering, move it toward the middle of the room.

▓ Plants for the bathroom
Ferns and other moisture-loving plants do best in vaporous rooms like bathrooms where they can lap up regular doses of mist.

▓ Water from the bottom
Water poured directly onto the soil may flood, or not reach the pot plant's roots. Instead, water plants bottom up by standing them in a dish and filling the dish with water. Delicate plants such as fuchsias thrive on this method. For the method to work, all pots should have holes in the bottom through which the water is absorbed.

▓ Keep away from drafts
If you don't want your plant to die of heat or cold, avoid placing it in drafty areas or near ducted heat or air-conditioning outlets.

▓ Do not overwater
Water your plants only when the potting mix feels dry to the touch—overwatering is often the cause of indoor plant death. Check by pushing your finger into the soil; if it comes out without any trace of soil on it, start watering. Remember that plants may need more frequent watering in summer.

▓ Plants like to be sprayed
Most indoor plants benefit from an occasional spraying of water. Make sure the water is at room temperature and use an atomizer or spray bottle. Spraying is particularly beneficial if you live in a centrally heated or air-conditioned house as the air can become very dry.

▓ Apply some fertilizer
Feed your plants with small amounts of fertilizer. The fastest and simplest solution is complete liquid fertilizer in the recommended dose, usually every two to four weeks—check the label.

▓ Use ice cubes
An efficient way to water your plants directly at a steady rate is to use ice cubes. Put a couple on top of the pot soil and leave them to melt.

Hanging and framing

Pictures contribute to the unique qualities of a room and will be preserved and enhanced if they are framed and hung thoughtfully.

▨ Firm and straight

Stop pictures from sliding from side to side on the cord by wrapping the cord with duct tape on either side of the picture hook. Keep frames straight by attaching loops of duct tape to the back of the frame at the corners, sticky side out, and pressing to the wall.

▨ The best hook ▲

Choose the appropriate hook for the picture's size and weight. Single-pin hooks will support a typical picture in a glazed frame measuring up to 24 x 35 in. (60 x 90 cm). A double-pin hook will support one measuring 35 x 47 in. (90 x 120 cm). Consider two hooks for bigger pictures.

▨ The weakest link

Whether a picture falls off the wall depends on the strength of the weakest link. This could be the cord or the hook but often it's the small eyes screwed into the frame to which the cord is attached, and which may penetrate the frame only slightly. Replace them with more substantial D rings.

▨ Get it taped

Tape pictures to their mounts with special linen tape, available from picture-framing stores. Ordinary sticky tapes can soak into the paper and damage the picture.

▨ Hung from the rails

To avoid marking and making holes in your walls, don't use hooks, use picture rails. They look great, especially in rooms with high ceilings (about 9 ft./2.8 m or more). Hang S-shaped hooks on the rail and suspend the pictures with unobtrusive nylon cord or fishing line, or with fine decorative wire if you like the visual impact.

Tape pictures to their mounts with special linen tape, available from picture-framing stores.

▨ Heavy pictures

You can hang a large or heavy picture on a solid masonry wall using a round-headed screw fitted with a wall anchor. The heavier the picture, the larger the screw.

GETTING THE **HEIGHT RIGHT**

The most common mistake people make when hanging pictures is to hang them too high. The following formula creates a great result and applies to pictures you wish to hang on the wall from a hook (i.e. not from a rail) and to which a cord has already been attached on the back.

1 Measure the height of the frame, divide the result in half and add 60 in. (1.5 m) (the subtotal).

2 Measure the distance between the picture cord at full tension and the top of the frame. Subtract this from the subtotal to produce the grand total.

3 Mark a spot on the wall equivalent to the grand total, measured up from the floor.

4 Fix an appropriate hook at the spot you marked on the wall. Now step back: your picture is perfectly positioned.

▓ Finding the spot ▶

Pinpointing the exact spot for a picture hook can be exasperating. Simplify the task by cutting a 10 in. (25 cm) length of wire off a wire coat hanger and filing one end to a point. Using pliers, bend the wire as shown to form a hook at the pointed end and a finger-sized loop at the other. Insert the pointed end under the cord and position the picture on the wall, holding it by the looped end of the tool. Push the point gently into the wall to mark the spot for the hook.

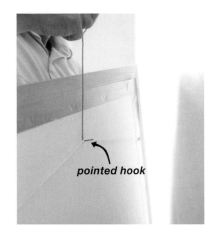

pointed hook

▓ Spread the strain ◀

Heavy frames can open up at the corners under their own weight. To prevent this, use D rings or drive two extra screw eyes into the bottom of the frame, then rig the wire through these and those near the top.

▓ Seal cord ends

Many picture framers use special braided nylon cord, guaranteed to be rot- and insect-proof. Always check that the knots are really tight before hanging a corded picture. To stop the ends fraying or the knots unraveling, seal the cut ends of the cord by holding them in a lighter or match flame for a moment.

What you will need

- Tape measure
- Two D rings
- Level
- Ruler
- Erasable marker
- Two screw-in wall anchors (toggle-type for heavier mirrors)
- Drill (masonry walls only)
- Two pan-head screws

Hang a heavy mirror

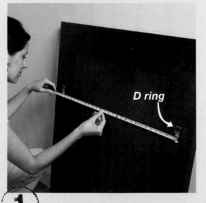

D ring

(1) Install D rings

Screw two D rings to the back of the frame on each side at an equal distance from the top and a third of the total height down. Measure the distance between the right edge of one D ring and the right edge of the other to establish the exact distance between their centers.

(2) Note measurements

Measure the distance from the top of the frame to the D rings. Make a record of this measurement as well as the one established in Step 1.

Handling heavyweights

The safest way to hang large and heavy pictures or mirrors is to use interlocking wall cleats. Make a 45° cut down the center of a 1 x 3 in. (2.5 x 7.5 cm) softwood board and screw one cleat across the back of the frame and the other to the wall. To hang the picture, hook its cleat over the one on the wall. ▼

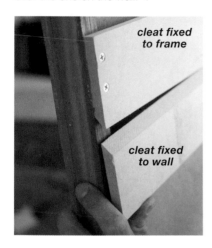

cleat fixed to frame

cleat fixed to wall

Washers take the strain

If you are installing a mirror with ready-made holes and its own screws, fit a rubber faucet washer on each screw between the mirror and wall. These stop the mirror from cracking as you tighten the screws. In steamy bathrooms they also hold the mirror away from the wall and allow air to circulate behind it, stopping condensation from forming and damaging the silvering.

Ever-straight pictures

For pictures attached to drywall, here's a way to keep them hanging straight forever. Push a pin into each lower corner of the frame, then cut off the heads so that ½ in. (1 cm) of the pin protrudes. Make sure the picture is straight, then push the pins into the wall. Alternatively, you can place a small amount of putty in the lower corners.

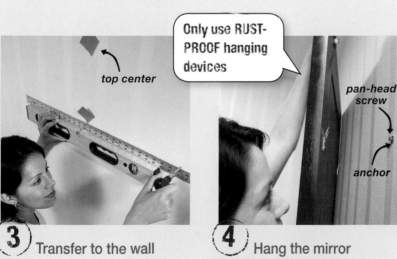

Only use RUST-PROOF hanging devices

top center

pan-head screw

anchor

③ Transfer to the wall

Choose a position for the mirror on the wall and mark the top center. Using a level, a ruler and the measurements referred to in Steps 1 and 2, mark the positions for the screws. Drive an anchor into the wall at each screw location, or drill and anchor into masonry walls.

④ Hang the mirror

Screw pan-head screws into the anchors. Allow each screw to protrude by about ¼ in. (6 mm), then hook the D rings on to it. If the top isn't level when you're done, wrap a few turns of duct tape around the D ring on the low side.

TOP TIPS FOR GROUPINGS

★ Don't cover more than two-thirds of the blank wall space. Use large pictures on long walls and small pictures on short walls.

★ Work out where you want the center of your grouping to sit and position the dominant piece (such as a mirror, a dark-toned work or one with a large, ornate frame) in the middle. Then select two or more major pieces, either larger or smaller than the central piece, and place them on either side of it.

★ If the outer works are small and horizontal, make the central piece a tall vertical. The central tall vertical can also be composed of two horizontal pieces, hung one above the other.

★ The bottom pieces in a group should be positioned at least 8–12 in. (20–30 cm) above any furniture situated near a wall.

★ Too much space between pictures disrupts the effect. A hand width is about right.

★ Pictures will have greater visual impact if mounted in a contrasting color to the wall. Choose a dark mount for a light wall and vice versa.

★ Add interest by varying the shapes and sizes of your picture frames. Also try to vary the mount sizes and colors. You can add impact by mixing the media or placing dramatic pieces next to plainer ones.

▓ Rattles and bumps

If your picture frames rattle on the wall when a car passes, or fall to the floor when someone slams a door, try securing the corners with a little putty.

▓ Breathing space

Place mounts around photos and prints to create a layer of air between the glass and the image. This will help prevent high levels of damaging humidity from building up and stop the artwork from sticking to the glass.

Frames and mounts should be chosen to match or enhance the picture, not each other.

▓ Mark the spot

To hang a picture frame right where you want it, make a guide for your nail. Tape over the head of a thumbtack and position it directly under the picture's mounting bracket with the sharp point of the tack facing outward. Hold the picture in place and push on the frame until the point pricks the wall. The tiny mark will show where to place the hook. ▼

▓ Wallpaper cover-up ▲

Don't damage your wallpaper with picture hook holes. Instead, make two slits in the wallpaper with a utility knife, creating a tab of paper where you want to install the hook, moisten the area, and very carefully peel up the paper. When it's time to rearrange your pictures, disguise the hole by gluing the tab back into its original position.

▓ Framer craft

When framing a picture, use push points—used for setting glass. They are less likely to split the frame and can be hammered in or stapled with a special tool.

▓ Room for fixing

The rabbet on a typical frame (the space enclosed by the molding) needs to be deep enough for the glass, the picture, its mount, a backing board, plus ⅛ in. (3 mm) of clearance space for the push points that will hold everything in place. You will have to use a thinner mount and board if you do not have this much clearance.

▓ Odd numbers look best

Uneven numbers of objects are more interesting than groupings of even numbers. For example, three pictures hung with equal spacing between them will look very stylish.

THE SEVEN DEADLY SINS OF **PICTURE HANGING**

(1) Using adhesive picture hooks —particularly in humid areas. They're not up to the job and your artwork could end up on the floor. When removed, they often bring a strip of underlying paint or wallpaper with them.

(2) Using a hook and cord that are the wrong weight for the picture. You can't catch marlin with a hook and line designed for shad, and pictures are no different. They won't hold. If in doubt about what you should use, ask for advice at your local hardware store or picture framers.

(3) Hanging pictures in areas where there are high temperatures (such as a sunroom) or frequent changes of temperature, both of which will accelerate the aging process of your pictures.

(4) Hanging pictures where they will be exposed to bright sunlight for long periods of time. This will fade both paintings and photographs.

(5) Hanging pictures in areas of high humidity, or extreme changes in humidity, such as kitchens and steamy bathrooms.

(6) Hanging pictures flat against a wall, which can encourage mold growth. Put something small and flat (like a matchbox) behind your pictures.

(7) Choosing an eye-catching frame and mounting. A frame and mounting should be chosen to match or enhance a picture, not make a statement of its own.

Home office

With a few small changes you can make your home office a pleasant place to be, as well as a tidy and efficient workplace.

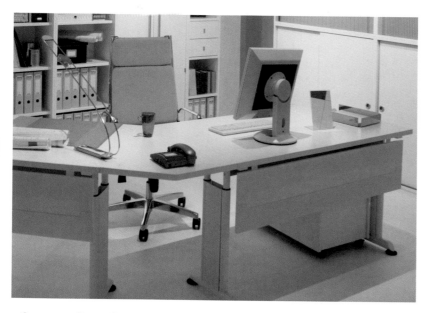

Create the illusion of a discrete work space by setting up a barrier made from screens or shelving units.

a discrete space by setting up a barrier made from screens or shelving units. Arrange the barrier so that it will shield the office as much as possible from the dominant traffic patterns in the rest of the house.

▦ Rugs and lights
When creating an office-within-a-room, use a large rug to help define the space, and install lighting that imparts a working atmosphere in contrast to the lighting in the surrounding room.

▦ Color and texture
Another way to define an office space is to choose colors, fabrics and textures for the furniture, fixtures, wall paint and wallpaper that are different from but harmonious with those in the surrounding room—and suited to the atmosphere of a working office.

▦ Desk shapes ▲
The traditional L-shaped work station is efficient for tasks involving large quantities of paperwork. Keep the computer and other desktop equipment on one leg of the "L" and the paperwork, office supplies, and phone on the other.

▦ Closet hideaway
An important feature of a home office is a sense of separation from other household activities and this is exactly what a large, converted closet can provide. Fit suitable lighting and electrical outlets and install shelving to store books, files and equipment. Folding doors will save space and hide the clutter when you're done working.

▦ Mark boundaries
If you don't have the luxury of a separate room in which to set up your office, create the illusion of

▦ Keep wires tidy
Collect that clutter of wires hanging down behind a computer desk in a "cable organizer." It keeps them neat and off the floor. ▼

Easy on the eyes

To cut glare, avoid painting the walls of your office or work area white. Pale colors are much easier on the eyes. White is fine for ceilings as they're out of the field of vision.

Get the light right

When working on a computer, it is important to keep overhead lighting no brighter than the computer screen, in order to prevent eye strain. Fine tune the overhead light source by installing a dimmer. Turn up the dimmer when reading or doing paperwork, and lower it when working at the screen.

The right angle

Angle a desk lamp so that it lights your work without dazzling you. If you use a lamp near a computer screen, make sure that the light does not reflect off the screen into your eyes.

Adding plants ▲

Good air quality is important for staying alert and fresh while you work. To improve the air in your home office or work area, add a few plants. Plants release oxygen, which improves air quality. They also emit water vapor, which restores the moisture to dry air.

Closets

The best closet has two features that allow you to dress with a minimum of fuss: a place for everything and everything in its place.

▦ The systems approach

Built-in closets are designed to help you organize your apparel methodically and access it easily. There are some great DIY systems that are quick and easy to install. Choose one with mirrored doors for reflection and an illusion of space.

▦ Closet basics

Store items that are only used occasionally (such as blankets, suitcases and travel bags) on the upper shelves, leaving room for the clothing and accessories you use regularly within easy reach.

▦ Made to measure

Mesh and plastic-covered wire shelving systems are easily customized to almost all closet requirements. Work out what you need, measure the dimensions of your closet, and take the information to a supplier so that units can be made up just for you.

▦ Open up some space

Save space in your closet by adding hooks to the inside door. It beats cramming items onto a crowded rail or piling them on the floor. The inside closet door is also a great place to fix a mirror. ▼

▓ Sagging clothes rail 1 ▶

Remedy a sagging clothes rail by adding a bracket halfway along. These usually project 3 in. (7.5 cm) from the top of the closet. You may need to refit the side brackets as well to ensure the clothes rail aligns through all the brackets.

▓ Sagging clothes rail 2

If adding a support bracket is not a practical solution for a sagging clothes rail, replace the rail with a length of galvanized pipe placed inside PVC piping. Remove the manufacturer's name from the PVC pipe with lacquer thinner.

▓ Double your space

Since few items of everyday clothing are ankle length, full-height hanging space in closets is a waste. Convert most of the space you have available to twin-level hanging, with a low-level rail midway between the top rail and the floor. Longer items can be stored elsewhere.

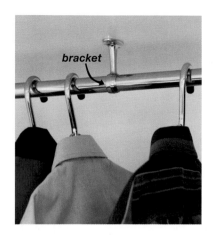

bracket

Mesh and plastic-covered wire shelving systems can be customized to almost all closet requirements.

▓ Aim for flexibility

Personalize the way you organize your wardrobe to suit your own needs. Look for equipment with maximum adjustability, such as moveable rails, organizers and freestanding drawers.

Storage

Don't despair about untidy possessions. There are many creative storage solutions on the market or awaiting discovery in your very own home.

▓ Recessed shelves

Shelving installed between studs need not be limited to places where the studs are exposed, such as an unfinished garage or workshop. By cutting into the drywall with a keyhole saw, you can create a space for recessed shelves inside an indoor finished wall or partition. Use shelves made of 1 x 4 in. (2.5 x 10 cm) pine boards supported with cleats nailed to the studs. If desired, conceal behind a painting hinged to the wall. Don't create recessed shelves inside exterior walls or walls that run with plumbing, ductwork or cables.

▓ Orderly bathrooms

Space-saving accessories for the kitchen can also bring order to your bathroom. Most kitchen stores stock turntable organizers (lazy susans) in single and two-tiered models. Before buying, measure the space inside the cabinet carefully, making allowances for drainpipe clearance if necessary.

Halls and ceilings

Install floor-to-ceiling shelving in wide halls. Leave at least 36 in. (90 cm) of the floor space clear so that people can move through easily. In narrower hallways, install a long high shelf for rarely used or decorative items about 12 in. (30 cm) below the ceiling. If a hall or room has high ceilings, create space for storage by installing a partial "false" ceiling accessible via hinged or retractable doors on the open side.

Don't discard old kitchen cabinets as they make great storage units for attics, workshops and garages.

Check that your cabinet is a STANDARD WIDTH before replacing the drawers

The case for baskets ◄

Replace full-depth shelves in kitchen cabinets with sliding wire baskets of different sizes. They make loading and retrieval easy, and are ideal for storing dry goods, cans, jars, fruit, vegetables and all kinds of kitchen utensils. You can store more things in baskets than on fixed shelves, as well as organize them more easily, like with like. With baskets, things are also far less likely to be pushed to the back and lost for years.

Raised beds

Beds take up a vast amount of floor space and some of it can be easily used for storage. Slide shallow drawers fitted with castors underneath beds with legs. To create secure storage under a divan bed, build a sturdy platform with sliding doors in the sides on which to elevate the divan. Alternatively, replace your bed with divans that have ready-made storage drawers in the base.

The suitcase solution

Pull out any empty suitcases you don't use very often and fill them with the clothes and shoes that you wear rarely or are currently out of season. This will free up your closet. Your luggage will take up no more space than it did before you filled it up.

Stackable bins

Transparent, plastic, stackable bins are ideal for storing pajamas, other foldable clothing and accessories such as handbags and shoes. When stacked, they take up little floor space, and the transparent sides help you to identify items quickly. Bins with drawer-type fronts make access easier.

Empty steps

Use the space inside the bottom steps of a hall staircase to store boots, sports equipment and other paraphernalia. Hinge the tread to make a lid, and secure it with a sturdy latch to prevent clattering from passing feet.

A use for old cabinets

Don't discard old kitchen cabinets. They make great storage units for attics, workshops and garages. The combination of drawers, shelves and cupboard space provides a tidy home for hardware, tools and equipment that are otherwise so easy to mislay.

Unused fireplace

Turn a disused fireplace into a handy storage space or a place for display. Cap the chimney to keep the rain out. Close off the flue with to minimize thermal loss. Create a faux fire by placing a series of candles in the fireplace. For maximum effect, ensure that the candles are of varying height.

ROOM AT THE TOP
STORAGE IN THE ATTIC

The space above the ceiling and beneath the roof is a convenient place to store seldom-used items. A little forethought and organization will enable you to store more things and find them easily when you need them.

Attic sense

Attics are less easy to access than most other storage spaces, so save them for seasonal items, or items you don't use but can't bear to part with. Check the roof regularly for leaks and don't exceed the load-bearing capacity of the floor.

Clean and dry

Consider packing clothes and other textiles in plastic garment bags sealable with a vacuum cleaner. They save space, are impervious to vermin, and being both airtight and waterproof, will protect the contents from damp and mold. The clear plastic means you can easily identify the contents.

Neat and tidy

Don't just heap things in piles. Use plastic storage bins (never cardboard boxes or garbage bags, which attract vermin). Consider bins with built-in wheels and arrange them in rows perpendicular to the ceiling to assist access. Leave aisles for easy maneuvering. Label everything so that when a container is needed, it can be easily identified.

Highs and lows

Temperature swings are more pronounced in an attic. These fluctuations will soon damage books, files and other paper documents as well as photographs and videos. Secure them in an insulated, airtight container, or store them somewhere else.

Painting and wallpapering

Choosing and buying paint

A coat of paint does more than simply add a splash of color—if chosen carefully, it can alter the sense of space and light in a room.

Watch the swatch

The quality of light in a room affects the appearance of the paint color. Try not to rely on paint swatches alone. If you can get a sample can, paint a large piece of light cardboard and make a super-sized swatch of your own. Hang the swatch on the wall and observe how the color responds to the light as it changes throughout the day. Also pay attention to how it looks under artificial light.

Manipulate the mood

Dark colors absorb more light and more heat than pale colors, so if you're after a room with a cozy, intimate feel, opt for something darker. Paler tones reflect light, which makes them a great choice for busy spaces such as living rooms.

Shape the space

To make a narrow room appear wider, paint one or both of the short walls a bright color and use a more subdued color on the other walls. If a room lacks a focal point such as a fireplace or large window, manufacture a feature by painting one wall in a striking accent color.

Lighten up

Paint colors tend to darken and intensify when applied across all four walls of a room. If you're attracted to a strong, bold paint hue, consider going a shade or two lighter. That way, when the whole room is painted, you'll end up with a color very similar to the paint swatch that first caught your eye.

Moving the walls

Warm colors advance toward the eye and trick it into thinking a surface is closer than it really is. As a result, a warm tone will make a sprawling room seem snug, while a cool hue will have the effect of expanding a smaller room.

Check the exposure

Rooms that face north, northeast or northwest receive little or no sunshine during the day, making them gloomy. Such rooms can be made more inviting with a coat of paint in a warm tone such as a sunny yellow or caramel. Conversely, a room that faces south and tends to be drenched in sunlight can be toned down with a cool color such as a gray or lavender. Be aware, though, that cooler colors have been shown to make people feel physically cooler. That's useful in a warm climate, or in the summer, but is not so helpful in an area where very cold weather is a challenge in the winter.

Instant blackboard

If you're painting a child's room, a playroom or a kitchen, think about brushing a couple of coats of blackboard paint onto a section of the wall. Your built-in blackboard will be handy for kids' drawings and family messages.

WHICH **PAINT FINISH** GOES WHERE?

Thanks to modern paint technology, there is a paint for every type of surface. In most cases professional painters will select a flat acrylic paint for the ceiling, a low-sheen acrylic for the walls and a semi-gloss or gloss acrylic for the woodwork.

Water-based is best

Water-based acrylic paints have a number of advantages over their oil-based enamel counterparts. When you're painting, drips and splashes can be removed with a simple wipe with a damp cloth. When you're finished, paintbrushes can be cleaned up in water. Unlike enamel paints, acrylic paints emit almost no fumes or vapors when applied, they dry faster and they usually cost less. Oil-based enamel paints can offer superior durability and are often favored for very high quality work. But for a DIY paint job, it's hard to do better than the acrylics. The types of paint below can be either acrylic or oil-based.

Flawless flat finishes

Matte (or flat) paint provides a soft, glare-free finish and tends to hide minor surface irregularities. It's easy to apply and is the best choice for ceilings, and walls in low-traffic areas.

Satin: a sensible choice

Satin finish paint combines the soft finish of flat paint with the washability of semi-gloss. It is ideal for walls in high-traffic areas that need to be wiped clean regularly.

Super-tough semi-gloss

Semi-gloss paint isn't as easy to apply as flat and low-sheen products, but provides a highly washable surface. It's usually used on windowsills, doors and trim, and in kitchens and bathrooms, where moisture resistance and washability are key.

High-quality high-gloss

High-gloss paint is highly reflective, which means it will highlight any flaws and defects in the surface; if you're going to use a high-gloss paint, you'll need to be meticulous about surface preparation. You will also need to take great care in how you apply the paint so that you end up with an even surface without runs. The advantage of high-gloss is its resistance to grease and moisture, which means it is easy to keep clean.

Special effects

There are numerous specialized paints on the market designed for particular jobs. Textured coatings are useful for covering up uneven walls and ceilings, but bear in mind that they are extremely difficult to remove. You can also buy paints for floors, tiles and melamine (for revitalizing kitchen units).

Camouflage the flaws

Gloss paint shows up every dent and scratch in a surface. If your woodwork isn't perfect or you don't want to spend long hours on preparation, use a less reflective flat or low-sheen finish instead.

White that won't yellow

Conventional white paint applied to hot-water pipes and radiators will eventually yellow. To avoid yellowing, use a special radiator enamel. It will give off strong fumes as it dries, so open windows wide.

Thirsty walls

Most paint cans indicate the average area of wall they will cover. However, some surfaces will require a lot more than this. Highly porous surfaces like bare plaster and rough surfaces such as untreated walls are very thirsty. Two or three undercoats may be necessary to cover a very strong base color.

For best results, buy a premium paint product recommended by a reliable paint retailer. Cheaper paints tend to have less coverage.

Pick healthier paints

Volatile organic compounds (VOCs) are a common component in paints. They help to make a product durable and workable, but can give some people nausea and headaches weeks or even months after a room is painted. In general, acrylic paints have a lower VOC content than enamels. You can now buy low-VOC and even zero-VOC acrylic paints. Ask for them in your local hardware store.

Primer choice

Primers are coatings that are applied to surfaces before they're painted to boost the adhesion of the paint product. For the best result, use a primer specifically formulated for the surface you're painting (such as plaster, wood or metal), rather than a universal primer.

Estimating paint

To estimate the amount of paint you'll need, first work out the surface area of the floor then add that to the surface area of the walls. Don't deduct anything for standard-sized windows (it's better to have too much paint than not enough). Check the can for the product's coverage (the amount of paint needed to coat a square foot or meter). Then add it up. Don't forget to multiply that by the number of coats you think you will need.

Awkward wall areas

Calculating surface area can be difficult when the room has an irregular shape. First, measure the length of each section of wall, including the sides of any recesses. Add up those figures and multiply by the wall height. Next, subtract the area of any doors (a rough guide is 19⅓ sq. ft./1.8 sq. m per door). Now add the surface area of the ceiling. The figure you end up with is the total surface area for the room. Multiply that by the number of coats you think you will need.

Keep mold at bay

Steamy kitchens and bathrooms are breeding grounds for mold because of the condensation that forms on wall and ceiling surfaces. Always use paints that have been specially formulated for those areas. These contain fungicides that retard mold growth.

Buying the best

For best results buy a premium paint product recommended by a reliable paint retailer. Cheaper products tend to have less coverage (so you'll need to buy more product anyway) and generally won't wear as well as a better paint (so you'll be painting again, sooner). Spend more now, and you will save in the long run.

Buy more than you need

Always buy more paint than you need; that way you'll avoid running out in the middle of the job, and you'll have some left over for touch-ups. Buy paint in 1 gal. (4 L) cans rather than 1 qt. (1 L) cans. A 1 gal. (4 L) can will usually cost about the same as two 1 qt. (1 L) cans, so the savings can be fantastic.

Washable walls

Traditionally, flat paints offered a beautiful soft finish but poor washability, meaning that handprints and scuff marks often became permanent features. Even if you did manage to scrub off the mark, you'd often be left with a tell-tale shiny patch. These days you can get flat-finish paints specially made to be more washable. In general, the higher the gloss level of the product, the easier it is to clean. In high-traffic areas, such as hallways and children's bedrooms, semi-gloss paint is the most sensible choice.

Start a color library

Record your color scheme on color wands made from wooden paint stirrers. Dip a stirrer into each different-colored can of paint, let it dry, and label it according to where the color was used. ▼

Surface preparation—stripping

Preparation is the key to a quality painting or papering job. Be meticulous now and you can sit back and enjoy a perfect finish down the track.

Eliminate build-up

Whether the existing paint is water-based or oil-based, wood trim usually looks best if the built-up paint is removed before the fresh paint is applied. If the trim already has up to five coats of an oil-based paint, you could probably get away with adding a fresh coat or two on top. But if the existing paint is water-based, there are no short cuts. You'll have to sand or strip the old paint away before applying a new coat.

Beware of melted paint

The melted paint produced by a hot-air gun or blowtorch can singe your skin and even ignite drop cloths. Always wear long-sleeved clothing and cotton or leather gloves to protect your skin when heat-stripping. Keep a container of water handy in case any drop cloths laid on the floor start to smolder.

Resisting gravity

Chemical strippers come in many forms, but the best choice for vertical surfaces is a gel-type stripper that will cling to the surface, maximizing the time the chemical has to work. Alternatively, thicken a standard stripper with some wallpaper paste.

Stay on the move ▶

The golden rule when stripping paint with a blowtorch or hot-air gun is to keep the tool moving. Too much heat on one spot will burn and char the paint rather than soften it. You also risk scorching the wood beneath.

Seal the knots

Beware of knots. If unsealed, the resin can seep through fresh paint. Always apply a stain-blocking primer to the whole surface first.

Catch the mess

Here's a way to contain blobs of paint and stripper as you clean your putty knife. Use tin snips or a hacksaw to cut a vertical slot in the side of a large coffee can. The slot should be just a little deeper than the thickness of the putty knife's blade, and just a little wider than its width. To clean, slide the putty knife down the slot, then pull it toward you, scraping the blade as you go. The residue will drop neatly into the can.

Scraping by

To remove a rough section of built-up paint, try wrapping some leftover screening (metal, not fiberglass) around a piece of scrap wood and using it as you would a sanding block. It will remove paint quickly and won't damage the surface.

Follow the contours

A way to preserve the definition of wooden moldings while removing layers of old paint, is to avoid sanding blocks and work with a shave hook or homemade tools instead. A small metal washer held between locking pliers, for example, is ideal for scraping concave sections. To finish the job, wrap fine sandpaper around a piece of wooden dowel and sand lightly up and down the grooves. Alternatively, use an abrasive sponge block.

What you will need

- Drop cloths and masking tape
- Putty knife
- Wetting agent (either chemical wallpaper stripper or hot water and dish soap)
- 4 gal. (20 L) garden sprayer
- Safety goggles (if using chemicals)
- 6 in. (15 cm) taping knife
- Commercial wallpaper stripper (if required)
- Scoring tool
- Bucket and sponges
- Bleach (optional)
- Acrylic primer

Removing old wallpaper

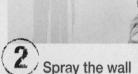
Work from the ceiling down to the floor

1 Peel off first layer

Modern, strippable wallpaper can be removed entirely in one piece. Old-style peelable wallpaper comes off in two layers: first the top vinyl coating, then the paper backing. To remove strippable wallpaper or the vinyl coating of peelable wallpaper, pry under a lower corner with a stiff blade, then peel gently upward until the entire layer is removed.

2 Spray the wall

Under the vinyl coating of peelable wallpaper, the paper backing will still be fixed to the wall. To remove, spray with a wetting agent (cover the floor with drop cloths, turn off the power and tape over electrical and telephone outlets first). Apply with a 4 gal. (20 L) garden sprayer (wear goggles if working with chemicals).

3 Scrape it off

Continue spraying the walls until the paper bubbles or begins to separate from the surface. Once that happens, start scraping the paper off with a 6 in. (15 cm) taping knife. Take care not to gouge drywall. If your scraper isn't doing the job, consider a commercial wallpaper stripper.

4 Wash clean

After all the material has been scraped off, wash the walls with a chemical wallpaper stripper, a mix of hot water and dish soap, or a mix of ¼ cup (60 mL) of bleach in 2 gal. (7 L) of water. Continue washing until all glue residue has been removed. Before painting or hanging new wallpaper, coat the walls with acrylic primer.

★ Get below the surface

Some types of wallpaper will resist the wetting solution. To help the solution penetrate, score the wallpaper's surface in a criss-cross pattern with a scoring tool and then spray with the wetting solution as before. Let it soak in, wait for the paper to bubble up or separate, then scrape the surface with a scraper or wallpaper stripper.

Vinegar vanishing trick

A solution of equal parts white vinegar and hot water does a good job of softening the adhesive behind old wallpaper—and it's much cheaper than a chemical remover. The vinegar has a pungent smell, however, so keep the windows open.

Scrub off the adhesive

Use a nylon brush or pot scrubber on hard-to-remove adhesive. Dip the brush or scrubber in hot water regularly to keep it clean.

Keep it dry

When removing wallpaper or washing down walls, make sure you cover the entire floor with protective drop cloths. Go for non-absorbent plastic sheets rather than canvas or plastic sheets backed with paper, both of which will allow water to penetrate.

Getting steamed up

A steamer can be awkward and even dangerous to use, but sometimes it's the only tool that will do the job. Steamers are effective on stubborn, old, non-strippable wallpapers, and on walls covered in multiple layers of wallpaper. Just don't steam drywall, because the moisture from the steamer can damage the surface.

Go straight to the top

When using a wallpaper steamer, start at the upper part of the wall. Any steam that condenses and runs down the wall will accelerate the adhesive-loosening process on the sections below.

Work in patches

Never wet more surface area than you can scrape off in 15 minutes. About 10 sq. ft. (1 sq. m) is enough.

▓ Wipe off the residue ▲

Use a window squeegee dipped in hot water to remove leftover wallpaper paste from stripped walls. Wipe the old paste from the blade frequently with a clean sponge.

▓ Watch the runs

When removing old wallpaper, be sure to place the waste on a plastic sheet, not on the floor. The solutions used to remove wallpaper can cause dyes to run, staining floors and other surfaces.

▓ Mind the scrapes

Whatever tool you use for scraping off old wallpaper, take care not to damage the wall surface beneath. Any scratches or gouges that you accidentally make while scraping will have to be laboriously filled in and repaired prior to painting or hanging new wallpaper. Be extra careful when working with drywall.

▓ Power up

Make a power wallpaper-peeler out of a power paint-roller. Assemble the power roller so that the tube feeds into a solution of hot, soapy water instead of paint. The motor will pump the suds through the tube to the roller as you work.

▓ Clear the carpets

Removing wallpaper is a wet and messy business, no matter what method you use. Waterproof plastic sheets are an essential part of the job, but even then you may find that some of the moisture you're generating makes its way through to the floor. If the room you're working in has particularly valuable carpeting, you should seriously consider removing it while the wallpaper is being stripped, and replacing it when the job is done.

▓ Test the water

You can test the porosity of the paper before you start stripping by spraying it with a little bit of warm water. If it absorbs the water easily, you can proceed. If it doesn't, you'll need to score the paper before wetting it with the stripping solution.

QUICK WET-DOWN

When wetting wallpaper, you'll find a sprayer gets the job done much faster than a brush or sponge. Use a hand-held sprayer, or, for an even more efficient job, a 4 or 5 gal. (20 L) garden sprayer.

A steamer can be awkward or even dangerous to use, but sometimes it's the only tool that will do the job.

▓ Step up to it

Wallpaper steamers produce both steam and a hot water runoff. To avoid having hot water trickling down your arm as you work, make sure you never hold the steam above shoulder height. When working on high sections, stand on a stepladder.

▓ Feather the edges

If a section of wallpaper backing just won't soak off, use a sanding block and 120- or 220-grit paper to sand the area. Be sure that the backing is dry before you sand. Continue until the transition between the wall and the backing is smooth.

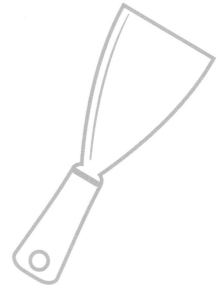

Surface preparation—clean, fill and smooth

The more time you spend on surface preparation, the better the finish—and don't underestimate the benefits of plain old soap and water!

Fix it with toothpaste
Crayon and ballpoint pen marks on walls will bleed through a fresh coat of paint. To remove them, rub with a dab of toothpaste on a damp cloth, then rinse with clean water. If some marks still remain, cover them with a stain sealer.

Choose a simple seal
Use a water-based acrylic sealant to fill cracks, scratches and seams in plaster and drywall before painting or papering. Apply it with a sealant gun or straight from the tube, and smooth it with a wet fingertip (while wearing plastic gloves).

Mold-free
To remove mold before repainting, use a mildew remover or a solution of one part bleach to two parts water. Don't use an olied-based household cleaner; the resulting oily patch may prevent fresh paint from adhering.

What you will need

- Masking tape
- Drop cloths
- Rubber gloves
- Clean rags and sponges
- Dish soap and warm water
- Household bleach and mild, non-ammonia detergent
- Paint scraper
- Sandpaper
- Patching compound
- Putty knife
- Hammer and nail punch (if required)
- Dust mask, goggles and respirator
- Deglosser (optional)
- Dustpan brush
- Primer or sealer

Preparing the surface

1 Wash it down
Remove all door locks and other fixtures. Cover and tape over light switches and fixtures, thermostats and electrical outlets. Cover the floor with drop cloths. Wearing rubber gloves, wash all surfaces thoroughly with warm water and dish soap. Remove any mildew with a solution of water, bleach and mild non-ammonia detergent.

2 Level the surface
Remove any loose or peeling paint with a scraper, and feather the edges with sandpaper. Patch large, uneven areas or deep gaps in the paint with a patching compound. Don't try to remove nails; instead, tap them in with a nail punch and fill the holes. Level any areas you have filled and, once dry, sand smooth.

▓ Shine a light on flaws ▲

Position a hand-held bulb or flashlight so it shines across the surface you're preparing to paint. The light will highlight flaws that aren't as obvious in daylight. Take a pencil (not a pen or marker) and lightly circle the spots that need work.

▓ Wash the walls

Always wash the walls and ceiling thoroughly before painting. A simple TSP solution will remove most grease and grime. Dampen your cloth, don't saturate: that way you won't have water trickling into electrical outlets. Rinse the surface and allow to dry before repainting.

▓ Dress for the job

When washing down walls and ceilings with TSP, always wear goggles and a long-sleeved top with the cuffs tucked securely inside a pair of rubber gloves. The eye protection is particularly important when you're working above your head.

▓ Go flat out

When painting new drywall surfaces, avoid reflective paint finishes as they'll highlight the seams and joints. Always apply a coat of primer first, followed by a coat of flat-finish paint. Low-sheen or gloss paints can be used for subsequent coats.

▓ Upwardly mobile

Instead of buying a pole sander for high, hard-to-reach areas, make a sanding stick. All you need to do is take the pad off a sponge mop, cover it with sandpaper, and slide it back into place. ▼

Check for lead paint using a test kit from a hardware store

③ Take the shine off

Sand glossy surfaces with fine sandpaper, wearing a dust mask and goggles as you work. Alternatively, use a commercial deglosser according to the manufacturer's directions. Make sure the room is well ventilated.

④ Sweep it clean

After sanding, brush away all the dust. Dusting will suffice for most ceilings, but kitchen and bathroom ceilings, which may be greasy or stained with mildew, need special cleaning. You can also buy primers and paints formulated with anti-mold agents in them.

⑤ Apply primer

Seal or prime raw wood. Also spot-prime any newly patched areas on the wall. You may want to tint the primer to cut down on the number of finishing coats that will be necessary. You will want to track your progress as you paint so don't make the primer exactly the same color as the finishing coat.

Cover-ups

It can be a challenge to keep the paint on the walls and off everything else. Some preparation will help keep fixtures and furnishings paint-free.

Paint-proof fixtures

Before painting, remove or loosen all fixtures, including the cover plates for plugs, switches and so on. If you can't remove them, rub them with a thin smear of petroleum jelly to keep them free of paint splatters.

DIY drop cloths

Professional painters use heavy canvas drop cloths. They absorb paint spills and provide a solid, non-slip footing, but they're too expensive for DIY work. Plastic sheets, on the other hand, are relatively cheap. To make them function more like canvas, cover them with a thick layer of newspaper. And try to remember to hold onto old plastic shower curtains: they make handy protective sheets in small areas.

Protect the edges

For a really thorough job of floor protection, lay plastic drop cloths on the floor, tucking the edges under the baseboards using a putty knife. If the gap is too small, apply masking tape around the perimeter of the floor.

Cover up the big items

Move heavy furnishings such as tall cupboards to the center of the room and cover with plastic sheets. They will need to be taped in place so that they won't slip off. ▼

▨ Answer the call ▲

When priming or painting, leave the telephone in an accessible place and cover the handset with a plastic bag. If the phone rings you'll be able to grab it without smearing it with paint. Similarly, wrap your cell phone in plastic wrap.

▨ Go wall-to-wall

Strips of old carpeting can serve as drop cloths when you're stripping, painting or making surface repairs. The weight of the carpet strips ensures they stay in place, and they can be used over and over again. If you don't have carpet scraps on hand, check local carpet retailers and installers; they're usually glad to give away carpet remnants.

▨ Press for a perfect seal

Have you ever peeled away masking tape only to find that paint has seeped underneath the edges? The masking tape will only do its job when the seal is perfect. To seal the edges, press the tape in place with the flat side of a 2 in. (5 cm) putty knife.

▨ Wrap against spatters

Anything that's been left uncovered in a room is subject to spatters and splashes when you're painting. Cleaning up all those drips can be enormously time consuming. To avoid the problem altogether, make sure everything is covered. Drop cloths can go over big objects, but smaller items including lightshades and doorknobs can be covered with plastic wrap. Plastic wrap is wonderfully sticky, but it can also be slippery, so you may need to secure it with tape.

▨ Stop the drops

When using a roller to paint walls or ceilings, don an old shower cap or hat—it will keep paint drips out of your hair and eliminate lots of tedious untangling in the shower later on.

Wear slip-on shoes while painting and take them off when you leave the room to avoid tracking paint.

▨ Food for thought

When preparing a kitchen for repainting, remember to tape around the door seals of fridges and freezers. If you don't, you may find dust makes its way inside and taints the food.

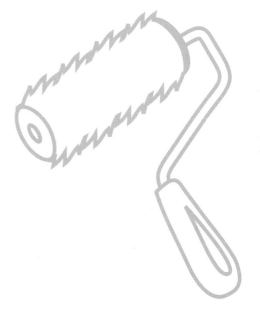

▨ Slip-on protection

Slip a protective plastic sleeve over doors to keep them clean. First, cut two pieces of heavy plastic sheeting slightly larger than the door (to leave room for the doorknob). Apply masking tape to all cut edges and then staple the sheets together along two short sides and one long side. Slide the sleeve over the door.

▨ Shoe saver

Pull an old pair of cotton socks over your shoes before you start painting. The fabric will absorb drips and splatters, leaving your shoes paint-free.

TOOLS FOR **PAINTING**

Poor-quality painting tools do a poor-quality job. You'll be rewarded if you buy the best painting tools you can afford, and learn how to take care of them.

(1) Brushes
Good-quality brushes improve with use. The only time you should be using cheap brushes is when you need to remove dust after sanding.

(2) Crevice brush
For awkward and hard-to-get-at places, such as behind pipes, use a crevice brush, which has bristles set at 45° to the handle.

(3) Cutting-in brush
Use a cutting-in brush for painting window sashes right up into the corners and against the glass.

(4) Nook and cranny rollers
Small rollers on long handles are useful for painting difficult-to-reach areas.

(5) Paint pads and tray
A paint pad comprises a fine layer of mohair bonded to a foam strip, mounted on a handle. Pads come in a variety of sizes and shapes for painting awkward spots such as corners.

(6) Rollers and tray
The quickest way to spread acrylic paint over large areas is with a paint roller. You'll need to put paint in a roller tray to load the roller.

(7) Paint shield
Use a hand-held plastic or metal shield to keep paint off glass when painting window sashes and carpet when painting baseboards.

(8) Extension pole
Most rollers have a hollow handle that will screw into a telescopic extension pole so you can reach the tops of walls or ceilings.

Mix and pour

Once you've mastered a few techniques for neat and accurate paint handling, your work will never be marred by drips or splashes again.

▓ Holey stirrer! ▲

A manual paint stirrer is more effective if it has several holes along its length. With each stroke the paint flows back and forth through the holes, allowing for faster, more thorough blending. You can buy a perforated metal stirrer, or make your own wooden one. To make your own, find a long flat piece of scrap wood and use a drill to make a series of small holes. Rinse your stirrer thoroughly after use to prevent the holes from getting clogged with dried paint.

▓ Watch the bubbles

An electric drill mixing attachment is handy for stirring water-based and oil-based paints, but don't use the attachment to stir lacquer, epoxy paint or shellac, or indeed any finish that has the words "do not shake" printed on its label. Power-mixing these sorts of products will stir up a mass of unwanted air bubbles that can spoil the final finish. Always stir them by hand.

▓ Make a DIY power-mixer

For small jobs you can make your own power mixing attachment by inserting a beater from an old kitchen mixer in your electric drill. This makeshift attachment will work well in 1 qt. (1 L) cans, but the shaft is too short to reach the bottom of 1 gal. (4 L) cans. Use on slow speed to avoid creating air bubbles.

▓ Mix with a milk carton

Cut off the top of a clean 1 qt. (1 L) cardboard milk carton and use it as a container for mixing (or holding) small amounts of paint. The paint won't stick to the wax-coated interior, and the corner of the carton makes a good pouring spout.

▓ Collar the news

Here's another way to contain the mess when stirring a full can of paint. Wrap folded sheets of newspaper around the paint can so they form a tall collar, and secure with tape. Spills and splashes will fall on the paper instead of your floor. ▼

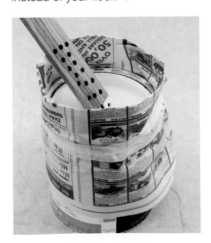

▓ In the mix ▲

Paint color may vary from one can to the next. If you have to open a new can in the middle of a wall, the difference may be noticeable. It's best to estimate the amount of paint you'll need and mix it in a single large container.

You can mix paints of various hues and gloss levels, as long as they have the same base: water or oil.

SECRETS
from the EXPERTS

To minimize that "new paint" smell, **chop a large onion** into chunks, throw them into a container of cold water and place in the newly painted room.

Painting with brushes

Buying the best brushes you can afford is the first step. After that, it's a matter of learning how to use them effectively.

▨ Drain the last drop ▲

When nearing the bottom of a 1 gal. (4 L) paint can, use an old-fashioned can opener to pierce a triangular hole in the side of the can and drain the last of the paint into a paint tray.

▨ Lose the lumps

To filter lumps out of old paint, first cut the leg off a pair of nylons and stretch it across the rim of a clean container, securing with a rubber band. Next, pour the old paint into the new container. The lumps will collect in the fine mesh of the tights as you pour. When you're done, carefully remove the nylons and discard. ▼

▨ Think small, stay clean ▶

Keep your paint supply fresh and clean by pouring it into a small container lined with foil or plastic wrap. Fill it with just enough paint to go halfway up the bristles of your brush. This will be the supply you dip into as you work. Meanwhile, put the lid back on the paint can to keep out dust and debris.

▨ Get a grip

A successful paint job begins with a proper grip on the brush. Hold the metal band, or "ferrule," between your thumb and fingers. This grip gives you the most control, especially when you switch the brush to your weaker hand. Dip about one third of the length of the bristles into the paint, then press the brush lightly against the side of the can. Don't drag the bristles against the rim of the can; that will cause bubbles. Let the paint pool on top of the bristles, but try not to overload the brush.

▨ Smooth strokes

To spread paint evenly, start with a few zigzag strokes, then spread the paint out to cover the gaps. To finish an area, use just the tips of the bristles to smooth out the brushstrokes. This is called "feathering" and removes any unsightly overlapping marks.

▨ Less is better

You'll be less likely to overload a brush if your paint can is only partly filled. The clear space at the top

What you will need

- Drop cloths (if required)
- Vacuum cleaner
- Piece of old card
- 2 or 3 in. (5 or 7.5 cm) paintbrush (for trim)
- 1 in. (2.5 cm) paintbrush (for picture rails)
- Paint

BEFORE YOU BEGIN
Fill damaged woodwork with fine surface filler, then lightly sand. Protect carpets with drop cloths.

gives you the room you need to remove any excess paint by gently pressing the brush against the side of the can.

Following orders

It is usually easiest to paint the ceiling first, then the walls, then finally the trim. Don't worry if paint gets on the trim when you're working on the walls: you'll cover that up later. If you've got a steady hand, you can try painting the trim with the outer bristles of the brush right in the joint where it meets the wall. Otherwise mask the wall with masking tape.

Smooth sanding ▶

The key to an ultra-smooth finish on trim is to apply several coats of paint, sanding with a sanding sponge (not sandpaper) between each coat. Sponges conform to the shape of the woodwork and get into

crevices where sandpaper can't reach. After sanding, vacuum, then wipe down with a tack cloth to remove the fine dust.

Clean line for trim

When painting trim, keep a flat-bladed screwdriver or putty knife handy, and a cloth dampened with the proper solvent. If some paint gets onto the wall or floor, fold the cloth around the tip of the tool and wipe it away.

If you're left-handed, it's best to paint from left to right. If you're right-handed, work from right to left.

How to paint wood moldings

Moldings look best painted GLOSS or SEMI-GLOSS

1 No dust, no drips
The gap between the baseboard and the floor is likely to be full of dust, so vacuum along the bottom edge before you start painting. A piece of cardboard slipped under the edge will help to keep paint drops off the floor.

2 Brush the board
Apply the paint with a 2 or 3 in. (5 or 7.5 cm) paintbrush, depending on the height of the baseboard. Paint so that the brushstrokes go lengthwise, following the run of the baseboard.

3 Paint the picture rails
Use a 1 in. (2.5 cm) brush for picture rails. For best results, apply two or three thin coats rather than one thick one, allowing ample time to dry between coats. Finish off with fine brushstrokes along the length of the picture rail.

Painter's mug ◄
Bolt a handle to a 500g coffee can, coating the bolts with silicone to seal the holes. On the opposite side, drill two holes just below the rim of the can, slide a length of coathanger wire through them, and use to scrape excess paint off your brush. Now you have the perfect paint pot.

Sock it to them
Turn old athletic socks into drip-catchers. Cut off the elasticized band at the top of the sock and stretch it across the body of the brush or around the can. The material will absorb paint trickles.

Preserve picture holes
A fresh coat of paint can fill in and hide small nail holes, which can be a nuisance if you're planning to rehang a picture in its old spot. To preserve a nail hole, stick a toothpick into it. Trim the toothpick until it protrudes by about 1/8 in. (3 mm) so you can brush or roll right over it. Remove after painting and reinstall the picture hanger.

Stop the drips ◄
When you wipe your paintbrush against the side of the can, paint eventually fills the rim and runs down the outside. Solve the problem by wiping your brush against a heavy rubber band stretched over the can. Excess paint will drip back into the can without making a mess or gumming up the lid.

Dump the bumps ▲
Before painting a textured ceiling, drag a flat screwdriver around the perimeter to scrape off a narrow strip of texture along all four edges (you'll never notice it's missing). With the bumps out of the way, you'll be able to achieve a crisp paint line where the ceiling meets the wall.

Hands-on painting
For those awkward spots that a brush can't reach, put your hand in a plastic bag, slip an old sock over the top, dip into the paint and let your improvised tool do the job.

Banish stray bristles
Remove a stray bristle from a window sash by stabbing at it with the tip of the brush and lifting up. To get rid of the annoying bristle for good, wipe the brush on some newspaper and throw it away.

DEALING WITH FLAWS AND SPILLS

Even the most fastidious painters make mistakes. Don't panic if your work looks a little messy, or even if you have a spill. There's always a solution.

Dealing with runs

Sags and runs are difficult to remove once the paint begins to dry. Avoid them by not overloading the paintbrush. If any do form, don't try to remove them while the paint is still tacky. Wait till they dry, then sand back and repaint. You may need to sand back to the bare wood.

Dab hand with spills

Act fast if you spill paint. Scrape up as much as you can with a flat-bladed tool, then dab off what's left with dry absorbent cloths. Lift off any remaining traces with clean cloths dampened with cold water (for water-based acrylics) or mineral spirits (for oil-based enamel paints). If you're cleaning a paint spill on fabric using mineral spirits, you'll need to clean off the residue with dish soap on a damp cloth.

Hard attack

Attack dried acrylic paint on carpets by repeatedly dampening the stain and teasing lumps of paint out of the pile with an old toothbrush. If you have a spill of oil-based enamel paint on your carpet or hard floor, you should be able to remove it with a water-based paint stripper. Test it on an inconspicuous corner first. Neutralize the stripper residue with water immediately afterward.

Surgical removal

If you spot a stray brush bristle as soon as it appears, lift it off the wet paint before it gets stuck. Otherwise, wait until the surface is thoroughly dry, then use a scalpel or utility knife to carefully cut it away from the hardened paintwork.

Rub insects off dry paint

Small insects sometimes land on wet gloss paint and get trapped. Don't try to remove them when the paint is tacky. Instead, wait until the paint is dry and rub them off with a rag dampened with mineral spirits.

Scrape paint off glass

The best tool for removing paint from a windowpane is a purpose-made plastic scraper fitted with a utility knife blade.

Super soaker

If you've spilled a large volume of paint and you happen to be a cat owner, then you can soak it up with kitty litter. Just heap it on the spill, leave it to absorb for a while, then scoop up and discard.

Painting with rollers

Paint rollers cover a large surface area much faster than a hand-held paintbrush. To get the best out of them, load sparingly and roll gently.

What you will need

- Paint
- Paintbrush
- Roller
- Paint tray

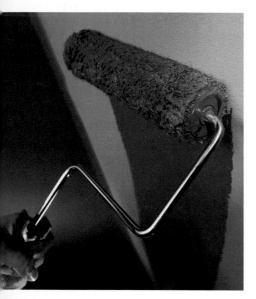

Dip, spin and roll

Don't submerge the roller in the paint to load it; paint will seep inside the roller cover and leak out while you're rolling. Instead, dip only as deep as the nap, spinning the roller against the tray and dipping again until the whole surface is coated.

Start on the inside

Never start against an edge such as a corner or molding with a full roller of paint. If you do, you'll end up with a heavy build-up of paint that can't be dispersed. Instead, start about 12 in. (30 cm) in, then gradually work back toward the edge.

BEFORE YOU BEGIN
For a neat finish, first paint around all the edges of the wall using a paintbrush. Only a brush can give you the crisp line you need where one surface meets another. This process is known as "cutting in."

Roll-on perfection

Areas at the edges and around the trim that are painted with a brush will have a different texture than those painted with a roller. Ensure a consistent finish: brush on the paint, then immediately roll it out using a 3 in. (7.5 cm) roller. Make sure the small roller's nap matches the roller used on the rest of the wall. ▼

When using a roller, roll upward at a slight angle with a light and even pressure.

Foil the mess

Line your paint tray with aluminum foil and you'll save on cleaning later. When you've finished painting, pour the excess paint back into the can, then you can simply remove the foil and throw it away.

Roll over the ceiling

To minimize lap marks when painting a ceiling, feather out the edges as you go. Apply the paint in one long roll from one end of the ceiling to the other, then roll the nearly dry roller in different directions along the edge to disperse the paint. Repeat the process until the ceiling is covered. If applying a second coat, paint in the opposite direction.

Using a roller

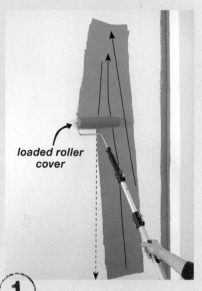

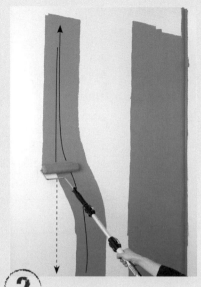

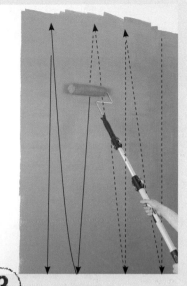

loaded roller cover

① Start near the floor

Load a roller with paint and, starting around 12 in. (30 cm) from the floor and 6 in. (15 cm) from the side, roll upward at a slight angle with light pressure. Stop short of the ceiling and roll down, working quickly to spread paint evenly.

② Continue in stages

Reload the roller and repeat from a starting point further across the wall, rolling up to a point just short of the ceiling and then rolling back down. Continue across the wall. Don't be concerned if you see roller marks; they'll be smoothed out later.

③ Overlap the strokes

Roll back over the entire area you've covered to smooth and blend the paint. Don't reload the roller with paint for this step. Use very light pressure and work the roller so that each new stroke slightly overlaps the previous stroke.

CHOOSING A **ROLLER**

A good roller gets a firm grip on the cover and prevents it from slipping. The roller should spin freely, have an ergonomic and solvent-resistant handle and a durable frame with a metal arm. Make sure it has a threaded handle to which you can attach an extension pole.

★ **Foam** gives a neat finish and is ideal when painting close to trim. For a seamless job, use foam pads when cutting in around the edges and a foam roller for the walls.

★ **Lambs wool** is tough and durable yet made from soft fiber that holds paint well with a minimum amount of splatter.

★ **Synthetic** fibers hold lots of paint, so you'll spend less time loading and reloading the roller.

★ **Microfiber** is suitable for most surfaces and tends not to shed.

★ **Mohair** is easy to clean and the extra-fine fiber holds and releases paint well. It's the best choice for use with high-gloss paints.

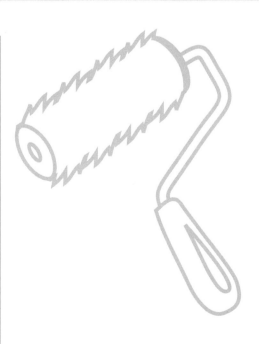

Paint storage and disposal

Be careful about how you seal and store your leftover paint and you'll be able to use it later for touch-ups and patch-ups.

Spray-on seal

To keep a skin from forming on oil-based paint, spray a thin film of mineral spirits over the surface before sealing the can. To apply the spirits, put the solvent in a small cosmetics sprayer (one teaspoonful is enough to seal a half-empty 1 gal. (4 L) can of paint). To keep the film intact, take care not to agitate the can as you seal and store it.

Make your mark ▶

Before you store paint, use a little to mark a line on the can at the level of the paint inside. The line will remind you what color the paint is and how much is left.

Pour and store

Funnel leftover paint into clean 2 qt. (2 L) cooking oil container when you're done. You'll see the hue of the paint through the plastic, and it's easy to pour it into a painting tray when you need it. ◀

Store leftovers in jars

A small amount of paint will keep better if you pour it into a jar with a screw-top lid. The less air in the jar, the better, so try to match the size of the jar to the amount of paint you'll be storing. Rub petroleum jelly around the neck of the jar before pouring in the paint; then any that spills down the outside won't make the lid stick. Label the jar with the date and shade of paint.

Line up the lid

When you open the lid of an old paint can that has been sealed up with dried paint, you'll usually be left with uneven, paint-clogged surfaces on both the lid and the rim. As a result, you'll find it difficult to seal the can the next time. To make the task a bit easier, grab a marker and draw a line across the lid and the rim at two different places before you open the lid. Then when you go to replace the lid, simply align the marks and press the lid down for a quick and easy seal.

Blow hard

When storing leftover paint, take a deep breath of fresh air and then exhale into the can before you snap on the lid. The carbon dioxide you blow out will prevent the paint from forming a skin.

An airtight seal

When storing leftover paint, put the lid back on the can, tap it in securely and then place the can upside down on the shelf. This produces an airtight seal and stops the paint from forming a skin.

Watch your waste

Your local authority can tell you how to dispose of waste paint responsibly in your area. In the meantime, don't let it get into the natural environment.

- Never wash your brushes, rollers or trays by flushing them under running water that will end up in the sewer, stormwater network or natural waterways.

- Never dispose of used mineral spirits or thinners by pouring them onto the ground or down drains.

- Let paint in cans completely dry before throwing it into your garbage and never incinerate paint cans.

Brush and roller care

Before storing brushes and rollers, make sure they're clear of all traces of soap and solvents. Do the job well and they'll last for years.

Suds saver

Oil-based paints often leave an oily residue in your brushes, even after cleaning them in mineral spirits. To get rid of the residue, try washing them in a cheap shampoo. Not only does it remove the oil, it also cleans out the last traces of color.

Comb your brushes

After cleaning your paintbrushes, try running a fine-toothed comb through them. This will remove any residual particles of paint as well as any loose bristles.

Bag the roller

If you're painting with a roller and have to take a break, slide a plastic bag over it and exclude as much air as possible before securing with a twist tie.

It's a wrap

You don't have to clean your brush every time you take a break. To stop it from drying out, wrap it tightly with kitchen foil or plastic wrap. When you're ready to restart, just unwrap and get to work.

In suspension ◄

To keep bristles from bending out of shape while soaking, suspend the brush from a length of stiff wire or thin dowel. Drill a hole in the brush just above the metal band, pass the wire or dowel through it, and then balance the rig on the jar so that the bristles are submerged in the mineral spirits below.

Soak it out

To soften a paintbrush that's stiff with dried water-based acrylic paint, soak it in a solution of equal parts vinegar and water for 10 minutes.

Roll and rinse

Getting all the acrylic paint off a paint roller is easy, but time-consuming. First, using an old blunt knife or screwdriver blade, scrape as much paint as possible back into the can. Next, run the roller over the

ribbed part of the paint tray and finally over sheets of newspaper to remove excess paint. Remove the roller sleeve if possible. Wash in cold or tepid water, working the paint out of the nap with your hands. You can also use a little soap, but be sure to rinse it all out before storing.

Keep bristles shapely

After you've cleaned your brushes, wrap them in plastic wrap, secure them with rubber bands, and hang them from hooks or nails. Next time you need to use them, they'll be clean and, most importantly, the bristles won't be misshapen.

Slip a plastic bag over your paint roller if you need to take a break

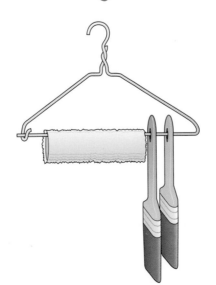

Drip-dry rollers

Making sure that paint rollers and brushes maintain their shape while they dry can be a problem, but a homemade hanger can help. Just cut a standard wire clothes hanger in one corner and shape the end into a hook. Bend the sides closer together so the arm will fit into the hook. Slide the roller and brushes on the wire and hang them out to drip-dry in a convenient place. ◄

Painting doors, windows and stairs

These tried-and-tested techniques will make easy work of painting doors, windows and stairs.

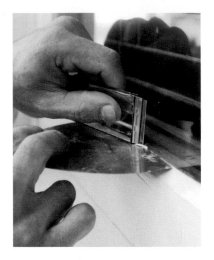

Fast door painting

The quickest way to paint a door is to apply the paint with a short ¼ in. (5 mm) nap roller, then to flatten out the stipple left by the roller nap with a paint-moistened, 3 in. (7.5 cm) synthetic brush. Take long, light strokes from the top and the bottom of the door, gently lifting the bristles off the door at the middle. The result will be a fast, smooth finish.

Keeping the edge

If a door is over-painted, it's likely to stick in its frame. To avoid the problem, sand all the edges of the door before repainting.

Masking the problem

When painting a door, you'll need to protect the hardware from drips. Before you start, cover each hinge leaf with masking tape, trimming off the excess.

Easy with the right brush

Painting multi-paned windows is a tedious job, especially if you have to put masking tape around all the woodwork to stop paint from getting on the glass. An alternative is to take your time and use a cutting-in brush to paint the woodwork. ▼

On a knife edge ▶

Here's an easy way to scrape paint from windows without damaging the glass. First, place a 4 in. (10 cm) putty knife blade against the putty or molding, then slide a razor blade scraper across the knife blade to make a perfectly clean edge.

Order of work

If you're painting windows, doors, and baseboards, start early in the day and do the windows first, followed by the doors, so they'll be dry before you need to close them at night. Paint the baseboards last, so any dust picked up on the brush from the floor as you work won't be spread to other surfaces.

Window short cut

Save time when painting multi-paned windows by "masking" them with lip balm instead of masking tape. Rub the balm around the edges of the glass, next to the trim, leaving a border of bare glass about

⅛ in. (3 mm) wide for a good seal. Any paint that ends up on the coated surface will be easy to remove when the paint is dry.

Smart stairs

Don't give up the use of your stairs during a painting job. First paint every other step and then, when they're dry, paint the alternate steps. This way you'll be able to use the stairs without spoiling the paintwork.

Connect the colors

If a door is going to be a different color on each side, paint the latch or lock edge the same color as the face that opens into the room. Match the hinge edge to the other side of the door.

PAINTING **BALUSTRADES**

The uprights and handrail of a staircase balustrade suffer a lot of wear and tear. It may seem like a tedious job, but giving them a fresh coat of paint will help to keep them in good condition.

★ Start by painting the balusters (uprights), working from the top of the staircase down, and from the top of each one in turn.

★ Paint the underside of the handrail next, then give the top and sides of the handrail two coats of paint for a hard-wearing finish.

★ Next paint the newel posts (the large posts supporting the handrail), again working from the top down.

★ Finish with the stringers (the boards that form the edges of the staircase), painting the outer sides first, then the inner sides.

What you will need

- Medium-grit sandpaper
- Lint-free cloth
- Primer (if required)
- Paint
- Small mirror
- Hammer and screwdrivers
- Paintbrushes (1 in./2.5 cm and 3 in./7.5 cm)

Painting a door

1 Sand the surface

Remove lockset hardware. Sand door with medium-grit sandpaper to dull the glossy paint, then wipe away any dust. Clean the door with a lint-free cloth and paint with primer, if necessary.

2 Paint the edges

Use a mirror to inspect the bottom edge of the door to see whether or not it has been sealed previously. If not, take out the hinge pins, remove the door and apply a primer. Proceed by painting all the edges of the door with a 1 in. (2.5 cm) brush before moving on to the panels.

3 Coat the panels

Paint the door one side at a time. For a panel door, first paint the molding using a 1 in. (2.5 cm) brush, then paint the panels themselves using a 3 in. (7.5 cm) brush. (When painting sliding doors, complete one door before starting the other. With flush doors, work from the top down.)

4 Finish the faces

Clean up any paint drips on the vertical stiles and horizontal rails (the flat faces of the door). Using a 3 in. (7.5 cm) brush, paint the center stile next, but only the areas between panels. Then paint the rails, feathering the edges wherever you meet a previously painted area. Finish with the two outside stiles.

5 Swing the color

When the door has dried, paint the trim with a 1 in. (2.5 cm) brush. On the in-swinging side, use the color of the in-swinging side of the door to paint the casing and the jamb up to the stops. On the out-swinging side, use the color of the out-swinging side of the door to paint the casing, the remaining jamb and the stops themselves.

How to paint a double-hung window

1 Clean and clear

Lay down a drop cloth, and clean the window glass, frames and trim. Remove any loose paint with a scraper or fine sandpaper. Take off locking hardware. Apply primer to any bare wood, and stain sealer if required. To guard against drips, apply masking tape or lip balm to the glass and low-tack tape to the adjacent wall surface.

2 Paint the sashes

Open both sashes halfway. Paint as much of the upper sash as possible, painting vertical surfaces first, then horizontal ones, and letting paint overlap the glass by ⅛ in. (3 mm). Reverse the sash positions, and paint the lower parts of the upper sash. Now paint the lower sash, again doing vertical surfaces first.

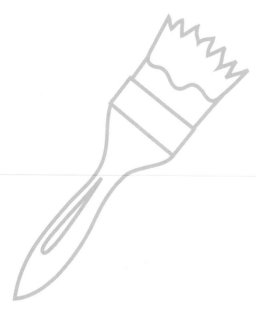

Stenciling

Stencils are a quick-and-easy way of decorating furniture, walls and floors. You can buy them pre-cut, or make your own.

DIY stencils

Copy your design onto a piece of paper and pencil a level line 1 in. (2.5 cm) from the bottom. This guideline will help you align the pieces of the stencil later on. Now trace the design onto clear acetate. If your design is multi-colored, you'll need one piece of acetate for each color. Tape one of the sheets of acetate to a cutting board and, using an art knife, cut out the areas for one color. Repeat for each color. Label the stencils to indicate top, bottom, right and left of the design.

Background check

Any type of paint can serve as a background for stenciling, but the most workable surface is a very low-sheen or eggshell finish. The background surface must be clean and completely dry before you start.

Test your combination

Before you start stenciling, always do a trial run on a piece of paper. You'll get to see exactly how the colors look together—and you'll get a chance to change them if you don't like the result!

> DO NOT paint aluminum tracks

③ Do the details

Use exterior paint on the bottom edge of the lower sash and the top edge of the upper sash. Check the sash corners and muntins for paint build-up and drips, and remove them by gently dabbing with a dry brush. When the windows are dry to the touch, slide them up and down a few times.

④ Take on the trim

Paint the casings, then the window stool and apron. Paint the window tracks last, if at all. If you must paint them be sure to strip or sand back all the existing paint first. Lower both sashes all the way so that you can paint the upper track. When that's dry, raise the sashes and paint the lower track.

⑤ A neat finish

Wipe off any lip balm and remove the masking tape and low-tack tape. If there's any excess paint on the window glass, use a scraper to scrape it off. After all parts of the painted window are completely dry, reinstall the window hardware.

▦ Protect the pattern

Spray the finished stencil with a coat of extra-pale matte varnish. This will protect the work and make it possible for you to wipe the stencil clean when necessary.

▦ Easy does it

When securing a stencil to the wall, use low-tack masking tape. Regular masking tape is strong and can damage the existing finish; low-tack tape has a weaker adhesive. Alternatively, spray the back of the stencil with artist's adhesive (do your spraying inside a clean box to contain the mess).

▦ Keep moving

It is best to choose fast-drying stencil paints or artist's acrylics when working on a multi-colored design. You'll spend less time waiting for the colors to dry, so you'll finish sooner.

▦ Pounce on it ◄

The characteristic stencil-look is created by the light dabbing of the tips of the brush bristles against the stencil. When stenciling, always try to dab from the edges of the stencil to the center.

Use a dabbing motion when applying paint to a stencil to prevent paint from seeping under the edges of the template.

Wallpaper preparation

If you want your wallpaper job to last, you'll need a well-prepared surface. Be ready to spend some time stripping before you start hanging.

Apply lining paper if the wall surface is rough; with liner in place you can paint or paper as you prefer.

Test for take-off

If there's only one layer of untextured wallpaper on the wall, and it's still adhering well, then you can paper right over the top of it. (If there are more than two layers, you'll have to strip them off, as the combined weight will be too great for the adhesive to bear.) Test the old wallpaper by running your fingertips over it; a crackling noise means it's loose and should be removed. Check the edges and corners, too, by prying them up with a putty knife. If large sections lift off, it will all have to go.

Covering old paper

If the old wallpaper passes the crackle and corner tests (above), stick down loose areas with wood glue or wallpaper paste, wash with dish soap or a mild solution of household bleach and water, apply a primer made for use under wallpapers and get ready to hang the new paper. Be aware, though, that papering over vinyl, foil or plastic-coated wallpapers is rarely successful; those papers are better off being removed.

All in good time

After you remove the old wallpaper and before you start hanging the new, paint the ceiling and all the trim. It's reasonably easy to remove wallpaper paste from woodwork and painted surfaces, but it's almost impossible to remove drips and splashes of paint from newly hung wallpaper. The wallpaper will also cover any paint on the walls.

Foolproof fabric

If you plan to hang fabric on the wall, it's a good idea to put up a lining paper first. To look good, fabric needs an especially smooth wall surface, and a lining paper is the quickest, and usually the easiest, way to achieve this.

Cure-all covering

Lining paper hides surface defects, which makes it a great problem-solver. If paint is peeling off your wall, sand off the loosest flakes, then cover with lining paper. If your wall is painted with hazardous lead-based paint that you mustn't disturb, cover with lining paper. For a rough surface like a brick wall, just cover with lining paper first. Once the lining paper is in place, you can paint or paper as you prefer.

Press test ▲

To test if lining paper is dry, press it lightly with your finger. If it doesn't indent, you can go ahead and paint or paper over the top. If it does indent, aim a fan at the wall to speed the drying process and check again in a few hours.

WALLPAPERING TOOLS

For any wallpapering job, you'll need a steel measuring tape, a pencil and a straightedge to act as a guide when you trim paper, plus a supply of towels and sponges for cleaning. You may also need some of the tools listed below.

1 Paste brush or roller
Use a roller or brush (5 to 6 in./12.5 to 15 cm) to apply paste. If you use an old paintbrush, make sure that it is clean. Wash the brush well in warm water after use.

2 Bucket
Any clean household bucket is fine for mixing the paste. Tie a piece of string across the rim, between the handle anchor points, and rest the brush on the string when you are not using it. Wiping the brush across the string will remove surplus paste.

3 Scissors
Paperhanger's scissors with 10 in. (25 cm) long blades are best for the main cutting work. The longer the blades, the easier it is to cut a straight line. Also keep a pair of small scissors handy for fine trimming.

4 Sponge
Use a clean damp sponge to wipe paste off equipment and to remove excess paste from the surface of vinyls and washable wallpaper.

5 Trimming knife
A good quality razor knife is useful for trimming and cutting vinyl wall coverings. It is also sometimes easier to trim pasted paper neatly with a knife and straightedge than with a pair of scissors—provided the paper is not too thin.

6 Plastic smoothers
A wide plastic smoother is used for smoothing out bubbles and creases in newly hung wall coverings. A small smoother is good for pressing down the seams.

7 Plumbline and bob
Use a plumbline to mark the true vertical on a wall before hanging the first length of wallpaper—few walls are straight. Buy one or make one by tying a small weight—a metal nut or a small screwdriver—to a length of string.

Hanging wallpaper

Wallpaper-hanging can be easy or challenging. It depends as much on your choice of pattern as on your paperhanging skills.

▦ Know your limits

Making sure the pattern matches across adjacent strips of wallpaper is a skill that takes time to master. If it's your first attempt at hanging wallpaper, choose one with no pattern match or a random pattern.

▦ Buy thick wallpaper

The heavier the wallpaper, the easier it should be to hang. Thin, cheap wallpapers tear and crease easily, making them hard to handle, especially for beginners. The strongest wall coverings of all are the vinyls. They're made from a tough printed plastic film bonded to a paper backing.

▦ Measure it out

If you're hanging wallpaper in a room with a typical ceiling height of around 8 ft. (2.5 m) and the paper doesn't have a repeat pattern, you'll probably get four lengths from each roll. If the paper has a large pattern repeat, you may get as few as three lengths. The vertical distance between repeats will be noted on the packaging; use it as a guide to calculate quantities.

▦ Just get this straight

The most important thing when hanging wallpaper is to hang the first strip perfectly vertical and straight. It's rare for the ceiling

SECRETS
from the EXPERTS

Make the job faster and easier by **marking key measurements directly** onto the pasting table. You won't have to constantly use your tape measure.

and walls to be absolutely straight, and a tiny difference at the beginning can turn into a major catastrophe by the end.

Starting smart

Using a plumbline, draw a vertical line on the wall parallel to the corner so that the distance between the two is equal to the width of the paper, minus ½ in. (1.5 cm). Now hang your first strip so that one edge is on the plumbline and the other wraps around onto the adjacent wall by ½ in. (1.5 cm).

Pick out the plugs

Before you hang your paper, place wooden toothpicks in all the wall anchors and attachment holes you want to retain, making sure they protrude by a tiny bit. The toothpicks will come through the new paper and you'll find it easy to locate the holes for repositioning those hanging or fixed items.

Fold and cut

To make a cutting line across a strip of wallpaper, make a mark at the right length, then fold the paper so the sides are precisely aligned, and crease. Unfold, then cut along the crease line. This method ensures your cut will be at right angles to the paper's edge. ▼

For a seamless look, remove the plastic plates of light switches, position the wallpaper, and replace.

ON THE **PAPER TRAIL**

Your wallpaper selection shouldn't be based on looks alone. When shopping around, consider these features.

★ **Vertical repeat**

The repeat is the distance from the start of a pattern to where it appears again. Some papers have repeats of more than 3 ft. (1 m). The longer the repeat, the more paper you're likely to need.

★ **Pre-trimming**

Most papers come pre-trimmed so the edges are perfect and ready to hang; stick to these if you're a beginner. Untrimmed paper is best left to the experts.

★ **Match**

The way the pattern aligns from sheet to sheet is called the "match." For some papers you'll need to slide adjacent sheets around to make the match and complete the pattern. A random pattern doesn't require such precision.

★ **Coverage**

To calculate how many rolls of wallpaper you'll need, find out the square foot (or square meter) coverage of the paper. Work out how many rolls you'll need, then add one more (or two if you have some tricky cuts or angles).

★ **Washability**

Some papers can be cleaned repeatedly before they start to show wear. The measure of this is called the "washability"—read the label.

What you will need

- Brush or roller
- Scissors
- Wallpaper paste
- Plastic smoother
- Razor knife
- 12 in. (30 cm) taping knife

BEFORE YOU BEGIN

Mark the position of each sheet with a pencil, using a wallpaper roll, tape measure and plumbline and bob as guides.

Hanging wallpaper

Hang the first sheet in the most visible corner

1 Put on the paste

Apply paste to the bottom half of your first strip, working from the middle to the edges. Next, fold the paper over so the pasted faces are touching. This allows the paste to cure without drying out. Repeat for the top half of the strip.

2 Hang the paper

Allow the sheet to rest for the time specified by the manufacturer. Unfold the top half and align the edge with your first pencil line, overlapping the cornice by 1 in. (2.5 cm). Leave the bottom half folded to keep the paste moist.

Cutting corners

When pasting wallpaper, remember to leave a small patch with no paste in each of the upper corners. Those patches will help you keep your hands clean for as long as possible while you're hanging up the strip.

Hang it high

It's not always easy to find a place to rest pasted paper before attaching it to the wall. A broom handle balanced between two chairs makes a great hanging rail.

Cut out confusion

One way to deal with doors and windows is to prepare the cut-outs in advance. Label them clearly to avoid confusion.

Brush out bubbles

To avoid air bubbles, always apply wallpaper paste with a wallpaper brush. Work from the center to the sides of each strip, and from top to bottom. Ensure you cover the paper well, but don't overdo it.

Eye the edges

Adjacent strips must be butted up, edge-to-edge, and a roller run over the seam from top to bottom to ensure the paper adheres well. Sometimes there isn't enough paste on the edges of the paper. Keep a pot of paste and a small, flat brush handy so you can apply touch-ups.

Play safe with scissors

Leave a 4 in. (10 cm) overhang at the top and bottom of each strip. Mark a crease at the cornice and at the baseboard with the rounded tip of a pair of scissors. Pull back the paper slightly, cut at the crease line with scissors, reglue and reattach. Overhangs can be cut with a utility knife, but cutting with scissors reduces the chance of a tear.

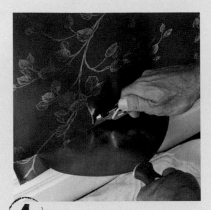

③ Smooth out

Run a plastic smoother across the paper to work out any imperfections. First move the knife up and down the edge aligned with the plumbline, then diagonally away from it. When you're done, align and flatten the bottom half of the sheet.

④ Trim and tidy

With a razor knife, trim overhanging paper, using a 12 in. (30 cm) taping knife as a guide. Slide the taping knife across the paper, leaving the edge in place until the cut is complete. Clean away paste deposits from baseboards and cornices.

⑤ Align and butt the joints

Prepare a second strip. When it's ready, unfold the top half and hang it so the pattern aligns with the first strip. Butt the second strip against the first and smooth. Continue working around the room, matching, smoothing, trimming and cleaning.

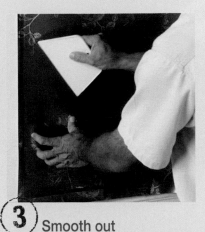

Turn off the power at the breaker first

▦ Fit for a frame

To hang paper neatly around a window or door casing, first hang a length of wallpaper so it overlaps the casing then make diagonal cuts at all the corners. Next, fold back the flaps of paper as far as the edges of the casing, then trim along the crease lines.

▦ Make the switch ◄

Papering around an outlet or a light switch is easier than you think. First, hang the paper straight over the top of the object, then make two diagonal cuts from corner to corner with a utility knife. Fold back the triangular flaps, mark with a crease, and then cut along the crease lines with scissors. Any overhanging paper can be tucked under the coverplate for a neat finish.

▦ An invisible repair

An air bubble that doesn't flatten out as the paste dries is usually caused by a dry spot on the back of the paper. To solve the problem, make two diagonal cuts across the bubble with a utility knife or sharp art blade. Peel back the flaps and apply a little paste to the back of the paper with a small paintbrush. Fold the flaps back and gently press into place. ▶

Furniture refinishing and repairs

Stripping

Reveal the beauty of a piece of wood furniture, with its natural grain and color, by stripping off ugly paints and varnishes.

▓ First, identify the finish

Clear finishes can be tricky to identify. If a finish has a low sheen and very little surface thickness, it's probably a penetrating oil. Otherwise you can identify the finish by testing a small, unseen spot. Rub the spot with a rag moistened with denatured alcohol. If the finish softens, it's shellac. If it doesn't, try rubbing with lacquer thinner. If the finish softens, it's a lacquer-based finish. If neither product affects the finish, it's probably a varnish.

▓ Go easy on antiques

Always respect the age of an antique and do as little as possible to change the original construction and finish. Stripping off a finish and replacing it with a new one could drastically reduce the value of an antique. If a chair is a little loose and creaky or a table's lacquer top is cracking, leave it as it is.

▓ Chemical stripper is best

The best way to take off old paint and varnish is with a chemical stripper. When you sand you also remove some of the wood and that can spoil delicate, well-defined moldings. When you use a hot-air gun or blowtorch, you risk charring the surface. Furthermore, abrasives and heat can pose a health risk when used on old lead-based paints; always strip these with chemical strippers.

▓ Beware of caustic dips

Furniture stripped in a commercial hot caustic soda bath is subjected to sudden changes in temperature—first, when it goes into the dip, then when it's hosed with water to remove the chemical. These sudden stresses can crack panels, weaken joints and raise grain, and may also discolor the wood. Neither cedar nor redwood reacts well to caustic dips.

What you will need

- Goggles
- Mask
- Chemical-resistant gloves or two pairs of rubber gloves
- Chemical stripper
- Paintbrush
- Plastic or metal scraper
- Brass brush or old toothbrush
- Steel wool (medium and fine)
- Mineral spirits
- Pointed tool, such as an old screwdriver or grout remover
- Cheesecloth or terry cloth
- Clean lint-free cloth
- Vacuum cleaner with brush attachment

Strip furniture

(1) Brush it on

To work safely, wear goggles, a mask and chemical-resistant gloves (or two pairs of rubber gloves). Brush on a liberal coating of stripper, working from top to bottom, one section at a time. Reposition the piece of furniture as often as necessary, and avoid going over any area with more than one brushstroke.

For easier access, place the piece on a table or a workbench

(2) Scrape it off

When the finish has bubbled up, use a plastic or metal scraper to remove it from large, flat surfaces. To get the finish out of crevices, use a brass brush or an old toothbrush. Repeat the process until all finish has been scraped away. Use medium steel wool to remove the very last of the finish, working with the grain to avoid scratches.

▦ Gel or liquid?

Gel strippers are effective on a range of surfaces, but are best on vertical surfaces, as they're easy to control and won't run to the floor. If you don't have a proprietary gel stripper, mix a little wallpaper paste into a water-based liquid stripper. Use liquid strippers on detailed woodwork, as they're better at getting into intricate carvings and moldings. ▼

TO STRIP OR NOT TO STRIP?

★ Clean up your act

Sometimes all that's needed to make a grimy garage-sale bargain look like new is a thorough cleaning. Mix equal parts of boiled linseed oil and mineral spirits. Warm the mixture slightly in a double boiler, then rub it on with some cheesecloth or terry cloth, or a coarser material depending on how dirty the surface is. After removing the bulk of the dirt, buff the piece with a soft, clean cloth.

★ Quick new finish

If the finish is showing a little wear and tear but is otherwise in good condition, restore it with furniture refinisher. Sold in home centers, refinisher melts and rejuvenates the existing finish without destroying the patina. Brush it on, wait the recommended time, then rub the piece with a soft cloth. The reworked finish will be lighter in color, but all the scratches and dirt will be gone.

★ The solvent solution

An old but otherwise solid finish can be rejuvenated with a dose of solvent. First identify the finish and the solvent that softens it (see opposite). Brush on the solvent, let it stand until most of it has evaporated, then rework the finish with a soft cloth. Always test a hidden spot first, and be prepared to strip and refinish the piece if it doesn't work.

Remove any loose steel fibers—they will CORRODE and STAIN the wood

③ Strip fancy legs

Brush the stripper on vertical surfaces one section at a time. After the finish has dissolved, use medium steel wool to remove it from turned pieces and small surfaces. For best results, unravel the steel wool slightly and rinse it often in mineral spirits.

④ Clean out crevices

Crevices usually require additional attention. Let the stripper do the work. Force it into crevices with the tip of a paintbrush, wait, then use a pointed tool such as an old screwdriver or a tool for removing tile grout (as shown here), to carefully scrape the dissolved finish from the crevices.

⑤ Restore the balance

To remove residue and neutralize the stripping chemical, rub the entire piece with a rag or towel dipped in mineral spirits, rinsing the pad often. Do not use water, which can raise the grain of the wood. After rubbing, wipe the piece with a cheesecloth or terry cloth, then vacuum with the brush attachment.

Clean up with vinegar

If wood has been left in a caustic dip for too long, the excess chemical may show up as salty white stains. To remove the stains, rub with a strong solution of white vinegar. Repeat this several times over a period of weeks until all the chemical has leached out.

Breathe easy

The safest place to work with chemical stripper is outside, in the open air. If you do have to work indoors, wear a mask and open the windows to avoid inhaling the strong fumes.

Start small

Stripping a piece of furniture well demands great patience, so start with something relatively small. A good rule of thumb for beginners is to only tackle pieces you can pick up by yourself. Stick to chairs and hatstands, and leave dining tables, wardrobes and four-poster beds until you have gained some experience.

Scrub up the details ▲

A wire-bristled suede brush is the ideal tool for removing softened paint and varnish from carvings and moldings. It's also good for scrubbing open-grained hardwoods such as mahogany and oak.

Take it in sections

If you're stripping a large piece of furniture, tackle it a section at a time. For example, strip the tabletop right back to bare wood before starting on the legs. Achieving the desired result with one section will encourage you to persevere with the project.

Stand tall as you work

Stripping a piece of furniture can take hours, so it's best to make yourself comfortable. If possible, stand the item on a steady platform so you're not bending your back as you work. You'll also be less likely to miss any nooks and crannies. And keep some water handy in case you splash stripper on your skin.

A job for old brushes

Stiff, old paintbrushes are ideal for applying paint stripper. Before you start, soak the old brush in a jar of the stripper. The dried-on paint will soon soften and separate from the bristles, leaving the brush pliable and ready to use.

Stripping a piece of furniture well demands great patience, so start with something relatively small.

▨ For a close shave ▲
With its straight and curved edges, a triangular or tear-shaped shave hook provides both straight and curved edges for stripping inside very tight corners.

▨ Handling the curves
Scrape out small inside curves with a washer clamped in locking pliers. If you can't find a washer that fits the curve exactly, file one back until it's the ideal shape.

▨ Scour off stubborn bits
Use a scouring pad dipped in paint stripper to remove any last vestiges of paint and varnish from the grain of the wood. Always rub in the direction of the grain to avoid scratching the surface.

▨ Save on scrapers
On flat surfaces, a plastic kitchen spatula is a perfect substitute for a plastic scraper. Just push it firmly through the dissolved stripper—it will scrape it off without scratching the wood.

▨ No sharp edges
Strippers soften the wood, so it's wise to round off your scraper's sharp corners with a file before taking off the dissolved finish. That way you won't score the wood. ▼

> Use a VISE if you have one—it will make this job a breeze

Plug before you strip

Prior to stripping, remove all the hardware from a piece of furniture and plug the screw and key holes with twisted newspaper. The plugs stop the openings from collecting stripper residue, which dries rock-hard and is difficult to remove.

Water can cause veneers to lift, so use a solvent-based stripper if you are working on veneered furniture.

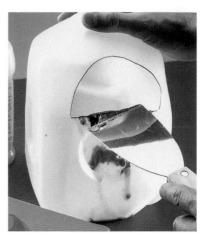

Recycle the gunk ▲

Some of the product that collects on your scraper while you're stripping can be reused. Make your own gunk-collector by cutting a semi-circular opening in the side of a plastic milk or juice bottle. Clean your loaded scraper by pulling it back over the cut edge so that the product drops into the container. When you have finished and you want to reuse some of the stripper, turn the bottle over and funnel the used product into another container.

Quick Fix

NET ADVANTAGE

After a stripping job, clean up around turned components such as table legs with a handful of the nylon netting that is used to bag fresh produce, such as apples, oranges and onions.

Save any clear drippings for a second coat

Catch the drips ▲

To protect floors while stripping, spread out plenty of old newspapers and stand the feet of chairs and tables in foil pie cases or baking trays to catch the runs. Test before using plastic tubs—stripper may dissolve them.

Soak the hardware

You'll also want to remove all traces of paint from hardware on wood furniture. To loosen water-based paint, soak it in boiling water. For oil-based paint, immerse it overnight in a bucket containing ½ lb (250 g) of ash from a wood fireplace mixed with 2 gal. (8 L) of water. Wear rubber gloves when reaching into the bucket.

Lose the lead paint

Don't recycle stripper if the old paint is lead-based. The residue could be harmful, and should be discarded as soon as possible. Scrape it into a container and take it to your local chemical waste drop-off point.

SECRETS
from the EXPERTS

Sticky stripper residue will slide easily off your scraper blade if you occasionally lubricate the blade's surface with a squirt of non-stick cooking spray.

Sanding

The secret to quality sanding is to match the tool you use with the task in front of you. Add a little patience, and you're set to go.

Hose it down

Sand the surfaces of tight inside curves with a sanding block made from garden hose. Take a 6 in. (15 cm) length of hose and slit all but 1 in. (2.5 cm) of it with a sharp knife. Wrap the sandpaper around the hose with the abrasive side facing out, tucking the edges into the slit.

Get organized

If you do a lot of sanding, it pays to file your sandpaper sheets by size, type and grade in the pockets of an accordion file.

Match the curves

Shaped trim is easier to sand with a sanding block that matches the contours of the wood. Surround a small sample piece of trim with scrap wood about ¾ in. (2 cm) higher than the surface. Liberally apply oil or lubricating spray to the trim and to the internal faces of the frame. Fill with a two-part filler, allow to dry before carefully removing the frame and trim. Now wrap sandpaper around the block and get to work. ▼

MONEY SAVER
Built to last

Sandpaper can wear through very quickly when you're sanding. To make it last longer, back the sheet with strips of duct tape.

Pencil it in

When you're doing a light sand over a large area, it can be hard to keep track of where you've sanded and where you haven't. To avoid the problem, scribble light pencil lines over the surface of the piece before you start, then sand away until they're all gone. You won't miss a spot. The finer the grit of sandpaper you're using, the lighter the pencil lines must be. ▶

SANDPAPER **BY THE NUMBERS**

★ Sandpaper is classified by a number reflecting the size of its grit particles. Higher numbers indicate smaller grains for finer sanding. Here are the common grades of sandpaper.

Grit	Texture	Use
40–60	Very coarse	Rough sanding and shaping. Removing paint.
80–150	Medium	Intermediate sanding after rough sanding. Sanding on previously painted surfaces.
180–220	Medium fine	Final sanding before applying finish.
240–360	Fine	Smoothing primer and paint. Smoothing before second coat of lacquer.
400 up	Very fine	Wet-sanding varnish or lacquer for an ultrasmooth finish.

Perfect your palette

Fine-tune the shade of a stain by adding artists' paint in small amounts. Use oil paint for an oil-based stain, and watercolor for a water-based one. When working with oils, mix the paint with a little linseed oil first, then dilute it with mineral spirits before adding to the stain. Do the mixing in a glass jar so you can keep an eye on color changes, and always test the mixture on a hidden patch first.

Check for compatibility

If you plan on mixing stains and dyes, make sure they're compatible first. Dyes are usually water-based, but stains can be either water-based or oil-based. For a successful blend, both products must have the same base, so check the labels.

Tricks for tiny spots

Use a cotton swab to stain intricate woodwork. The swab can get into tiny crevices, making easy work of finely detailed jobs.

Make a DIY dust-magnet

You'll need a sticky "tack cloth" to collect fine dust from a sanded surface before staining. Make your own by wetting a cloth with mineral spirits, then dripping a little varnish onto it. Fold the cloth and squeeze to disperse the varnish and wring out the excess mineral spirits. Store it in an airtight container.

> Stains can vary in color from batch to batch. Always buy enough stain to finish the job.

What you will need

- Rubber gloves
- Wood sealer (if required)
- Medium-grit sandpaper (if required)
- Tack cloth
- Wood finish
- 2 in. (5 cm) paintbrush
- Lint-free cloth
- Fine-grit sandpaper (if required)

BEFORE YOU BEGIN
Always check the manufacturer's instructions before applying finishes to wood furniture.

Sneak a preview

To get an idea of how a wood surface would look when coated with a clear varnish, just dampen a rag with mineral spirits and wipe it on an inconspicuous area. If you're not satisfied, change the tone with a stain before varnishing.

Stir but never shake

Do not shake a tin of varnish. Shaking creates air bubbles that will spoil the finish. Instead, stir the contents of the tin slowly and gently with a clean, flat stick.

Banish the bubbles

Air bubbles can spoil the finish of a fresh coat of varnish. To work bubble-free, pour varnish into a

---

Spontaneous combustion

Rags that are still wet with oil-based finish can burn your house down! As the oil dries and changes from liquid to solid, it absorbs oxygen. This process generates heat. When this heat is trapped in a wad of rags, the heat feeds on itself until the rags ignite. Be sure to hang rags until they're completely dry before you throw them out.

SAFETY FIRST

Apply the finish

> Brush in line with the wood grain

1 Prepare the surface

Check the product instructions for the finish you're using and, if necessary, apply a sealer first, wearing rubber gloves. When the sealer dries, smooth the surface with a medium-grade sandpaper, then wipe with a tack cloth. If no sealer is required, simply clean the wood with a tack cloth.

2 Apply the product

Brush on the finish from top to bottom, working on one section at a time. If it's a polyurethane or varnish product, brush on just enough for an even coat. If it's a penetrating finish, wipe off the excess with a cloth before it dries.

3 Work on a perfect finish

Check the manufacturer's instructions in case you need to sand between coats. If sanding is necessary, let each coat dry before sanding with fine-grade sandpaper, then remove dust with a tack cloth before applying the next coat. Let the final coat dry for 48 hours.

brand-new paint pail or a container kept solely for varnish. Load your brush, then press it against the side of the pail. This action will remove any air trapped in the bristles.

▦ Leave no bristles behind

Cheap brushes tend to lose bristles, which then stick to the wet surface of a fresh coat of finish, ruining it. For a professional finish, apply varnish and lacquer with a good-quality paintbrush or varnishing brush—but even a quality brush can have some loose bristles when it's new. To get rid of them, dip the brush in a mix of solvent and varnish, then brush vigorously on some paper or scrap board.

▦ Finish before fitting

Remove wooden knobs and handles before you varnish or lacquer a piece of furniture. Apply the finish to the knobs and handles separately, then reattach them when all surfaces are dry. ▼

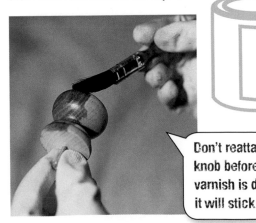

> Don't reattach a knob before the varnish is dry— it will stick

FINISHING TOUCH:
FURNITURE FINISHES

Lacquer, polyurethane and varnish are all readily available in satin, semigloss and gloss—but as furniture finishes, they have different benefits and disadvantages.

 ## Clear acrylic

SOLVENT

- Water

CHARACTERISTICS

- Genuinely clear, thin, hard film with no amber tones. Moderate resistance to wear and spills.

HOW TO APPLY

- Usually sold in a spray can. To apply, spray or, if necessary, brush on two or three thin coats.

 ## Oil-based varnish

SOLVENT

- Mineral spirits

CHARACTERISTICS

- Hard film with a warm, amber tone. Moderate to good resistance to wear and spills.

HOW TO APPLY

- Brush on two to three coats, sanding between coats. Recoating is easy but spot-repairs are problematic.

 ## Lacquer

SOLVENT

- Lacquer thinner

CHARACTERISTICS

- Thin, hard film. Very good spill and wear resistance. Often used on commercial furniture.

HOW TO APPLY

- Usually professional equipment is used to spray on two or three coats. If using a slow-drying product, apply with a brush. Don't use over other finishes.

 ## Penetrating oil

SOLVENT

- Mineral spirits

CHARACTERISTICS

- Soaks into wood fibers for natural-looking finish.

HOW TO APPLY

- Wipe or brush on, let stand for 30 minutes, then rub vigorously. Usually three coats are required. Wet-sand the surface before applying the third coat.

 ## Polyurethane

SOLVENT

- Mineral spirits

CHARACTERISTICS

- Very hard oil-based film has a warm, amber tone. Water-based is crystal clear. Excellent resistance to wear and spills.

HOW TO APPLY

- Brush on two coats for oil-based; three for water-based. Recoat within the specified time; spot finishes are problematic. Don't use over shellac.

 ## Shellac (white or orange)

SOLVENT

- Denatured alcohol

CHARACTERISTICS

- Thin, lustrous film, either clear (white shellac) or amber-toned (orange shellac). Wears well but easily marred by spills.

HOW TO APPLY

- Brush on two or three thin coats. Spot-repairs are easily done.

Hands-free finishing

Applying finish to knobs can be tricky. To avoid having to handle the knob, use a clothespin to grasp it by its screw, then set the upright peg on a steady base.

Lift the legs clear ▲

Drive a screw into the bottom of each chair leg, adjusting as required to keep the piece from rocking. Now you can apply the final coat, all the way to the leg ends.

Buff on a sheen

When the last coat of an oil or varnish finish is completely dry, buff it with polishing cloths made from old jeans (avoid seams). The denim leaves a lovely lustre.

Don't let dust spoil the job. Always sand in one workplace and finish the piece in another.

Apply with paper

Use paper towels, not rags, for applying penetrating oils. When you work with rags, lint can become embedded in the finish, but paper towels are lint-free. Oil-soaked towels can spontaneously combust in a garbage can, so leave them to dry thoroughly before throwing them out.

Turn the can over

After you've put the lid back on a can of varnish, invert it for about half an hour before storing it the right way up. This creates a better seal and prevents a skin from forming.

Painting furniture

A coat of paint can transform a tired or tatty piece of furniture into something splendid. Do your best to prepare it properly and give it an even coat.

Avoid a sticky situation

When priming and painting drawers, coat only the fronts and their edges. Applying paint to the sides will make drawers stick. Coat the sides with a clear finish.

Patience makes perfect

Don't pick out stray brush bristles, dust particles or lint from a painted surface once a skin has started to form on it. Instead, wait for the surface to dry, then buff out the flaws with a damp paper towel.

Warm up the spray can

You'll get a better result with spray paint if you rest the can in warm water for about five minutes before using. The spray will come out in a finer mist for more even coverage.

Spray like a pro

To spray-paint without mess, use a makeshift spray booth. All you need is a large cardboard box—the kind that fridges and ovens come in. A local store may be able to give you one they've discarded.

Handle the corners

When spray-painting the exterior of a piece of furniture, spray the corners first, aiming directly at each corner and coating both sides evenly. When spraying the inside of

What you will need

- Mineral spirits and cotton cloths
- Fine- and medium-grit sandpaper
- Tack cloth
- Wood filler (as required)
- Grain filler (as required)
- Sanding block
- Primer
- Paintbrushes
- Paint

Paint furniture

Bright lighting will help you perfect your work

1 Fix the flaws

To clean wood, wipe it down with mineral spirits. Sand to dull all shine, then wipe with a tack cloth. Repair any damage with wood filler. If the wood is open-grained and you don't want to see it through the paint, rub in a grain filler.

2 Prime it

Sand the filler lightly with medium sandpaper on a sanding block. Wipe with a tack cloth. Apply a primer. First turn the chair upside down and paint areas that are hard to reach, then turn it right side up and paint from the top down.

a cabinet, don't spray into the corners at all. Instead, spray straight onto the flat surfaces, doing the back first, then each side.

▒ Get an angle on it
You'll get a more even finish on open-weave materials such as cane if you hold the spray can at an angle of roughly 45° above the surface. When painting wicker, spray first from one side, then from the other, so that you penetrate the weave as much as possible.

▒ Reverse your instinct
When spray-painting a flat surface such as a tabletop, we tend to hold the can at an angle, resulting in overspray. Always work from the near to the far side, covering the overspray as you go. If you work the other way, the overspray will leave a pebbly texture on areas already coated.

(3) Paint to perfection
When the primer is dry, lightly sand with fine sandpaper. Wipe with tack cloth, then apply 2 to 3 coats of paint. If using gloss paint, sand between coats with fine sandpaper and clean with a tack cloth.

Antiquing and distressing

A coat of glaze and a few artful scratches and scuffs can turn any piece of furniture into an "antique" with shabby chic flair.

▒ Antique at home
An antiquing treatment can transform a shabby piece of furniture. Just give the piece a base coat of satin or semigloss enamel and let it dry for at least a day. Then make a transparent glaze by mixing clear wood-sealer or thinned varnish with a dark tinting color. Apply the glaze and then wipe it off, taking more off the flat, exposed surfaces than the grooves and recesses. This will simulate natural wear. Experiment on wood offcuts first to be sure of the results.

▒ Mock the ravages of time
Before antiquing a brand-new piece, give it an artificial appearance of age by "distressing" it. Round corners and edges by sanding or filing. Dent edges with a ball-peen hammer, and scuff flat surfaces with a bunch of keys. Make worm holes and irregular scratches with a sharp awl. When you've finished, sand the distressed areas to soften the look. ▼

▒ Flick on the freckles ▲
One way to heighten the effect of glazing is to splatter some fly specks of very dark color on the surface after wiping off the glaze. Make some of the glazing solution deeper in color, dip a toothbrush into it and flick it over the surface. The effect varies, depending on how close you hold the brush to the surface and how quickly you move it.

▒ Strip for wear and tear
Give a new piece a well-worn look by applying paint stripper to the base coat in irregular patches. If you want a crackling effect, wait until the paint begins to lift or bubble, then remove the stripper. Leave the stripper in place longer if you want to remove the paint completely. Neutralize the stripper with water or solvent as directed, and leave to dry thoroughly before applying an antiquing glaze.

▒ Show the cracks
There are several ways to give your antiquing project some patches of crackled paint. One of the simplest is to brush on some wood glue thinned with water and let it dry thoroughly before applying a base coat of oil-based paint.

Surface repairs

Small imperfections on a handsomely finished surface are surprisingly easy to fix. The solution could be as simple as a steam iron ... or a crayon.

Cut through grime
Clean away layers of dust-ingrained wax with a homemade furniture cleaner made from equal quantities of vinegar, mineral spirits and water. Pour the mixture into a household sprayer with a squirt of dish soap, then spray on and wipe off the solution before the liquefied residue hardens.

Find a shellac
You can find out if a piece of furniture is finished with shellac by rubbing an inconspicuous part of it with a cloth dipped in denatured alcohol. If the surface softens in seconds and leaves smears on the cloth, you'll know you're dealing with shellac.

Do the spirit test
Before you start repairing a piece of furniture, you'll need to find out if the wood is waxed or oiled. To test, dampen a cloth with a little mineral spirits and wipe it over a hidden corner. If the surface finish dissolves and leaves a smear on the cloth, it has been waxed; if it turns slippery and doesn't smear, an oil finish has been applied.

Look at the color
Cellulose lacquer and acrylic varnish are almost completely clear when dry, while polyurethane varnish yellows with time, so simply looking at the discoloration can help you work out which finish has been used. Alternatively, rub some lacquer thinner on a hidden spot: lacquer and acrylic varnish will rapidly dissolve, but polyurethane varnish will be unaffected.

Say nuts to scratches
Camouflage a fine scratch on a piece of furniture by rubbing it with the flesh of an oily nut (such as a pecan) or even a little bit of smooth peanut butter. It's the oil in the nut that's doing the job, so if you're a little wary of rubbing your furniture with nuts, then rub vegetable or olive oil into the scratch with your thumb, and then polish the surface with a soft, clean rag.

Conceal it with crayon
Small scratches and nicks in a wood surface are easily treated. Find a wax crayon that matches the wood color, run it over the scratch, then rub lightly with a soft cloth to blend it in. If you can't find a perfect color match, consider using a combination of crayons.

Cover up with coffee

To obscure scratches on a dark furniture finish, mix one teaspoon of instant coffee in one tablespoon of water or vegetable oil, and apply it where necessary. Don't use this on shellac or a valuable antique.

Follow the experts

Disguise superficial scratches on french-polished surfaces with an old-fashioned concoction used by antique restorers. Pour equal volumes of mineral spirits, denatured alcohol and linseed oil into a jar and shake the mixture thoroughly before using. Apply it to the scratched area with a soft cloth, rubbing in a circular motion.

Make scratches vanish

Use Danish oil to disguise scratches on a surface that has been finished with polyurethane varnish. Once the oil has dried (about four hours), wipe the surface with clear wax.

Wipe up white rings

A wet drink container will leave a white ring on a polished surface. If you catch it early, wipe up the excess moisture and leave it to dry—sometimes the ring will disappear. If not, set a hair dryer on low heat and pass it over the surface, making sure you keep the

Use cigarette ash, which is a gentle abrasive, to remove watermarks from a finished surface.

nozzle at least 12 in. (30 cm) away and letting the wood get warm, but not hot. If a trace remains, rub with vegetable or olive oil, then buff hard with your palm and wipe clean.

Rub out ink blots

Oxalic acid is often used to bleach ink stains out of furniture, but it is a severe remedy and can be dangerous. On bare wood, try the gentler solution of rubbing salt and lemon juice over the stain. On a finished surface, inkblots are best ignored, especially if the piece of furniture is an old desk or bureau. ▼

For the best result, treat an ink stain as soon as it occurs

Quick Fix

SOLVE IT WITH STEAM

Dents in wood can often be raised with steam, which swells the compressed fibers back to their normal size. Prick the dented area with a pin repeatedly, then cover with a wet towel. Now give the dent several shots of steam from a hot iron, being careful not to scorch the wood.

Settle the scorch

To treat a surface burn, scrape out the charred wood with a trimming knife or chisel, fill the resulting depression with clear nail polish and then refinish as necessary. If the surface is just scorched, rub with a paste made of fine fireplace ash and lemon juice, then wipe clean and touch up with the appropriate finish.

Polish up a serious burn

Mask around the burn with tape, then use a knife with a rounded blade to dig out the damaged wood. If necessary, stain the exposed wood to match the tone of the surface wood. Mix equal parts of clear nail polish and acetone-based nail polish remover and apply one thin coat at a time until you fill the hole. Make sure each coat is thoroughly dry before applying the next. Sand the surface with extra-fine sandpaper, then remove the masking tape.

Mark the spot

Treat worn areas on chair arms and table edges with a wood marker—a felt-tip pen product available from wood-finishing suppliers that seals and refinishes the surface. Wipe the area with mineral spirits, sand with superfine sandpaper, then color it in using an appropriately colored marker. Rub gently with a finger to blur the edges of the spot repair. Repeat several times to build up the new finish.

After a retouching, let the new finish harden a few days, then buff with fine steel wool to blend the edges into the old finish.

This will be extra-effective if the vinegar is warm

Peel off the past ▲

You can easily remove the stickers and decals often used to decorate children's furniture when they're no longer wanted. Just soak them in vinegar, then peel them off cleanly.

Wipe up a water stain

To treat a large area of water damage, smear on a generous coat of petroleum jelly and leave to stand overnight. In the morning, wipe clean to reveal a rejuvenated finish.

Hands off nail polish

Don't wipe up nail polish spills! Nail polishes contain solvents that can soften a finish, so wiping up a spill could mean wiping up a finish, too. Instead, let it dry, then scrape it off with a credit card. Touch up as necessary.

Paint over plastics

Once plastic furniture has been scratched, quite often there is little that you can do to remedy the situation. But one simple solution is to paint the damaged plastic furniture. The latest paints cover plastic easily and smoothly, with no need for a primer coat. And if you're in a hurry to get the job done, use spray paint.

Veneer fixes

Fine layers of decorative wood grain are often used to dress up unremarkable woods, but their delicacy means they must be treated with care.

Evaluate the veneer

If you have a piece of furniture with a veneer that's more than 1/8 in. (3 mm) thick, then you probably have an antique. Back in those days, the veneers were hand sawn. The machine-cut veneers of modern reproductions tend to be much thinner. Repair a piece of modern veneered furniture by all means, but leave the antiques to the experts.

Tap for soundness

To test whether or not veneer is loose, tap it with a fingernail. If it makes a hollow sound, it's probably come loose. If it makes a dull thud, the chances are it is solidly stuck to the core stock.

Patch up a problem

One way to deal with damaged veneer is to patch it. Prepare a patch of new veneer that covers the damage and matches the line of the surrounding grain. Hold the patch over the problem area and cut around it carefully, then pry out the old, damaged veneer. Scrape away any old glue and stick the patch in place. ▼

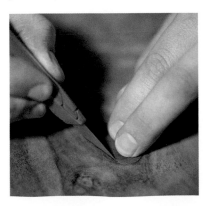

Stop the gap

Repair very small holes in veneer with wood filler. Fill a hole so that the wood filler sits just slightly above the surface. When it has hardened, rub it down with fine wet-and-dry sandpaper. ▼

Fatten it up

If a patch of veneer is too thin for the hole it's filling, glue it to another piece, with the grain on top running at right angles to the grain on the bottom. For a perfect fit, sand the bottom piece before gluing.

Pop the bubble

To flatten a veneer bubble, use a sharp razor or craft knife to make a slit in the direction of the grain, then use a glue injector to squirt glue beneath the veneer. Press the bubble flat, weighing it down with a brick or heavy book for at least 12 hours.

Iron out problems

If slitting and regluing doesn't remove the bubble, cover the area with aluminum foil and press with an iron set on low, applying heat for no more than 10 seconds at a time. Continue until the bubble flattens (checking for scorching as you work). Clamp the repair overnight.

Cracks and gouges

The deeper the scar, the more substantial the repair. Shallow flaws can be handled with fillers, but serious wounds may need solid wood plugs.

Disguise nicks

To artfully conceal nicks and gouges on a table leg or cabinet side, use a wax or putty furniture filler stick and some dark furniture wax (both are available at wood-finishing suppliers). First clean the area with mineral spirits, then take a filler stick in a shade to match the lightest tone in the wood and use it to fill the larger gouges. Smooth the filler with a craft stick and buff lightly with superfine steel wool. Now use the dark wax to fill the smaller scratches and nicks. This treatment looks wonderfully natural, but it's not durable enough to withstand hard use, so don't try it on a tabletop.

Patch like a pro ▼

Shellac sticks are sold for repairing damage and stopping up holes in furniture finished with shellac. But if you're not experienced at working with this material, you will be better off fixing the problem with liquid shellac. Pour it into a saucer and leave it for 30 minutes or so to thicken. Pick up some of the viscous shellac on the end of a matchstick and trickle it into the damage. Build up the repair layer by layer if necessary, then carefully scrape off the excess with a sharp blade before rubbing down with superfine wet-and-dry sandpaper and a little baby oil. Practice your technique before trying this on a valuable piece of furniture.

Stick fast

Here's a tricky fix for small nicks. Paint on some wood glue, let dry until tacky, then sand. The sanding dust will combine with the glue to make an invisible patch. After the glue dries, re-sand for a smooth finish. Some woods turn black on contact with wood glue, so test first.

Watch out for woodworm

Woodworm are the larvae of wood-boring beetles, most commonly the furniture beetle (*Anobium punctatum*). To check for active woodworm, look out for tiny piles of gritty sawdust, called "frass," at the bottom of cupboards and drawers, and around any parts of a piece of furniture that haven't been painted or varnished. If you suspect an infestation, seek advice from a pest controller.

Keep track with wax

Some people like the look of wood spotted with old woodworm holes, but if you don't, you can easily disguise the holes with wax or a wood filler—the damage will be less conspicuous and fresh infestations will be easier to spot.

Liquid shellac has a SHORT SHELF LIFE— always check the use-by date

Break out the car filler

For an inexpensive alternative to wood filler, try car body filler, which will work with particleboard and MDF as well as solid wood. Before applying the product, drive small screws into the damaged area. This will help the filler to bond and stop it from cracking.

Block out the repair

You can make a mold for an awkward filling job by using small blocks of wood. Line the blocks with a clear plastic tape to prevent the filler sticking to them, then tack them into place around the repair site. Shape the final layer of filler with a sharp chisel while it is roughly soap-hard, then when it is fully hardened, smooth it with fine sandpaper. ▼

Put a plug in it

If you have a suitably sized plug-cutter attached to a drill, you can neatly cut out a flaw in a piece of furniture and replace it with a matching plug of wood. If you try to cut your plug from a piece of wood that closely matches the grain and color of the surface you are repairing, then the patch will be virtually invisible.

Do it with diamonds

Diamond-shaped inserts also make good plugs. Plane a slight bevel on the edges of the plug to ensure a really snug fit, then hold it over the damage and mark out the piece to be removed. Cut and remove the flaw, then tap the plug into place. ▼

Car body filler makes an inexpensive alternative to wood filler. It will work on particle-board, MDF and solid wood.

Doors and drawers

Drawers and doors tend to go unnoticed—until they stop working. Fortunately, there are some simple ways to get them running smoothly again.

Tighten the screws

Loose hinges often cause cabinet doors to sag or stick. Sometimes simply tightening the screws will lift the door and solve the problem. If the screw holes have loosened and the screws have pulled free, try plugging the holes with toothpicks or matches and refastening the screws. If the hinge is bent, replace it with a more robust one.

Ensure a smooth run

A quick way to improve the action of a drawer on wooden runners is to take the drawer out and then spray the runners with aerosol furniture polish. The wax in the polish will reduce the friction between the wood surfaces and help the drawer to run freely.

Stop a spinning knob

To prevent a wooden knob from spinning, drill a hole in the base of the knob, clip a small nail in half, and insert the lower half in the hole with the point facing out. When you tighten the screw to secure the knob, the point will bite into the wood, stopping the knob from turning. ▼

> Make it a rule to always repair damage and fix broken furniture as soon as you can.

Quick Fix

FIX STICKING DRAWERS

To stop a worn drawer from sticking and scraping, tap large thumbtacks into the frame it slides on, just under the drawer's edge on each side. The tacks will raise the drawer to the proper height and provide a new low-friction surface for the drawer to slide on.

▓ Stay on track

Some metal drawer tracks are not fixed to the cabinet sides and can become bowed. Fix them by gluing a small wooden block between the cabinet side and the track. This will prevent the drawer roller from slipping out of the track.

▓ Dry out a binding drawer

Drawers often stick simply because high humidity has caused the wood to swell. When a drawer sticks, take it out and dry it in a warm place. After a couple of days, test it for fit and sand or plane any areas that stick. Then seal all wood surfaces with a coat of clear polyurethane to retard future moisture absorption. Don't keep antiques in rooms with persistently high relative humidity.

▓ Wax with a candle ▲

Need to get a wooden drawer sliding more smoothly? Try sanding the bottom edges of the drawer sides and the tops of the runners with 150-grit sandpaper, then waxing them with the stub of a plain household candle.

▓ Unstuff a stuck drawer

When a drawer is stuck, usually something in the drawer is sticking up above the sides. Remove the drawer above, then empty and repack the contents of the drawer.

▓ Battle the bulge

Sometimes a drawer will jam because the bottom is warped out of shape and the bulge is catching in the cabinet frame. To fix it, disassemble the drawer, turn the bottom over, and reassemble. If the drawer bottom is in really bad shape, consider replacing it.

▓ Find the key

The locks on old pieces of furniture are usually simple mechanisms, so replacing a missing key can be surprisingly easy. Just unscrew the lock from the back of the cupboard door or drawer front and take it to a secondhand furniture dealer. Most dealers keep a selection of old keys, and chances are one of them will fit your lock. Otherwise ask a locksmith to make you a new key, using your lock as a template.

▓ Deal a card trick

If the edges of a pair of cupboard doors aren't meeting neatly, then the latch that secures them can't engage properly and the doors are likely to swing open. One way to improve the connection is to shim the hinges of one or both doors. To shim a hinge, unscrew the flat leaves and line the exposed recesses with one or more pieces of thin cardboard, then screw back into place. If a door has been jamming along its top edge, just shim the upper hinge. If it's the bottom edge that has been catching, shim the lower hinge.

▓ On the level

Before you do anything structural to repair a door that swings open or sticks shut, check to see the piece of furniture is standing level. If a level shows the floor is sloping, cure the problem by shimming under the base with cardboard.

When restoring furniture, try to remove any metal fixtures first

Pin it down ▲
Tack small, intricate brass fixtures onto a scrap of wood when you're cleaning them. It's much easier than cleaning them in your hand.

Soak it in ketchup
Restore badly tarnished brass hardware by soaking it overnight in ketchup. In the morning, scrub it with an old toothbrush and rinse in water to restore the lustre. If the piece has been coated in paint, soak it in paint stripper overnight, then scrub it clean with the type of small brass wire brush used for cleaning suede shoes. ▼

Fix wobbles

There's no need to put up with chairs, tables and cabinets that rock and teeter when the solutions are so easy to achieve.

Even out the problem ▶
Fix wobbly furniture by installing levelers. For each one you'll need a coach bolt with a mating T-nut and an ordinary nut. Drill a hole into the underside of the corner or leg that needs a leveler and tap the T-nut into it; then screw in the bolt with the nut on it. After you level the piece, tighten the nut against the T-nut to secure the bolt. Put a caster cap under each leveler to protect the floor.

Get a leg up
To build up the leg of a tubular metal table on an uneven floor, slide cup-shaped leg tips onto all four legs, then pack one or more washers inside the tip of the leg you want to lengthen. The washers will raise the height of the leg.

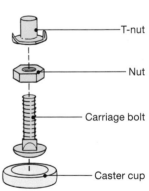

- T-nut
- Nut
- Carriage bolt
- Caster cup

Cure for the wobbles
Place a wobbly chair or table on a flat surface and wedge the shorter leg with a wood shim until the wobble stops. Next, take a wooden block the same height as the shim and use it as a guide to make pencil marks around the other three legs. Finally, trim those legs with a handsaw to make all four legs even.

FIVE RULES FOR
FIXING FURNITURE

1 **Don't use nails, screws, metal mending plates or angle irons to put broken furniture back together.**
Wood furniture parts should be joined by glue—metal add-ons are just a temporary fix before the total failure of a joint. But there are exceptions. Some pieces of wooden furniture are put together with screws, and some that are predominantly glued have screw joints—for example, where chair arms attach to the backrest. And some drawers are held together with small nails.

2 **Fix it before it breaks.**
Some breakages are the result of accidents, but most are caused by the stresses of everyday use on loosened joints. For that reason it's vital to fix a joint as soon as it becomes loose. One loose joint leads to another and, as you continue to use the piece, the wobbling will wear, weaken, distort or crack the wood. The next thing you know, a problem that could have had a simple fix becomes a major issue.

3 **Remove all of the old dried glue.**
Glue adheres by soaking in and attaching itself to wood fibers. It's extremely strong on wood, but has almost no holding power on old glue. Take the joint apart and scrape off any old glue with a sharp knife, chisel, file or small paint scraper. Coarse sandpaper only works on glue that is fairly loose or flaky.

4 **Use the right glue for the job.**
For most furniture, you can use ordinary wood glue, or a high-strength wood glue. Before the 1960s, animal glue was used in furniture making. If you want to keep your furniture original, you should reassemble with animal (or hide) glue. It's tricky because it has to be heated—and it's smelly! Avoid epoxy glue or the super-bond glues for routine fixes, as these will not penetrate the wood fibers.

5 **Always hold a glued joint together under pressure until it dries.**
An unclamped joint is a lost cause. Hold glued-up parts together using weights, sticks or boards used as wedges; or ratchets or elastic straps. Clamping pressure must be sufficient to bring the two pieces of wood together securely and accurately, just as they were in the original construction of the piece.

Fix joints and splits

Repairs to joints and splits may look like jobs for the professionals, but take heart! Some advice and common sense will take you a long way.

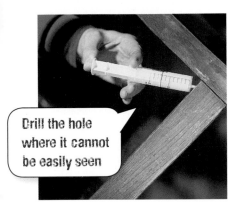

Drill the hole where it cannot be easily seen

▓ Squirt a joint with glue ▲

Before you start pulling apart a loose joint, see if you can fix it with a simple injection of glue. Drill a small hole into the joint, then use a plastic syringe to force fresh wood glue into the gap. Plug the hole with a blob of putty until the glue has set.

▓ Avoid a jigsaw puzzle

After you've taken a chair apart for regluing, it can be difficult to tell one leg or rung from another. To avoid confusion, put masking tape labels on all the different components before you start. After you've reassembled the piece, you'll be able to peel the tape off without damaging the finish.

▓ Dig out sneaky tacks

If you miss one of those little tacks that hold wood parts together, you risk splitting the wood when pulling the piece apart. Carefully examine the joints and search for small holes plugged with wood filler. To remove a hidden tack, use a flat-bladed screwdriver to first file a groove and then to dig it out.

▓ Use an old-timer's trick

After taking apart a piece of furniture for regluing, dab hot vinegar on the exposed joints to loosen and remove the old glue. It usually works in a few minutes, but if the glue is particularly thick, it could take up to an hour. The vinegar will leave a white film that can be wiped off easily.

▓ Wrap up the wobble

If a mortise and tenon joint is so loose it's wobbly, then glue alone may not solve the problem. If the joint is worn down, try coating the tenon with glue, then wrapping it tightly with cotton thread. When the glue is dry, apply some glue to the outside of the wrapped tenon and insert it into the mortise.

▓ Wedge for a tight fit

To firm up a very loose joint, cut a slot in the tenon and drive in a wedge. The wedged tenon will fit more tightly in the mortise when the joint is reassembled. Make sure you cut the slot at right angles to the grain, and experiment to get the right length and width for the wedge before you proceed. ▼

Fill and fix the damage

Some joints may be too badly damaged to make a tight glue joint—especially those areas that may have been repaired several times already. One solution is to repair the joint with some 24-hour epoxy, which will serve as both a filler and a bonding agent. Keep the joint upside down while the epoxy is setting so it doesn't run out. ▼

Scrape off excess epoxy while it's still soft

Make your own mortise

If the damage to the mortise is irreparable, chisel out the affected wood and glue in a wood plug. Drill a hole to accept the tenon.

Brace sloppy corners

You can reinforce loose corner joints in inconspicuous places (at the back of a bookcase, for example) and keep them square with small triangular braces made from plywood. Simply glue and screw the braces into place across each corner.

Test the fit first

Before you glue all the joints, reassemble the piece and check that you have all the right pieces of wood sitting in all the right places and that everything is sitting as it should. It's better to discover a problem now than to have to undo clamps and remake joints later.

Don't let the jaws bite

Before you reassemble, note where the clamps are going to sit. Tape wood cleats, corrugated cardboard or pieces of hard rubber at those spots to spread the pressure of the clamp jaws and stop them biting into the wood. Don't over-tighten clamps, otherwise you might force the joints out of square.

Waterproof the joint

Ordinary white wood glue is water-soluble, so it's not suitable for use on any joints likely to be exposed to moisture. If you think that any joints are likely to be exposed to dampness, use waterproof wood glue, resorcinol or urethane adhesive.

What you will need

- Scraper, wood rasp or sandpaper
- Dowel (if required)
- White carpenter's glue (for indoor use away from damp)
- Resorcinol resin glue (for outdoor furniture)
- Small paintbrush
- Notched spreader or old hacksaw blade
- Nail and string (if required)
- Tape, clamps, nails, tacks or weights for pressure
- Wet cloth

Overhaul a wobbly chair

Apply glue to both surfaces and let soak for one minute before reassembling

① Get rid of the old glue
Scrape, file or sand all the old glue off the joints. To get the glue off the inside of dowel holes, wrap some sandpaper around a piece of dowel, insert and twist. Leaving the old glue in the joints could prevent the new glue from penetrating the wood fibers.

② Apply fresh glue
For a narrow surface, run a bead of glue along the wood and spread it with a brush. For a larger surface, use a notched spreader or an old hacksaw blade. The teeth will spread the glue easily and to an even depth.

Mask now, relax later

Before regluing an inside corner joint, run some masking tape along the wood edges that form the line of the joint. After the glue dries, peel off the tape, and watch the excess glue come off with it—a lot easier than scraping excess glue away from the bare wood of the joint.

Fix a split panel

To fix a split in a thin panel of wood, glue blocks of scrap wood onto the underside or back of the panel, on either side of the split. When the blocks are firm, squeeze glue into the split, then tighten C clamps across the blocks to force the split closed. When the glue has set, knock the blocks off with a mallet and chisel. If the panel is thick, fix the blocks with screws, but don't let them penetrate the face of the panel.

Apply a tourniquet ▲

When regluing stretchers between the legs of a wooden chair, use a home-made tourniquet to hold the joints fast. Loop a length of cord around the legs (protect the wood with corrugated cardboard), then put a stick or screwdriver through the loop and twist until the cord has no slack and the tourniquet is tight.

SECRETS from the EXPERTS

For **no-mess mixing**, put both epoxy components in a plastic bag and knead until smooth, then cut off the corner and dispense the adhesive straight from the bag. When finished, throw the bag away.

> Too much clamping pressure can FORCE GLUE out of a joint

③ Set any splits

To repair split wood, wedge the split open with a nail, inject glue into the gap, and then draw a piece of string back and forth inside the gap to spread the glue. Remove the nail, and apply clamping pressure while the glue sets.

④ Apply pressure

After you've glued a joint, keep firm pressure on it with clamps, tape, small nails, tacks or a heavy weight until the glue dries. If you're setting a chair leg, try a web clamp or a tourniquet-style clamp.

⑤ Wipe away the ooze

Don't worry if glue oozes from the repaired joint—just make sure you remove the excess. If the piece is to be painted, one wipe with a wet cloth should do. If clear finish or stain is to be applied, rinse the cloth thoroughly and wipe again to remove all glue residue.

Upholstery

The basics of upholstery are easy to learn, so don't hesitate to pick out a fabulous new fabric and recover that sad old seat!

Work with ELASTIC WEBBING if you are new to upholstering

Quick Fix

LET IT BE

If the old upholstery is smooth and in good condition, then save yourself the time and effort of removing it and reupholster directly over the top. If the fabric is torn, it will need to be removed.

Web like a pro

To re-web a seat base, get some webbing, fold it under by 1 in. (2.5 cm), and fasten it to the center of the frame's rear edge with five tacks in a zigzag pattern. Pull the webbing as taut as possible, and anchor with four tacks along the front edge of the frame. Cut the strip, leaving about 1½ in. (4 cm) excess, then fold it back on itself and tack down with three tacks. Attach other strips in the same way, from back to front. Finally, do the interweaving side strips, again starting with the central strip. ◄

Tack it in time

Replace old staples with flat-headed upholstery tacks, especially when re-covering with heavy fabric or plastic. Stapling is easier, but the tacks will hold more securely.

Give yourself a hand

If you're having trouble keeping the fabric taut while you work, try using duct tape to hold the fabric edges in place. Once the fabric is positioned to your satisfaction, you can start tacking, removing the tape as you go. ▼

Stop the slips

Glue foam padding to the seat base with household glue to stop it from moving around or bunching up when you're tacking down your fabric. This is especially useful when working with slippery fabrics.

Learn from the past

Remove the old seat covering carefully and you'll be able to use it as a template for the new one. Iron the old fabric flat, pin it to the new fabric, then cut around the pattern for a precise fit.

Choose tough fabrics

Cottons or synthetics that have the pattern woven throughout the fabric will be much more durable. Polished cottons with surface-printed patterns are pretty, but not nearly as tough.

Protect your handiwork

Dining chairs are susceptible to food and drink stains at every meal. After going to all the trouble of reupholstering, you'd be foolish not to spray the new seat covers with one of the many fabric protectors that are available.

Plan ahead ▲

Store any fabric scraps and leftover tacks in a large manila envelope, and staple it to the bottom of the furniture piece. Later, when you need a patch, the materials will be at hand.

BEFORE YOU BEGIN

For a first-time reupholstery project, select a solid-colored fabric or one with a small overall print.

Upholster a slip seat

1. Prepare the seat

Unscrew the seat from its frame and remove all staples or tacks with a tack puller. Check that the seat support is stable and the filling in good condition, then lay fabric upside down on a clean table. Lay the seat on top, also upside down. Cut the fabric, using the seat as a template and allowing 3 in. (7.5 cm) extra on each side.

2. Tack on the cover

Take one side of the fabric and fold it over onto the bottom of the seat, tacking the center point. Pull the cover just taut, and fold over the fabric on the opposite side, again tacking the center point. Working from these points, tack outward on both sides to within 3 in. (7.5 cm) of the ends.

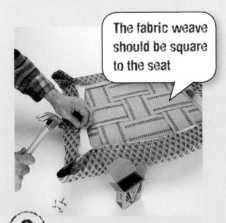

> The fabric weave should be square to the seat

3. Square up the fabric

Now tack the other two sides, using the method described in Step 2. Tap in the tacks so they lie between 1 and 1½ in. (2.5 to 4 cm) apart, stopping about 3 in. (7.5 cm) short of the ends. As before, pull the fabric taut, but not so much that it distorts the weave or wrinkles the fabric.

4. Fold the corners

Pull the fabric into a neat corner, smoothing into a tight fold as you go. Cut away any excess fabric, then tack down the fold, starting at the outside edge and working in. Place the tacks about 1 in. (2.5 cm) apart. Be sure to keep the fabric firm as you work.

5. Finish with a dust cover

Make a paper template the exact shape and size of the seat bottom. Using the template, cut out a dust cover from suitable fabric, then fold the edges under by about ½ in. (1 cm) and iron flat. Place the dust cover on the underside of the seat and tack it into place, making sure the tacks go through both layers of the folded edge.

Repair a wicker chair

1 Snip out a strand

To repair wicker, use scissors or pruning shears to snip out the damaged strand from the back, cutting the ends at an angle over the nearest spokes or cross-strands. Take a new, presoaked strand and trim it so it's 3 in. (7.5 cm) longer than the space to be filled.

Work from the UNDERSIDE or BACK

2 Weave it back in

Weave in the new strand following the original pattern, keeping it taut. When finished, trim the new strand so the ends butt up against the ends of the old, surrounding strand. Apply glue between the ends and clamp the joints with spring clamps.

Wicker

Maintain it well and make repairs as soon as they're needed, and your wicker furniture will be in good shape for years to come.

Wet your wicker

Wicker furniture made from straight-grained fibers such as rattan will be more resilient if you give it a damping down twice a year. Move the furniture into the shade and spray lightly with a garden hose. Allow the wicker to dry thoroughly before moving it back into the sun.

Know your fiber

Wicker is a loose term applied to both straight-grained fibers (including reed, rattan and willow) and twisted fibers (such as those made from sea grass or paper).

Advice on how to care for the wicker varies according to the material—for example, twisted fibers should never be stripped or hosed down.

Rethink reed

Repairs are usually done with presoaked strands, but soaked reed can be hard to work with, as the fibers tend to swell and may even split or fray. The solution? Try working with dry strands of reed, and if you do dampen them, never soak them for more than 20 minutes.

Give dirt the brush-off ▲

Use a soft-bristled brush to wash wicker, and an old toothbrush for getting into nooks and crannies.

Get a grip

Removing nails from wicker furniture can be tricky. To make the job easier, dig out material from around the nail head, then remove the nail with pliers.

③ Remove a spoke

If a spoke needs replacing, use diagonal-cutting pliers to snip it off at either end. Line up each cut so it sits a few strands deep into a section of horizontal weave. Remove the spoke and cut a new, dry spoke to the same length as the removed piece.

④ Feed in a new spoke

Grasp the new spoke with needle-nosed pliers and feed it into place, following the original pattern. If working with the dry spoke proves difficult, soak it to make it more pliable. Secure it by applying waterproof glue to the ends of the new spoke and the exposed ends of the surrounding spokes.

⑤ Rewrap a chair leg

If binder cane has unravelled, cut off the loose piece, then take a new piece of presoaked cane and glue it over the exposed end of the old cane, nailing to secure. Wind tightly and evenly around the leg until ½ in. (1 cm) from the end, then apply glue and nail the rest of the strand, trimming off excess material.

▓ Tape to the rescue

After installing fresh binding cane, wrap the assembly with masking tape. This will keep the binding in place until the glue dries.

▓ A better bond

Before repainting wicker, brush it with a liquid wood cleaning product to remove grease and grime. This process will also soften old paint, allowing good adhesion between the old and new coats.

▓ Brush on brightener

If cleaning won't lighten moldy or mildewy wicker, try dosing it with a solution made from one cup of household bleach mixed with 4 cups (1 L) of water. Wear rubber gloves and brush on the solution with a paintbrush. Let the wicker air-dry in the shade, then rinse off.

▓ Survive the sea air

In coastal areas, protect wicker and other outdoor furniture from salt damage with a coating of external acrylic paint. The weather-resistant coating is available in both spray and liquid formulations.

▓ Take a different angle

A sprayed-on finish will be finer and more even if you hold the spray can at about a 45° angle above the wicker. To ensure that the paint penetrates all the crevices in the wicker weave, first spray from one side and then the other. ▶

▓ Contain the spray

Spray finishes can pass through the open weave of wicker and onto nearby surfaces. When working indoors, use large pieces of cardboard to confine the spray.

▓ Go two-tone

Give your painted wicker furniture an extra dimension by adding a second color. First, spray on the undercoat and leave it to dry thoroughly. Then apply a second color and, while it is still wet, wipe the paint with rags until you have achieved the desired effect.

Recane a spline-cane seat

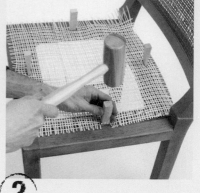

1 Pry out the spline

First take out the spline that secures the cane to the seat. Use a utility knife to score the spline on both sides, breaking any bond with the surrounding glue or finish. Pry out the spline with an awl, softening the glue with a 50:50 solution of vinegar and water if necessary. Remove the cane, then scrape out the groove to remove all glue or finish residue.

2 Fit the new cane

Soak the new, pre-woven cane in water, then lay it over the frame, glossy side up, so the weave is parallel to either the front or back edge. Tap a wooden wedge into the center of the groove along the back edge, then lightly stretch the cane toward the front edge, wedging it in the center of that groove. Repeat for the left and right sides.

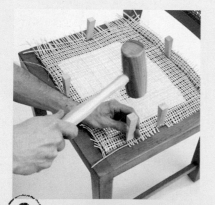

Allow the new seat to DRY COMPLETELY before using it

3 Get into the groove

Using a mallet and a wedge with a blunted tip, tap the cane into the groove, working first along the back edge of the frame then the front, then one side and then the other. Remove the central wedges and use a sharp chisel to cut off the protruding cane just below the top of the outer edge of the groove.

4 Secure with spline

On rounded seats, use one length of spline; on square seats, use one piece for each side. Measure the dry spline against the groove, then use a chisel to cut the ends at a 45° angle. If necessary, soak the spline to make it pliable, but do not over-soak. Place a bead of carpenter's glue in the groove and gently press the spline into place.

5 Seal the seat

Tap the spline into the groove with a wedge and mallet until it's flush with the surface of the frame. Leave to dry for 24 hours, then lightly sand the cane to remove any loose fibers. Starting with the underside, seal both sides of the seat with a clear lacquer sealant.

Cane

If you think cane furniture repairs are too hard to tackle at home, think again. Prewoven cane can make the job surprisingly easy.

▦ Say goodbye to sags ▲

To fix a sagging cane seat, use a sponge to wet the seat from underneath (the underside is more porous and will absorb moisture better), then leave out in the sun to dry. As the water evaporates, the cane will shrink and tighten.

▦ Finish first, cane second

If a piece needs to be refinished as well as recaned, do the refinishing first. The project will be faster and much less tricky if you don't have to work around brand-new caning.

▦ Cut cane to size

To make a template for a new round or square cane seat, tape a piece of paper over the frame and then run a pencil along the inside wall of the groove. Cut the cane about 1 in. (2.5 cm) larger than the pattern.

▦ Be generous

When buying recaning materials, leave room for trimming. Make sure prewoven cane is about 2 in. (5 cm) larger all around than the seat and the spline is an inch or two (2.5 to 3 cm) longer than the groove.

▦ Read the past

Before you re-cane an antique, check the frame. If there's a groove running around the edges, then it was made with a prewoven cane seat and can be easily re-caned. If it has evenly-spaced holes then it was hand-caned—a job for the experts.

Always keep prewoven cane flat, even when soaking it. Don't roll or fold it. Instead, soak it in the bath.

▦ Let salt do the work

Scrub grubby canework with a solution of one tablespoon of salt mixed with 1 qt. (1 L) of hot water. The salt helps prevent stickiness and keeps the cane from darkening. After scrubbing, wipe the cane with a clean cloth, then dry it with a hair dryer set to Medium.

▦ Peg the groove

Need some wedges? Pull apart sprung wooden clothes pegs and use the pieces to hold cane in the seat groove. ▼

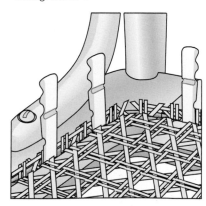

▦ Remember the rules

Carry cane chairs by their frames, not their seats. Don't expose them to dry air or direct sunlight for long periods, or use them as stepladders.

▦ Brush off the flakes

The canework on old furniture is often coated with varnish. As it ages, the varnish will start to peel off. To remove those scaly flakes, use some fine steel wool to gently brush away the loose varnish.

▦ Raid the pantry

Use baking powder to clean up dirty canework. Wet the cane with warm water, then apply the powder with a paintbrush. When the cane dries, brush off the powder, rinse with cold water and let the piece air-dry.

▦ Mind the spline

When dampening a cane seat, try to keep water off the spline. Water could dissolve the glue in the groove and loosen the spline.

Appliances and fixtures

Low-voltage systems

Devices that run on low voltages are often powered by batteries. They are generally cheap to run and very safe.

Quick Fix

THE USUAL SUSPECT

The first item to examine in any malfunctioning battery-driven device is the power switch. Check it carefully to make sure that the contacts are meeting as they should, and that they are free of rust. Clean off any corrosion with fine sandpaper.

▓ A shocking experience

If you experience even the slightest shock from an appliance, run one multimeter wire to a reliable ground, and touch the casing of the appliance with the other probe. If any voltage is present, don't use the device until the fault has been fixed.

▓ Which current?

There are two types of electricity: alternating current (AC) and direct current (DC). In domestic situations, household alternating current is 120 volts, while direct current is supplied by batteries, usually of 1.5 or 9 volts each.

▓ Back in contact ▲

Over time, oil and dirt build up inside the mechanical components of electrical equipment. Volume controls and switches become erratic and "noisy." If they cannot be

How to use a multimeter

BEFORE YOU BEGIN

A battery-operated multimeter allows you to test whether an electrical circuit, plug, switch, element or battery is fully functional. Compact digital models are much simpler to use than old-style analog meters, and will automatically sense and set the range in ohms, amps or volts, as relevant to the particular test.

1 Test a plug
Unplug the appliance and turn it on. Ensure the meter is set to its lowest range in ohms (usually RX1) and touch the probes to the plugs. A reading in the range 20 to 100 means the circuit is functional. Above or below that range, replace the plug and cord, or buy a new appliance.

2 Test an element
Remove the element from the stove. Ensure the meter is set to its lowest range in ohms (usually RX1) and touch the probes to both terminals. A reading in the range 20 to 100 means the element is functional. Above or below that range, replace the element.

reached for direct cleaning, it is sometimes possible to do the job with a spray cleaner made specially for the job. The can comes with a nozzle extension that directs a jet of cleaner to where it is needed. Disconnect the power before spraying, and wait a while before reconnecting.

Out of touch

Dirty or damaged battery contacts are a common cause of equipment failure. Using fine sandpaper, polish the contacts within the equipment as well as the battery ends themselves.

Resurrect a remote

If new batteries don't bring a dead remote back to life, try cleaning the contact points gently with an eraser, followed by a squirt of electronic contact cleaner. Reinsert the batteries and test it again.

Shine a light ▲

Dropped a part and can't find it? First, turn off the lights. Then turn on a flashlight, hold it close to the floor, and rotate it in a circle. Like a searchlight, the beam will cause small objects to cast large shadows, making them easier to find.

Tidy up

If your remotes are cluttering up your coffee table and getting lost behind sofa cushions, here's how to tidy them up. Apply adhesive-backed Velcro to the underside of the coffee table and to the backs of the remotes. Put the soft (loop) side on the remotes. The remotes will be hidden from view but you'll always know where to find them.

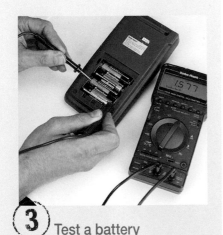

(3) Test a battery

Ensure the meter is set at a slightly higher DC voltage than the battery. Then, with the battery inside the device, touch the terminals with the probes (red to +, black to −). If the reading is 20 percent or more below the battery voltage, replace the battery.

If new batteries do not resurrect a dead remote, try cleaning the contacts with an eraser and some contact cleaner.

Electricity is dangerous

If you have no electrical training, confine your repairs to battery-powered systems, where there is little or no chance of receiving an electric shock.

SAFETY FIRST

▦ Back in contact ▲

Most remotes have electrically conductive paint on the bottom of each rubber button. The more you use each button, the more the paint wears off. If one of the buttons on your remote doesn't work, and you want to avoid the high cost of a replacement, fix it yourself with some fresh conductive paint, available from electronic stores. Disassemble the remote by taking out any screws and carefully prying the case open with a butterknife. Locate the conductive buttons. Paint all of them while you have the case open. The paint dries in about 24 hours, but it needs a full 72 hours to cure completely.

▦ Give a remote a cleaning

If you've spilled anything sticky on your remote, open it up, dunk the rubber buttons sheet, plastic case and any hard plastic buttons in a bowl of warm water and dish soap. Brush off the debris, rinse all the parts with warm water and let them dry.

▦ Hot spots

Install smoke detectors in living and play rooms, outside bedrooms, at the top of the stairs, in the attic and the garage. Use more than one in a large open-plan area. If bedrooms are 40 ft. (12 m) or more apart, install a detector outside each one.

MONEY SAVER
Give it a try

When old electronic equipment gives up the ghost, repairs generally cost more than the item is worth. Before throwing it away, however, take a look to see if you can spot the problem. Often it is simply a matter of a loose wire that needs reconnecting—a very simple job.

What you will need

- Battery-operated smoke detector kit
- Broomstick and colored chalk
- Ladder
- Pencil and ruler
- Screws and anchor (supplied with kit)
- Electric drill and bits
- Screwdriver

BEFORE YOU BEGIN
Read the instructions. Choose the best location and mark the spot with chalk applied to the end of a broomstick.

▦ Give it space

A smoke detector may not work properly if it is positioned in the where the walls meet the ceiling. Install smoke detectors on ceilings away from walls. Always check with your local fire department for right distance. ▼

Installing a ceiling smoke detector

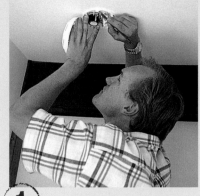

Most alarms will "beep" when the battery is low

(1) Positioning
Open up the detector and using a pencil, mark the positions of the detector's screw holes onto the ceiling. This will show you where to drill pilot holes for the screws.

(2) Drill holes
Drill holes for fixing screws and insert plastic anchors supplied with the kit. Tighten screws fully into the plastic anchors and then loosen them off two turns. Put smoke detector in position over screw heads, turn to locate, and tighten screws.

(3) Install battery
Install battery per instructions, close cover and press the test switch to make sure the alarm is working properly. Test the alarm regularly and replace batteries annually or when the alarm emits a warning beep every minute or so.

▦ Broomstick to the rescue

Bathroom steam or cooking smoke can accidentally set off a smoke detector. To silence a detector, depress its test switch with the end of a broomstick. If you hear a short beep at regular intervals, replace the battery. Replace the detector if it continues to malfunction.

▦ Spots to avoid

Avoid installing smoke detectors where airborne particles will set them off constantly, such as near showers and stoves, or where smoke is easily dispersed, such as near windows and air conditioners.

▦ Memory prompt

Replace smoke detector's batteries at least once a year. If you live in an area that uses daylight savings time, change the batteries when you change the clocks.

Make sure you have enough smoke detectors for your home—one in each bedroom and above staircases.

▦ Fix a doorbell button ▶

When a doorbell stops working the most likely fault is a push button failure. Doorbell buttons are connected to low-voltage wires, so there's no danger of electrocution with this repair. Begin by removing the screws that hold the button in place. If your push button isn't fastened with screws, pry it out with a putty knife. Disconnect the two wires from the button and touch them together. If the doorbell rings, the button is the problem and you can solve it simply by connecting a new button.

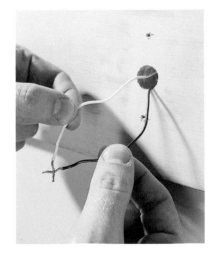

Refrigerators

Is your fridge noisy, leaky, smelly or rusty? Don't throw it away—many of these problems can be easily fixed or, better still, prevented.

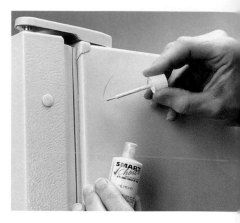

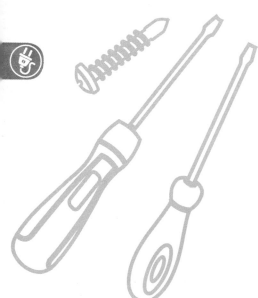

Quick Fix

WHAT'S THE BUZZ?

If your fridge "buzzes" while the motor is operating, it's probably the condenser coils vibrating against the wall or against the mounting bracket. Move the fridge slightly away from the wall and check for loose mountings.

▨ Messy puddles

The suction tube linking the evaporator coils inside your fridge with the compressor located under or at the back can sometimes get frosty. As the frost melts it makes puddles of water. Prevent frost build-up by covering the suction tube with a foam sleeve or wrap-around insulation. Consult the owner's manual to find the suction tube as its position varies between models.

▨ Defrost a freezer drain

If the drainage system of your fridge freezes over, water will condense and run down the back wall, often collecting in the bottom of the fridge and spilling out every time you open the door. To fix the problem, remove everything from the freezer and store it temporarily in a cooler. Switch off the fridge and use a hair dryer to melt any ice in the lower back portion of the freezer compartment.

▨ Grateful muscles

Moving a large fridge can be hard work. Make the job easier, and protect floor surfaces, by slipping a section of carpet, pile side down, under the appliance. It will slide across the floor with a firm push.

▨ No more stains

If the exterior of your fridge is stained or rusty, rub the area with a rubbing compound, available from car accessory stores. Applied in a circular motion, the mild abrasive will remove any stains without damaging the paint.

▨ No more chips ▲

To repair scratched or chipped surfaces on your fridge, first clean the area with soapy water. If the damage is deep, sand to feather the edges. If rust is evident, remove with sanding, or use a rust treatment to neutralize the corrosion. Once the surface is dry, dust and apply appliance touch-up paint with a spray or brush.

What you will need

- Screwdriver, wrench or socket set
- Replacement seal

BEFORE YOU BEGIN

Replacing a damaged seal around the perimeter of your fridge door is a low-cost way to save energy.

▓ Keep compressors clean

Efficient compressors are vital—they release the heat that would otherwise spoil your food. If the compressor coils are clogged with dirt and dust, they cannot release the heat efficiently. Clean the coils twice a year, or more often if you have pets that shed lots of hair. If the compressor is at the back of the fridge, unplug the fridge and pull it away from the wall. If the compressor is under the fridge, just snap off the grill at the front. Suck up the dust with a non-conductive plastic vacuum attachment. ▼

If your food is spoiling, use a special fridge thermometer to check the actual temperature inside the fridge.

Install a new door seal

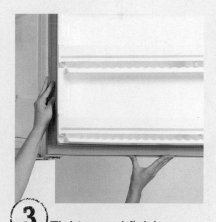

① Remove old seal
Most seals fit into a retaining strip or liner held in place with screws. Lift the edges of the seal to locate the screws, loosen them, release the lip of the seal, and carefully remove the seal—there's no need to remove the screws completely.

② Install new seal
Make sure the new seal is the right type and fit. If it is crimped, soak it in hot water for a few minutes. Then, starting at a top corner, carefully press the lip under the rim of the liner. Continue all the way around the perimeter.

③ Tighten and finish
Smooth the seal around the door, making sure it's not too tight or too loose. Tighten the middle screws on each side, then tighten the remaining screws just enough to hold the seal in place. Finish by firmly tightening all the screws.

Deodorant for fridges

Deodorize a fridge by putting a few cotton balls saturated in vanilla in the food compartments. If a bad smell remains, and there is no spoilt food in the fridge, check the back of the fridge and the drip pan for decomposing matter.

Give your fridge space

When deciding on the layout of your kitchen, take some time to consider the best position for your fridge. Never place it next to an oven, as the heat from the oven will affect the cooling mechanism of the fridge, causing it to be overworked. There needs to be ample ventilation all around the fridge. When planning the installation of fitted counters, make sure there is ample space behind the fridge. Fridge manuals normally specify the minimum clearance required.

Ovens and stovetops

Whatever the level of your culinary expertise, there are two vital ingredients for successful cooking: a reliable stove and a convection oven.

Clean jets

If the jet on a gas burner becomes clogged, clean it with a straight pin or a pipe cleaner. Don't use a toothpick—it might break and get stuck in the hole.

Clean ignition

Ignition lighters must be clean to conduct a spark, but are easily soiled by boiled-over food and other burned-on mess. By cleaning the igniter and its metal "ground," you can solve most ignition problems. Use a cotton swab to remove the gunk, then clean thoroughly with an old toothbrush. ◄

It's elementary

Old-style electric ovens only had one element, located at the bottom of the oven. Today, ovens have elements at both the bottom and top, and sometimes a separate element at the rear. You can use the elements one at a time or in combination to suit the style of meal you're cooking. Of course, it's tempting to turn on all the elements for maximum action, no matter what you're cooking. But by using the different settings you'll make more targeted use of your energy and probably get a better result, too.

Don't use foil

Don't cover the floor or racks of your electric oven with aluminum foil to catch drips. Foil reflects and intensifies heat, damaging the lining and glass doors and causing elements to burn out prematurely.

Reverse a refrigerator door

(1) **Remove upper door**

Unplug the refrigerator, empty the shelves, and remove the base grill or base panel. Remove the top handle and hinges with a wrench. Take off the upper door by opening it slightly while lifting up and out. Don't loosen any of the washers or shims.

(2) **Remove lower door**

Take off the lower door by lifting the handle while loosening the middle hinge pin. Remove the handle and hinge hardware from both doors and reinstall them on the other side. The handle-mounting screws may be hidden under caps.

(3) **Install the doors**

Install the reconfigured doors, tightening the hinges until they are snug. Align the doors, and tighten the top hinge screws at least a half turn more. There may be a plastic filler on the grill that needs to be removed and reversed before you can reinstall the grill or base panel.

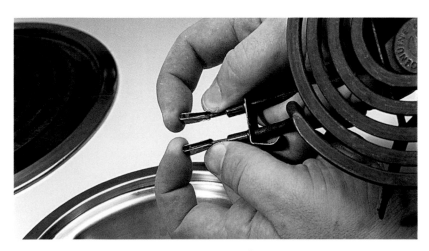

Heat trapped by foil in the bottom of an oven cannot reach the heat sensor near the top, altering cooking times considerably.

▓ Warning sign

A bright spot on the side of a stove element is a tell-tale sign of impending failure. Buy a replacement before it fails.

▓ Cool burner ▲

If a burner on your electric stove won't heat up, turn it off, remove it from its socket, plug it in again and wiggle it around. If it feels loose, remove it again and very gently bend the two connector prongs slightly outward. This should create a tighter connection when the element is replaced.

SECRETS
from the EXPERTS

Appliance repair technicians say they are frequently called out to fix a broken oven when the problem is simply an **inadvertently set timer**. If your digital display reads "hold," "delay," or "time cook," then the timer is engaged. On ovens with dials, be sure the knob is turned to "manual."

Microwave cleaner

It's easy to clean spills and baked-on food from inside your microwave. Partially fill a cup with water and add a slice of lemon. Boil the water inside the microwave for a minute. Leave the door closed and let the steam loosen the mess. After 10 minutes, open the door and wipe clean with a soft cloth. ▼

> Never try to clean a microwave with products meant for a conventional oven

How much is left

To check roughly how much liquid is left in an propane tank, wet your hand and slowly move it down the outside surface. When you reach the liquid level the cylinder will feel cooler than it did when it passed over the empty part.

New use for spaghetti

The pilot light of ovens and gas barbecues without automatic ignition can be hard to reach with a match. Solve the problem safely. Light one end of a piece of dry spaghetti to create a long match.

Degreasing

To get rid of stovetop grease stains, first wet them with a little water and cover them with a sprinkling of bicarbonate of soda. Then rub off with a damp sponge.

Grease guard

Catch spatters before they hit the wall with a metal splash guard. Drill two small holes in the guard and suspend it from cup hooks inserted into the wall. When grease builds up, remove the guard and clean it with soap or ammonia.

BEFORE YOU BEGIN
Screwed-in elements should be replaced by a qualified repairman but plug-in elements are simple to replace yourself. Elements are available from the manufacturer and appliance parts specialists. Take the burned-out element with you and make a note of the model number of your stovetop in case this is needed.

Replace a stovetop element

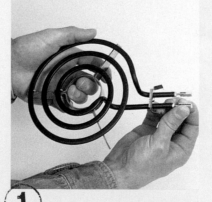

① **Remove and inspect**
Switch off the stove. Gently raise the end of the element opposite the connector and pull it out—it may be a bit stiff. Examine the ends of the element for evidence of corrosion.

② **Install new element**
If the ends are corroded, the connector will need to be replaced by an expert before the new element is installed. If not, reverse the order of removal to install the new element.

Dishwashers

The sweetest music to anyone who ever faced a load of dirty dishes is the chug and churn of a dishwasher. Keep yours in tune.

In the nick of time

One small nick in a vinyl-coated rack can start off a rust invasion that will stain your dishes and cookware and eventually ruin your dishwasher. Act quickly. Get a new rack or repair the vinyl coating.

Plastic rack repair

If the vinyl coating on the racks of your dishwasher is nicked or peeling, cover the racks with flexible clear plastic tubing. For most racks, tubing with an outside diameter of ¼ in. (6 mm) and an inside diameter of ⅛ in. (3 mm) works well. Cut the tubing into ¼ in. (6 mm) lengths and slip them over the ends of the racks.

Another rack saver

If the racks in your dishwasher have begun to rust, you may be able to avoid further damage with a special paint made for coating damaged areas on dishwasher racks. Unlike other paints used for containing rust, it won't come off on your dishes. It's heat-resistant, has a rubberized finish, and comes in a range of colors. Buy it in small bottles with a brush in the cap from appliance parts suppliers.

Lime wash

To remove the chalky mineral deposits from your dishwasher, empty the machine, fill it up again, add a cup of white vinegar, and run it through a cycle. Then add normal dishwashing detergent and run it through another cycle. Don't do this too often, however—vinegar is an acid and will cause damage to the materials inside the dishwashing machine if used excessively.

Beware of sharp edges

Arrange items in the cutlery basket—especially sharp knives—with their blunt ends uppermost so they won't damage the racks or the door seal. Other items that have sharp edges such as pans and colanders are best washed by hand.

Blotchy stains

Iron in the water is the usual cause of blotchy stains in a dishwasher. To remove stains, let the empty machine fill, add half a cup of citric acid crystals, and run it through a cycle. For a permanent solution, put an iron filter on your water supply.

Black marks

If your dishes have mysterious black smears, it may be the result of metal utensils rubbing against them in the dishwasher. Separate pots and dishes when you load. Also, don't put in throw-away aluminum containers. The thin aluminum material tends to break down in the heat of the washing cycle and marks the dishes.

189

Clean a dishwasher's spray arms and strainer

What you will need

- Screwdriver, wrench or socket set
- Unwound paperclip or pipe cleaner

BEFORE YOU BEGIN

A regularly cleaned dishwasher will work more efficiently and last longer. Check your appliance's manual for specific advice.

① Start at the bottom

Some lower spray arms have clips or tightly fitted screws. Others simply lift off, or have screws that you can remove by hand. Once the arm is removed, lift out the strainer (filter or screen) on the floor of the dishwasher and clean it.

② Go to the top

To remove the upper spray arm, unscrew the retaining clip, then disconnect the arm from the water channel by removing the center screw. On some models, you'll need to remove the tray and unclip a protective grid before you remove the center screw.

③ Clean arms and reinstall

Clean any blocked openings in the spray arms with an unwound paperclip or pipe cleaner. Flush water through the arms while tilting them back and forth to wash out foreign objects. Reverse the removal procedure to reinstall the arms.

Washing machines

If your clothes emerge from your washing machine less than clean, it may be the machine that's at fault, not the detergent.

▦ Keep it light

Overloading your machine may not ruin it, but it will compromise the cleaning of your clothes and linens, and create additional wear and tear on certain parts, such as bearings and the suspension, making them prone to premature failure. Be sure to always follow the manufacturer's suggestions for load size.

▦ Lint trap

If the hose from your washer discharges into a sink, avoid blocking the drain with lint by securing the foot of an old pair of nylons to the end of the hose with a strong rubber band. Turn the foot inside out to clean out the lint after every wash.

▦ Fabric snagger

Are your clothes catching on something in your washing machine? Rub an old pair of nylons over the agitator and the drum surface to locate any rough spots and smooth them off with very fine sandpaper.

▦ Car tool to the rescue

The agitator in washing machines is held in place with a tightly fitted cap. If you cannot turn it with a regular wrench, try a wrench used to remove oil filters in cars. These have an adjustable strap for a firmer grip.

▦ Bridging the gap

If your washer and dryer aren't installed one above the other, it's easy to put things on their tops, which then drop or spill into the space behind. The machines must sit away from the wall to accommodate hoses and vents, so to solve the problem, cover the gap with a shelf mounted on brackets. Use the shelf to store detergent, bleach and other laundry products.

▦ Sort it out

It may seem like a waste of time to sort clothes into whites and colors, or lightly soiled and heavily soiled, but to use less energy (and save money) when you wash your clothes, start sorting. Heavily soiled garments, for example, will need a long warm wash, but the lightly soiled clothes will be fine with just a quick, cold-water wash.

▦ Cold water

It takes energy to heat water—up to 90 percent more energy—which is why cold-water washes are always more economical than warm or hot washes. Use cold washes as often as you can, or at least favor warm washes over hot.

Upgrading to a more energy-efficient washing machine is not your only energy-saving option.

▦ Get a clean machine

Detergent build-up can affect the performance of your washing machine. Run the machine through a wash cycle with a cup of vinegar to remove soap scum, then again with a cup of baking soda to neutralize any sour residue.

Replace a washing machine's inlet hoses

What you will need

- Bucket
- Multigrip pliers or adjustable wrench (if required)
- Wire brush
- Toothbrush
- PTFE (Teflon) tape

BEFORE YOU BEGIN
Failed inlet hoses on your washing machine can spell disaster, so keep an eye on them and replace worn hoses before they burst.

1 **Release the pressure**
Shut off the valves fully, then place a bucket beneath them to catch remaining water in the hoses that will leak out. Unscrew the hose fittings by hand, or using a pair of multigrip pliers or an adjustable wrench if it is hard to turn.

2 **Clean the threads**
Unscrew the hose fitting from the machine inlet in the same way, draining any remaining water into the bucket. Use a small wire brush to remove any PTFE tape that may remain on the valves.

Powdered detergents work better in cold water if you dissolve them in a little bit of water first.

Touch up a tub
A chipped drum in an older-stye washing machine can eventually rust and ruin your clothes with unsightly marks. Cover chips or scratches with clear nail polish, silicone sealant or an epoxy touch-up paint made specially for the purpose. To get a perfect touch-up every time, tear out a match from a matchbook, dip the torn end into the paint, and apply it to the chip.

Muffle banging pipes
When an inlet valve shuts suddenly, the water rushing through the supply hose comes to a slamming halt. The result is a loud banging noise. Keep things quiet by installing a water-hammer shock absorber between the hose and the inlet.

Turn the taps off
If your washing machine hoses are permanently attached to the laundry valves, turn the valves off after each wash. If you don't, and a hose bursts while you are out, it could be a major disaster.

Motor maintenance
Accumulated dust and dirt on motor windings restrict airflow and can cause burnout. Once a year, unplug the machine, pull it away from the wall, and gently vacuum the windings or vents in the motor casing.

Clamp a leaky hose
If you detect a leak coming from a washing machine hose, you may not need to replace the entire hose—just the clamp connector. Often they

Always wind the PTFE tape on CLOCKWISE

SECRETS
from the EXPERTS

If your machine has hot and cold inlets but the temperature of **the mix is never quite right**, make sure the inlet valves are fully open and the hoses and the mixing valve are not blocked.

(3) Clean the filters

Clogged inlet filters can result in low water pressure, no water or the wrong water temperature. Gently clean the inlet filters using an old toothbrush. If mineral deposits are present, soak the filter in vinegar for a few hours.

(4) Secure the new hoses

Wrap about two turns of PTFE tape, available from hardware stores, onto the valve thread. Screw on the new hoses until hand-tight. Do not use pliers as an overtightened plastic hose is easily damaged. Open the valves fully, then wind them back one turn.

become loose through wear. Using pliers, remove the old clamp and replace it with a new worm-drive clamp. To a certain extent, you can trim rubber hoses, but you are probably better off replacing the hose if it is old and cracked. ▼

Wash and wear

Overloading the drum increases wear on the machine and results in poor washing and damage to clothes. Take time to observe the wash cycle closely. The clothes should be circulating freely in the water, not sluggishly in clumps or in bunches around the agitator.

Get an earful

If your machine emits an ominous sound during the wash cycle but you cannot work out what the sound is, improvize a stethoscope by holding the handle of a screwdriver near your ear and placing the blade on the machine near the suspect noise. Alternatively, use a mechanic's stethoscope, available from car accessory suppliers.

▧ Carpet quiet

Subdue annoying rattling sounds by standing your machine on a piece of fire-resistant carpet.

▧ Front loader?

If you have a front-loading washing machine, make sure you buy the right washing detergent—or you could face an avalanche of suds.

▧ Fresh air

Damp breeds rust and rust ruins machines. After every use, open the lid or door so that moisture inside the tub can evaporate.

▧ Gummed up

To clean a gummed-up automatic detergent dispenser, flush it with a strong, steady stream of cold water.

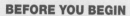

What you will need

- Level
- Scrap of wood
- Adjustable wrench

BEFORE YOU BEGIN
Not only will an unlevel washing machine make a racket during the spin cycle, but the components inside will wear out fast. Balancing the legs will solve the problem.

Dryers

Sunshine is a natural dryer and disinfectant. Save energy with sun drying if you can, and keep your dryer for wet days and big washes.

▧ No heat?

If your dryer drum turns but the air doesn't seem to be heating up, the machine's thermostat may be faulty. Turn the machine off for a while and try it again. If the air still won't heat, call a service technician to check the thermostat. You may need to replace it.

▧ Safe air flow

If you are attaching an air duct to your dryer, use only an approved, non-flammable duct, and avoid any crushing, dips or elbows. This is where lint or other material could collect, thereby blocking the airflow and creating a fire hazard. In any case, the duct should be under 20 ft. (6 m) long.

▧ Lint and fluff

Always remove the lint and fluff from the accessible places in the dryer where they tend to collect—the back, air vents, around the mouth of the lint filter and around the door. Once a year, it may be worth getting a service technician to give the whole interior of your dryer a professional clean.

▧ Fresh air

Dryers need fresh air to work properly. If the dryer is installed in a closet or other tight area, keep the door open during dryer operations or the appliance will overheat. Alternatively, install a louvered door that will allow air to circulate even when it is closed.

Quick Fix

WORN STARTER BUTTON

If the dryer doesn't start after closing the door, the button switch that activates the motor may have worn down. Taping thick cardboard to the inside of the door will fill the gap and activate the button until you can have a new switch installed.

Leveling a washing machine

1 Measure the imbalance

Place a level on the washing machine—first side to side, then front to back—to find out how much the legs must be adjusted. On most models, you can adjust only the front legs. The rear legs are self-adjusting.

2 Adjust front legs

Tilt the washing machine back and prop it up with a piece of wood. With an adjustable wrench, loosen the lock nuts on the front two legs. Then raise or lower the feet as needed by turning the legs clockwise or counterclockwise by hand.

3 Test and tighten

Remove the piece of wood, and check to see if the washing machine is level. If it is, use the wrench to tighten the lock nuts. If it isn't level, repeat Step 2. If the rear legs won't adjust, tilt the machine forward about 1½ in. (3 cm) and let it drop gently.

Fit a vent hood

Insects, and even rodents, find clothes dryers an ideal nesting place. They're warm, cozy, and until the wet clothes go in and the drum starts to spin, apparently secure. Install a vent hood with tight-closing louvers or flaps to stop them making their way through the vent and into the drum. ▼

> Never SCREEN a dryer vent—it will quickly clog-up

Vent out

Always direct the air vent on your dryer to the outdoors, using a duct if necessary. An interior vent can bring enough moisture into your house to warp paneling, flake ceilings, and create moldy patches.

Keep it plumb

A wall-mounted dryer should always be level and plumb. If a dryer is mounted at even a slight angle, the bearings and brushes in the motor will quickly wear out.

Protect sensors

Fabric softener and the residue from antistatic sheets can coat the dryer drum, preventing the sensors from shutting off when clothes are dry. If you use these products, protect the sensors by regularly washing the inside of the drum with hot water and dish soap (not an abrasive cleaner).

When fitting an air duct to your dryer, avoid crushing, dips or elbows, where lint can collect and become a fire hazard.

Video and audio

Sophisticated vision and sound systems are electronic extensions of our eyes and ears, and benefit from similar care and attention.

If you have access to analog channels, boost the signal with a pre-amplifier.

▓ Amplify hearing

There are many devices available that enable people with a hearing impairment to enjoy television without disturbing fellow viewers and neighbors. One of the most effective is a loop amplifier, consisting of a cable that runs around the room (under the floorboards if necessary) and attaches to an amplifier and then to the television. The listener picks up the amplified sound by switching their hearing aid to the "T" (telecoil) frequency. They can then adjust the sound to a comfortable level using their hearing aid.

▓ Amplify reception

If you have access to analog channels, boost the signal with a pre-amplifier, available from

Moving a television

Always carry an older-style cathode ray tube TV with the screen facing toward you—this is the heaviest part—and hold the plug and cable well away from the floor to prevent tripping.

SAFETY FIRST

Hang a big-screen TV

What you will need

- Painter's tape
- Tape measure
- Level
- Drill
- Spade bit (if required)
- Spare length of cable
- Electrical tape

BEFORE YOU BEGIN
Unless your TV is small and light, you will need to screw the brackets into the wood studs—not to the drywall alone.

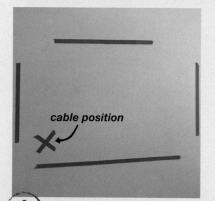

cable position

1 Mark the position
Determine the position of the TV, considering the viewing angle and power and antenna outlets. Use painter's tape to make a silhouette of the outer casing on the wall, marking cut-outs for the cables to go through the wall behind the TV and exit at the base.

2 Attach the brackets
Fit the mounting brackets to the TV monitor, measure from the top of the monitor to the brackets and use this distance from the top mark on the wall to position the wall bracket, checking with a level. Remove the brackets from the monitor and use a drill/driver to secure them with the supplied screws.

electronics supply stores. Some mount next to the TV set, but for a really effective result you need an amplifier with two components, one that attaches to the antenna mast, and one mounted inside the house that attaches to the power supply.

Installing a splitter for multiple TVs

Splitters let you view multiple TVs through a single receiver whether that's an aerial antenna, a satellite dish or an underground cable connection. Splitters are customized for each of these modes, so take care to choose the right one, including, in the case of an aerial antenna, the type of cable that it uses to conduct the signal (flat ribbon or coaxial). If the reception from an aerial antenna or satellite dish is weak, the number of TVs served by a single splitter will be limited to two, maybe three at the most. When installing, minimize the cabling because extensive cabling diminishes the picture.

Keep a distance

An aerial antenna that comes in contact with an electrical power line (in a strong wind, for example) could deliver a lethal electrical charge inside the house. Set it up so that the distance between it and the nearest power line is at least twice the length of the antenna.

To the point

Antennae are directional pick-up devices, so to be effective they must be pointed at the transmitted signal. If your antenna has a "V" configuration, direct the twin points of the V toward the transmitter.

For a BRICK CAVITY WALL, use a core drill with hammer action

core drill

③ Make the cable cut-outs
Cut a hole behind the TV and another low on the floor. If there is a block in the wall between the two holes, remove a section of drywall in front of it then use a drill with a spade bit to cut a notch in the wood. Replace or patch the drywall after the cable has been pulled through the notch.

④ Thread the cords
Feed a spare length of cable through the top and out the bottom, attach it to the cables with electrical tape and draw the guide cable out through the top to easily pull the cables through.

⑤ Connect the TV and test
Cut the cables free of the guide cable. Connect them to the TV to tune and test the set-up. When the TV is tuned, lift it onto the wall bracket, inserting the locking devices in the wall bracket.

▦ Easy wire hiding ▲

In rooms with wall-to-wall carpet, you can often force wire between the carpet and the baseboards. This is the fastest, easiest way to hide wire. The only way to know if it will work is to give it a try. There may be enough space for heavy-duty cable, or you may find it tough to push in even the smallest wire. If there's a doorway between the power source and the speaker, run the wire all the way around the other side of the room to avoid it. A ruler makes a good wire-pushing tool. Don't use anything sharp that might cut into the wire's insulation.

▦ Slim down cabling

The usual way to hide the bundles of rope-like, ugly cabling that comes with TVs and the like is to stuff them under the furniture. Now you can replace them with ribbon-like cabling as slim as foil, which adheres to the walls. It looks very discreet, but if you add a coat of paint, it'll disappear altogether. ▼

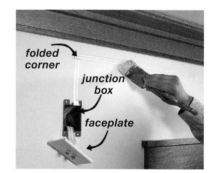

folded corner
junction box
faceplate

▦ Adjust the brightness

Manufacturers often maximize the factory settings for brightness and contrast to make sure that their TVs look nice and bright when they go on display beside competing models in the showroom. Bring those settings down a bit and not only will you get a better picture, but you could reduce the set's energy use by as much as 30 percent.

▦ Fit a TV interference filter

Interferences such as CB radio signals can be eliminated with a television interference (TVI) filter. Choose one that matches the conducting cable on your antenna.

RECTIFY **POOR DIGITAL TV** RECEPTION

Digital TV has many advantages over analog sets, offering more channels, a crisper picture and even 3-D viewing. Reception can be a problem, however, leaving a picture that freezes or no picture at all. Try these simple remedies before calling out a technician.

★ Be wary of signal amplifiers

If you have an aerial antenna and interference from non-TV signals is causing problems, an aerial amplifier won't help. The amplifier will strengthen both the interfering signals and the TV signal. Most reception problems are not due to signal strength anyway.

★ Check the cables

You can improve signal quality by making sure you have RG-6 shielded cables (which block out interference) running from the TV set to the wall socket and from the wall socket to an outdoor antenna. Use screw-in F connectors to make sure you have solid connections all round.

★ Check signal splitters

Remove any unnecessary signal splitters as this weakens the signal. It might be worth checking in the attic to see what a previous owner has rigged up. If you need to use a splitter, opt for a powered one. Consider reducing the number of TVs in your home.

★ Check for interference

Local interference can be caused by other electrical devices in the house such as computers, fridges, washing machines and any wireless equipment such as cordless phones and laptops. Your wiring could be the problem if you see speckles running through the TV picture. This can be solved with an isolated power conditioner.

CREATE A
HOME THEATER

Building a home theater in your house need not be a huge expense. Almost any room can be turned into private movie theater with just a few simple alterations. The key is knowing the factors that make a room more or less suitable.

Choose a room for optimal sound

Sound is an important part of the cinematic experience. You will want it loud enough to create atmosphere but not so loud that it upsets your neighbors. For the best sound, choose a room with these characteristics:

AN ENCLOSED SPACE

▥ Four walls and a door form the best home theater room. An enclosed room lets you nudge up the volume without disturbing others and limits the area that has to be filled with sound, so you'll get a more powerful effect from your system. Positioning speakers is easier, too.

A RECTANGULAR ROOM SHAPE

▥ Shape influences how sound bounces around the room. Perfectly square rooms or rooms that are twice as long as they are wide can create muddy sound patterns. The perfect room is about 1½ times as long as it is wide, with the screen and front speakers placed against one of the short walls.

LARGE ENOUGH

▥ You don't want a large screen in a small room. Sit too close to a large screen and you'll see the individual dots that make up the picture. Ideally, the eye-to-screen distance is about three times the screen size (measured diagonally).

CENTERED SEATING SPACE

▥ You don't just need seating space; you need it in front of the screen. An onscreen image is sharpest when viewed straight on. The farther you move off center, the dimmer it gets. Most screens present a good picture within an arc of 60 to 90 degrees.

Furnish the room for sound and screen

When furnishing the room, keep lighting and sound in mind. For a vibrant picture, you want very little light in the room. For better acoustics, choose soft furnishings that absorb sound, not hard surfaces that reflect it.

COVER HARD FLOORS

▥ Wall-to-wall carpeting is ideal, but a large rug over wood or tile flooring is almost as good. Decorate walls with sound absorbers. Heavy fabric wallpaper is an acoustical improvement over bare walls, and cloth wall hangings are even better. A bookshelf against a wall is also an effective sound absorber.

BLOCK OUT LIGHT

▥ Heavy curtains that completely cover windows are best (for both light and sound). Window coverings that fit inside window openings, such as blinds or shutters, block light pretty well but sometimes allow shafts of light to pass around them. Subdue any light the does enter by choosing darker colors for walls, carpet and other furnishings.

REDUCE LIGHT REFLECTIONS

▥ For picture clarity (and less eye strain), avoid reflective surfaces in the room, especially mirrors, picture glass, table tops or cabinet doors. Even paint sheen has a noticeable effect. Choose flat or semi-gloss instead of satin or gloss.

Natural temperature control

These simple measures help you to stay cool in summer and warm in winter without the financial and carbon costs of powered appliances.

▓ The first line of defense

In a hot climate, stopping heat from entering a house is better than removing it once it's in. Overhanging eaves or exterior shades or awnings deflect the summer sun without impeding a flow of warmth in the winter, when the sun shines from a lower angle.

▓ Curtain off heat

Curtains provide some protection against summer heat. For best results, line them with light-colored insulation fabric to deflect some of the heat, and open or close them as the day progresses according to the position of the sun.

▓ Veranda days

A veranda is traditionally protected by a roof and may be shielded by blinds or awnings to make it a cool retreat in summer. Facing south, and with the blinds or awnings raised, it also makes a cozy spot in winter. For summer cooling only, choose a northerly orientation. A west-facing veranda will get hot in the afternoon.

▓ Trees for shade

Deciduous trees supplement a pergola, their shadows extending the area of shade. Plant large trees well away from the house to avoid blocking the light and the gutters.

DESIGNED FOR **COMFORT**

★ Temperature control is subject to many factors. Here are five of the most important. Consider how your home is affected and the action you may be able to take to improve your comfort.

Factor	Action
Orientation	Ideally, the main living areas should face south. It is then easier to exclude the sun in summer, when it is hot, and to make the best use of it in winter.
Insulation	Insulate the floor, roof and walls to keep the heat out in summer and conserve it in winter.
Glazing	Tailor the size, position, glazing and protection of your windows to suit their orientation (sun or shade).
Thermal mass	Internal brick and stone walls, as well as a concrete slab, can all be used as heat sinks. Warmed by winter sun, they re-radiate the heat at night, while in summer they stay cool during the day.
Ventilation	Maintain access to fresh air by directing airflow using vents, exhaust fans or air collectors, and carefully positioning outdoor plants and fencing.

Quick Fix

WRAP UP OR STRIP OFF

Don't forget that one of the simplest ways to stay warm or cool is to dress for the weather. Add or remove layers of clothing to keep yourself comfortable.

What's your angle?

If your house is surrounded by plenty of space but is situated in such a way that it misses out on the prevailing summer breezes, coax the breezes in the right direction with fences and trees. Work out the angles, and site the barriers so the breezes deflect to the area in your house where they will be most beneficial. The barriers will also buffer cold winds in winter.

Keep the heat in

In the winter, heat is easily lost through windows. Double glazing keeps most of the heat in, but if your windows are single glazed, you can help prevent heat-loss by drawing the curtains. The thicker the curtains, the better. You can also back your curtains with thermal liners, designed to keep the heat from escaping.

On hot summer days find a shady spot outdoors where you can make the most of the fresh air.

Double benefit

Plant a pergola or trellis with grapes or tomatoes and reap a double benefit of cool shade and an edible crop. If you want the sun's warmth in winter, choose a fruit or vegetable that will drop its foliage.

Stick to the sunny side

Most houses have a sunny side and a cool side. Keep this in mind when deciding on the layout of your house. Positioning a home office or living room, for example, on the sunny side will save hours of expensive daytime heating and lighting in the winter.

Ventilation

One of the most important aspects of a well-designed home is that the interior spaces are ventilated adequately.

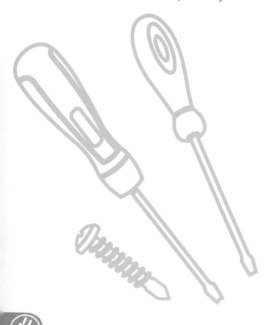

Cool your house by installing wind turbines near the apex of the roof.

▓ Secret of a healthy home

Good ventilation is vital to the health, comfort and running costs of a home, whatever the season. It reduces energy consumption, prevents the build-up of toxic chemicals in the air, reduces visible and hidden moisture damage, helps to prevent termite infestation and eliminates odors.

▓ Warning signs

How do you know if the ventilation in your house is inadequate? In the winter months watch for frequent allergy problems among family members, lingering smells and musty odors, and condensation on windows and walls.

▓ Air collectors

Infuse your home with warm, dry, fresh air from solar-powered air collectors attached to the roof or walls. Air collectors can also be used instead of vents to ventilate enclosed areas like attics.

▓ Try a solar chimney

A "solar chimney" installed on the sunniest side of the house and painted black to absorb heat creates constant air movement by drawing warm air from inside to outside. Combine with vents on the shady side of the house to create a natural air conditioner.

▓ How to clean a fan vent

Remove the grill and wipe the blades with a paper towel soaked in an ammonia-based liquid cleaner. Wash the grill to remove grease and grime, and vacuum any dirt from the motor housing.

▓ Vent to the outside

Rot and deterioration will likely occur if condensation gathers in the attic and on the underside of the roof. Prevent the problem by venting ceiling exhaust fans to the outside, especially if the roof has a metal cover.

▓ Vent airless spaces

Any subfloor space, attic, false floor or cupboard must be provided with ventilation so that there is a flow of fresh air. Always vent to the outside. If the space is seldom used, attach screens to the vents to stop rodents and birds from moving in.

▓ Combustion appliances

Combustion relies on oxygen. Dangerous oxygen depletion may result if the air supply to stoves and heaters is inadequate. An air intake vent or duct may need to be installed to ensure safe operation.

▓ Cool breeze

If you don't want to go to the expense of a specially designed "solar chimney," try installing wind-turbines near the apex of the roof instead. Careful manipulation of doors, windows and vents will achieve the same "chimney" effect, with cool air being drawn into the house to replace hot air expelled from the vents.

SECRETS from the EXPERTS

Good ventilation depends on **two basic principles**: air cannot flow into a building if it cannot get out; and hot air rises. Once you know this, the task of improving your ventilation should be easy.

Install a wind turbine

① Position the vent

Place the vent near the ridge line of the roof where it can catch breezes from any direction. Rest the base flashing with its top edge slipped under the ridge cap of the roof. Make sure the base flashing is centered so that it covers the corrugations or ribs of the roof equally, then trace a hole, using the base as a template.

② Position the throat

Use aviation shears to cut a hole in the roofing. Turn up the ends of the corrugations with the pliers so the hole will be weather-tight. Mold the flashing to the roof and attach with pop rivets. Position the throat and rotate until the top is level—check with the level.

③ Lock the throat

Fasten the throat to the base flashing, inserting the provided screws into the ready-made holes. Check that the top of the throat is still level, then screw on the bracket that locks the throat into position.

④ Seal seams

Use silicone sealant to seal all seams and joints, working from the inside of the adjustable throat. Position the rotating vent on top of the adjustable throat, line up the ready-made holes and fasten the vent into place using the screws provided in the kit. Check that the vent rotates freely.

⑤ Seal flashing

Seal around the base and sides of the flashing to ensure that it is completely waterproof. Remember that, for efficient operation, under-eaves soffit vents should also be fitted so that cool air can be drawn into the attic to replace that expelled through the roof vent.

Insulation

Insulation keeps a house cool in summer and warm in winter; and the investment will eventually pay its way in saved energy.

▦ Tarzan of the attic

As you put more insulation into the attic, you will have to heave yourself time and again from the ladder through the ceiling hatch. Make it easier by securing a stout rope to the rafter directly above the hatch and grab the rope firmly to give yourself a hand. Add a couple of knots for a good grip.

▦ Dust to dust

Dust is the enemy of reflective foil insulation. Once the shiny surface is obscured it loses its effectiveness. Clean it to restore its insulating properties, or else replace.

▦ Plug the leaks

Before laying insulation, look for holes around wires, pipes and air ducts through which air could flow beneath the insulation. Plug holes with an injection of fireproof sealant or expanding foam.

▦ Something to reflect on

Reflective foil insulation can be an important component in domestic insulation systems as it helps to deflect heat away from the living space. Tack it to the underside of the rafters. If it has only one shiny side, make sure the shiny side faces toward the sky.

▦ Allow breathing space ▼

If your insulated attic is unvented, keep a space between the batts and the eaves with plastic ventilator trays fitted between the joists. Without ventilation, warm moist air rising from the house will condense in the attic and settle as moisture. This can cause the wood to rot, saturate the insulation and leak

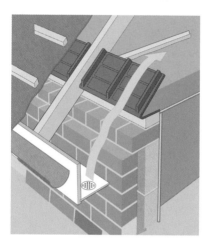

What you will need

- Respirator or dust mask
- Goggles
- Gloves
- Tape measure
- Insulation batts
- Walking plank (2. x 8 ft./60 cm x 2.4 m piece of plywood)
- Straightedge
- Utility knife
- Soffit vents
- Drill
- Jigsaw or keyhole saw
- Screwdriver
- Stainless-steel self-tapping screws

Insulate an attic

① Measure and cut

Turn off the power supply and check the attic for wiring problems, water damage and vermin. Measure the distance between the joists to determine the width of the batts to buy. Cut the batts to fit with a utility knife, compressing them between a straightedge and wood.

② Install batts

Press the batts between the joists, taking care not to compress them. Leave a 10 in. (25 cm) space around flues, chimneys and heat-producing electrical fixtures.

through and ruin the ceilings in the rooms below.

Upstairs, downstairs

A well-insulated roof can cause the warm air in a house to collect in upstairs rooms. Keep them from overheating with adequate ventilation and adjustable heating.

A clean sweep

Use a broom to push fiberglass batts under the eaves where headroom is limited. Wear protective gear and don't tear the insulation or place it over soffit vents.

Insulation cutting jig

Cut insulation batts easily with a jig made from two lengths of wood and an old hinge. Cut lengths of 2 x 4 in. (5 x 10 cm) and 2 x 8 in. (5 x 20 cm) wood, 4 in. (10 cm) longer than the width of the insulation. Attach

them with the hinge. Slide the batt between them, press down on the 2 x 4 in. (5 x 10 cm) to compress the insulation and slice with a utility knife using the edge of the 2 x 4 in. (5 x 10 cm) as a guide. ▶

The value of air

It's the air trapped in the tiny spaces within the insulating material that provides the insulation. Compress it too much and it will be less effective.

Avoid creating a fire hazard

Keep insulation at least 10 in. (25 cm) clear of flues, chimneys (particularly metal chimneys for open fires) and heat-producing electrical fixtures, such as recessed lights, fans and transformers. To contain loose insulation, tack a board or a sheet-metal shield between the joists on each side of a fixture.

Check for ASBESTOS before you drill or cut

(3) Position vent

Exterior soffit vents help to dissipate moisture and hot air. Position the vent so air flows into the attic, up the underside of the roof and out the ridge vent. Place the vent on the soffit. Trace around it, then measure 1 in. (2.5 cm) in and draw that outline. Drill out the four corner holes.

(4) Cut the hole

Using a jigsaw or keyhole saw, cut along the outline you drew in Step 3. This process creates a lot of dust so wear eye protection.

(5) Install vent

Place the vent in the opening and, if necessary, screw it into place with stainless-steel self-tapping screws. Some vents snap in place and do not require fastening.

Fireplaces and woodstoves

An open fire takes time and effort to get going and requires a fair amount of upkeep, but the crackling pleasure of dancing flames is worth it.

Ash sifter

Fires burn longer when the coals are separated from the ashes. Cut a piece of metal mesh (available from most hardware stores) and fit it over the grate. The openings in the mesh will let the fine ashes fall through, and at the same time hold the glowing coals closer to the flames.

Open up

Often the only air supply for an open fire is the warm air from the house. Warm air rises and can interfere with the natural convection that keeps your fire burning well, so leave a window open just a crack—about 1 in. (2.5 cm). Strengthen the updraft and reduce smoking by choosing a window on the windy side of the house.

Ash insulation

A ½ in. (1 cm) bed of ash left in the fireplace after cleaning is an excellent insulator that will prevent heat from being absorbed into the hearth. Instead, the heat will be reflected upward, giving you a better-burning fire. ▼

Cold prevention ▲

To warm up a cold chimney and prevent wintry drafts from chilling the room before a fire is lit, light one end of a piece of newspaper and hold it high in the damper opening. The warm gases will quickly counteract cold air flowing down.

Poisonous air

Carbon monoxide can be a problem in a room with a fireplace. The danger signs are headaches and drowsiness. Avoid the potentially serious consequences by providing adequate ventilation. Keep any wall vents free from dust and obstructions and leave a door or window ajar.

Free firewood

Save money on firewood by visiting construction sites. There are always scraps that are ideal for burning. Builders will usually let you take wood free of charge, but always get permission first. Make sure it hasn't been treated though, as the chemicals could be toxic.

The final cut

Dry firewood generally has darkened ends with visible cracks or splits, is relatively lightweight, and makes a "clunk" sound when you bang two pieces together. Always have firewood cut to length and split six months before you use it so the wind and sun can dry it out properly.

The right wood

Don't burn painted, stained or pressure-treated wood in a fireplace or stove. It will introduce harmful chemicals into the air.

Spring cleaning

Clean your chimney in spring, or at least every other spring depending on how often and for how long you use the fireplace in winter. The task calls for steadiness, time and some special equipment. Consider hiring a professional chimney sweep to ensure a thorough job.

Make sure you always use dry wood for your fire and it will burn brighter and give out more heat.

How to clean a fireplace

Remove excess soot from the brickwork with a vacuum or brush, then scrub it with clean water using a stiff bristled brush. Lighten burn marks by dabbing them with vinegar and rinsing off. Clean the tiled fireplace hearth with an all-purpose non-abrasive household cleaner and rinse off with clean water. If the hearth is marble, use a pure soap solution only, then rinse with clean water.

Soot eraser

Clean stubborn soot with a solution of six parts water to one part muriatic acid. Add acid to water and wear protective clothing and gloves.

Replace a woodstove door gasket

What you will need

- Screwdriver, chisel or knife
- High-temperature sealant
- New gasket
- Utility knife

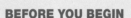

BEFORE YOU BEGIN

If your stove is losing its "oomph," check the door gasket. All gaskets deteriorate as time goes by but they're not difficult to replace.

1 Remove the old gasket

Starting at the seam or a break in the old gasket, gently pull it away from the door. Once that is done, clear away the remains of the gasket and all the old sealant, using a screwdriver, chisel or knife. It is important to get the surface as clean as possible to ensure a good bond between the sealant and the door channel.

2 Apply sealant

When the gasket channel and its surrounds are completely clean, fill the channel with a liberal amount of high-temperature sealant—check first to see if a particular sealant is specified by the manufacturer of the woodstove. Wear protective gloves when handling sealant.

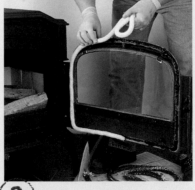

3 Fit new gasket

Press the new gasket firmly into place, making sure it is seated completely in the bed of sealant. If trimming is necessary, cut carefully to ensure a tight fit at the butt joint. Close door, and wait 24 hours in order to maintain pressure on the seal until it is thoroughly cured.

▓ Too hot for comfort

Before you buy a stove, calculate the volume of the area you wish to heat and seek advice on the most efficient option. Biggest isn't always best—overheating can be even more uncomfortable than underheating. At least you can put on a sweater if you are too cool.

▓ Annual maintenance

Service your stove once a year, at the end of winter. Check seals and joints for leaks, including the seals where the flue passes through the roof, and replace or reseal them as necessary. If you are cautious about cleaning the flue yourself, employ a professional chimney sweep.

▓ Enameled stove cleaner

To clean an enameled stove, remove dirt or soot with a solution of equal parts vinegar and warm water. Repair chips and scratches with a touch-up kit, available from the manufacturer.

▓ Watch your backdrafts

Because the air is warmer, chimney updrafts tend to be weaker in autumn and spring than in winter. Consequently, backdrafts (which cause smoke to collect in the fireplace) are more likely. During those seasons, light smaller fires that let more air into the firebox, thus creating a stronger updraft.

▓ Test for leaks

Check the door gasket once a month during the heating season. When the stove is cold, hold a dollar bill in the door and close the door on it. Tug on the bill. If you can easily pull it out, adjust or replace the door gasket. If the bill won't budge, the gasket is good. Check for loose spots all around the stove's door gasket.

Ceiling fans

Ceiling fans are easy to use, look charming, and are a graceful way of keeping your house cool and dispelling moisture.

▧ Cut the wobble ▲

If the blades of a fan wobble after they have been cleaned, attach small weights such as washers or coins to the top of each blade with masking tape. Test one blade after another, repositioning the weights until the blades cease to wobble, then glue the weights into place.

▧ Assume control

Want to change the settings on your ceiling fan from your favorite easy chair? Not a problem. Conversion kits that enable most fans to operate by remote control are available from hardware stores.

▧ Bad vibes

There is nothing worse than a noisy fan. If your ceiling fan includes a light fixture that vibrates and rattles, first of all check that the screws are tight. If they are, try fitting a large rubber band around the neck of the glass fixture. This will act as a noise buffer between the bulb and the screws that hold the fixture in place.

▧ Cool people

Fans cool people, not rooms. Running a ceiling or any other kind of fan in an unoccupied room wastes energy.

▧ Which way to turn

Most modern ceiling fans have a reverse mode, enabling the blades to turn counterclockwise during the summer and clockwise during winter. The winter direction helps distribute heat more evenly around the room by forcing warm ceiling air downward. Put the fan on its lowest speed to avoid a draft.

If a ceiling fan with a light fixture vibrates and rattles, first check that the screws are tight.

▧ Dimmer damage

Install a variable-speed control device designed for ceiling fans to control the speed on your fan. A standard dimmer switch could damage the motor.

▧ Clean sweep

Clean the blades on your ceiling fans regularly with a dry lint-free cloth. Dirt can upset blade balance and cause the fan to wobble.

▧ Check your ceiling

Before fitting a ceiling fan, check that a fan-rated electrical box is available. You may need to install a block or bracket between two joists in the ceiling and add a new box.

MONEY SAVER
Cool trick

Air moved by a ceiling fan makes your body feel cooler, even when the temperature is relatively high. Save energy by raising the air conditioner's thermostat a few degrees above your normal setting and running the ceiling fan, too.

What you will need

- Ladder
- Stick and pencil
- Angle finder (if required)
- Screwdriver or wrench (if required)
- Replacement blade or blades (if required)
- Small weights, duct tape and glue
- Cleaning cloth

BEFORE YOU BEGIN

Almost all problems with ceiling fans are caused by unbalanced or damaged blades. Turn the fan off before you check.

Repair a ceiling fan

1 **Check balance**
If your fan wobbles, it's probably due to unbalanced blades. Hold a stick against the ceiling at right angles to one of the blades. Mark the spot where the blade hits the stick. Rotate the fan by hand, noting the hit points of the remaining blades. If the hit points don't align, the blades are out of balance.

2 **Check angle**
Check that the blades are all at the same angle (normally 13 to 15 degrees). You'll need an angle finder for a precise measurement. Grasp the blade with both hands and gently bend the mounting struts up or down as necessary. Alternatively, tape a small weight on the upper side of the blade, test, and glue when the angle is right.

MONEY SAVER

Turn it off

To save energy, confine air conditioning to where it's most needed. Shut doors to areas that do not need to be cooled.

Air conditioners

Natural climate control isn't always possible but smarter ways with air conditioning can still make a difference to your energy costs.

Clean and cool

Being cool will cost you less if you clean your air conditioner regularly. Whether you have central air conditioning, a split system or window units, dirt and debris will restrict the airflow through the filter and around the cooling elements, forcing the unit to work harder and use more electricity.

Spring check-up

Every spring, inspect the seals and gaskets around a window air conditioner to check if they're leaking air. Seal up any gaps by repairing or replacing parts that appear to have deteriorated.

The higher the better

Hot air rises and accumulates near the ceiling. So the best location for your air-conditioning unit is also near the ceiling, not lower down or near a window.

Too cold to function

Don't run a window air conditioner when the temperature is too low—it could damage the compressor.

③ Are blades damaged?

Even if your fan doesn't wobble, check the blades for signs of damage such as corrosion. To remove damaged blades, undo the mounting attachments with a screwdriver or wrench.

④ Replace blades

Make sure the replacement blades are a precise match. If they are too large or small, the fan will wobble. When replacing a blade, make sure that all screws and fixtures are securely fastened.

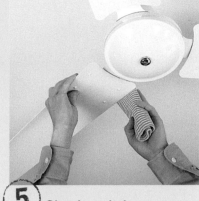

⑤ Check and clean

Check the fan at all speeds. If you have replaced a blade or blades and the fan still wobbles, check the alignment (Steps 1 and 2). Finish by cleaning all the blades, paying particular attention to the leading edges of metal blades, where corrosion is common.

▦ Keep it cool

Window air conditioners operate less efficiently in direct sunlight. If you cannot install the unit on a shaded wall or an east- or north-facing wall, you will need to shield it with a protective awning. ▼

▦ Reduce humidity

When the weather is hot and humid, set the air-conditioning fan on "low." It won't be quite as cool as when the fan's on a "high" setting, but it will be less humid.

▦ Blowing hot and cold

Some modern wall and window air conditioners on the market not only cool the air—they can act as heaters, too. And a central air system circulates hot air around the home much more efficiently than a baseboard or fan heater.

▦ Thermostat position

Make sure the thermostat of your air conditioner is not close to heat-producing items such as lamps. The unit will be "fooled" into running for longer than is necessary.

An energy-efficient model may cost more to buy, but it will be cheaper to run and likely to pay back the extra cost over time.

Wiring, lighting and plumbing

Electrical wiring

Electricity is a shock that can kill, and provide the spark for a fire. Don't unleash it. Follow the electrical codes, and always be careful.

▓ Know your breaker panel

The main switch on your electrical panel controls the electric current passing into your home. The current's rate of flow ("amp") depends on the application, be it lighting, appliances or the stove. Each of these applications has a circuit in your electrical panel. If something goes wrong, a circuit breaker disables or trips the affected circuit by releasing a switch or a button. In electrical panels without circuit breakers, a fuse for the affected circuit burns out or "blows." Many fuses are protected by porcelain fuse carriers.

▓ Add a circuit

The power used by individual electrical fixtures and appliances is measured in "watts" (that is, volts multiplied by amps). Some electrical appliances overload a circuit because they have too many watts, leading to repeated circuit failure. For a permanent fix, get an electrician to add an extra circuit.

▓ No foreign objects

Never replace a fuse with one of higher amperage, or any other type of wire or object, as it could cause an electrical fire or inflict a potentially fatal electric shock.

Circuit breakers and fuses

Branch circuits that distribute electricity throughout your house are typically rated from 15 to 50 amps. When a circuit draws too much current, wires can overheat, insulation can degrade and fail and the risk of fire greatly increases. To prevent this, each circuit is protected at the service panel by an overcurrent protective device. Most pre-1965 panels have fuses, and newer panels have circuit breakers (older stoves also have fuses). If a circuit draws excess current, the breaker will trip off or the metal strip inside the fuse melts open, stopping current flow.

Circuit failures are often caused by overloads, short circuits and ground faults. Overloads are caused when too many lights or appliances are on a circuit. Short circuits occur when a hot wire touches the neutral wire or another hot wire. A hot wire that touches a grounded metal box would be a ground fault. Before resetting the breaker or replacing the fuse, identify and correct the problem.

A heavily used circuit that fails when you turn on a high-wattage appliance is probably overloaded. The solution is to move portable appliances to a different circuit with unused capacity. If the circuit still fails, check for a short circuit or ground-fault condition.

Standard Edison-base plug fuses (15 to 30 amp) can only be used as replacements in existing installations. Many local requirements mandate upgrading to type S plug fuses.

Screw-in circuit breakers
These can replace existing standard plug fuses. When a breaker trips, its buttons can be replaced.

Reset a circuit breaker ▲

Check which switch has flicked to "off," or which button has popped out, and make a note of the affected circuit. Flick the affected breaker off, then on again to restore power. Then switch on all the appliances in turn.

Circuit breaker panel

Consider replacing your old fuses with circuit breakers. If a circuit fails, you can restore it instantly with the flick of a switch or the press of a button. Make sure you buy breakers with the correct amp rating for the circuit.

Find the culprit

After you have reset a tripped circuit breaker, disconnect and then re-connect each item on that circuit. If one is faulty or overloading the circuit, the breaker will trip again.

Avoid fried chips

Most modern electrical appliances and equipment—particularly computers—are easily damaged by power surges, especially those caused by lightning strikes. To prevent your expensive electronic equipment from being instantly reduced to junk, put surge protectors between your equipment and the wall plug. But check before you buy, as some protectors will handle lightning strikes, while some of the cheaper models will not.

Time-delay plug fuses

(15 to 30 amp) will tolerate the quick burst of a high motor-starting current without blowing and needing replacement.

Type S plug fuses

These fuses and their matching permanent adapters prevent the wrong-size fuses from being used.

Ferrule-type cartridge fuses

Rated up to 60 amps, usually protect large-appliance circuits.

Knife-blade cartridge fuses

Rated up to 600 amps, usually protect service or feeder wires.

RULES AND REGULATIONS

★ **Apply for a permit**

The installation of electrical wiring and equipment is governed by electrical codes. You must get an electrical permit to install fixed wiring and associated lights, outlets and fixed appliances such as electric stoves. You do not need a permit to replace bulbs, fluorescent lights and fuses, reset circuit breakers, check cords and plugs for damage, and install low-voltage recessed lights, provided you follow the instructions.

EXTENSION **CORDS** **UNTANGLED**

If tangled cords annoy you, here's a great trick, especially if you own extension cords that are too long to coil into a neat "figure eight."

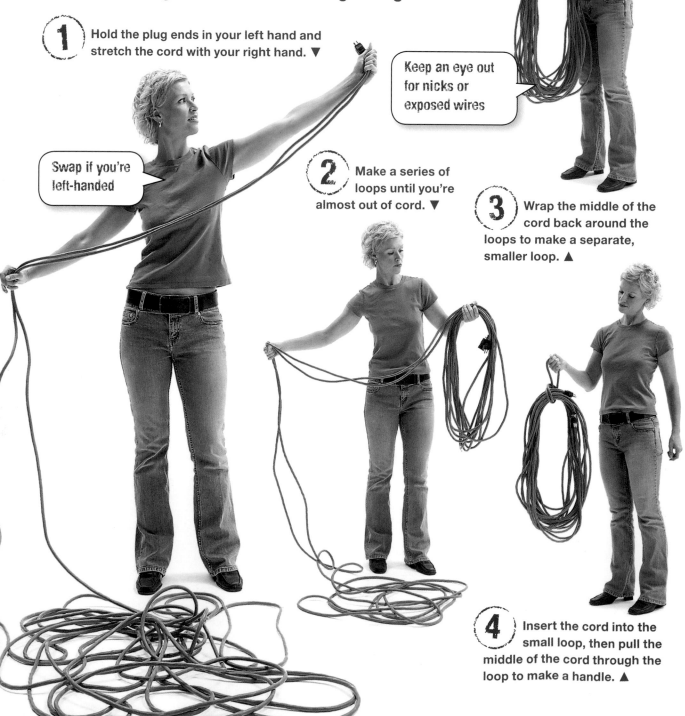

1 Hold the plug ends in your left hand and stretch the cord with your right hand. ▼

Keep an eye out for nicks or exposed wires

Swap if you're left-handed

2 Make a series of loops until you're almost out of cord. ▼

3 Wrap the middle of the cord back around the loops to make a separate, smaller loop. ▲

4 Insert the cord into the small loop, then pull the middle of the cord through the loop to make a handle. ▲

Outlet tester ▲

Check the safety of outlets with an inexpensive tester available at any hardware store. Lights come on in various combinations to alert you to any problems with polarity, grounding or incorrect wiring.

Switch to safety

Some extension cords come with built-in on-off switches. These are recommended for use with portable power tools operated outside with an extension cord. It is also best to opt for power strips or surge protectors that have on-off switches, as flipping the switch can be an added level of safety, especially near windows, where a stray gust on a rainy day can wet the floor.

Baby beware!

Babies and toddlers are fascinated by electrical sockets which, to their innocent eyes, are custom-made for the insertion of tiny objects. Sockets at floor level are an obvious hazard. Keep your little ones safe with childproof safety plugs. This is especially recommended if you don't have circuit breakers on your electrical panel. Look for plugs with smooth rather than hard edges, as they are much harder for little fingers to grasp and pull out.

Lend a hand

Before your electrician begins an installation, discuss where the wires are to go and how he or she intends to hide them, such as running cables to outbuildings in a deep trench and "running" wires through a masonry wall. Offer to help with the unskilled labor, such as digging ditches, lifting floorboards, drilling holes or removing plaster. This will save the electrician time and effort just as it will save you some money. As long as you carry out the work to the electrician's specifications, there is unlikely to be any objection.

Figure-eight coil

Here's an improvement over the elbow-and-thumb method most people use when winding up an extension cord. Coil the cord in a figure-eight motion and it will unwind without tangling. ▼

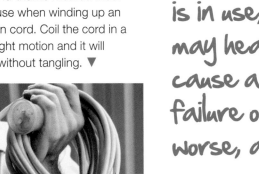

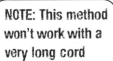
NOTE: This method won't work with a very long cord

MONEY SAVER
Plugging electrical leaks

Up to a fifth of the energy used by televisions, stereo equipment, computers and printers is consumed while they're in standby mode. To save power, turn them off when they're not in use.

Never leave an electrical cord coiled up when it is in use, as it may heat up and cause a power failure or, even worse, a fire.

Warning shocks

If you receive a minor shock from an electrical light or appliance or an associated cord, plug or other electrical accessory, stop using it immediately. Don't use it again until an electrician has checked it for safety, and any unsafe items have been repaired or replaced.

SAFETY FIRST

BRIGHT IDEAS FOR
SAVING ON LIGHTING

Be brighter! Energy-efficient bulbs have revolutionized lighting, but there are other simple ways to reduce both your lighting use and costs.

Reduce the wattage

An overly lit room not only wastes power, it can also make you recall places that are overlit for functional purposes, such as factories and offices. Choose bulbs whose wattage matches both the purpose of the room and the atmosphere you would like to create.

Avoid multiple fixtures

Don't be fooled by the idea that you can trade a single incandescent light for multiple lights with low-wattage bulbs and come out ahead. You almost certainly won't. The more lights you have, the more power you use.

Use multiple switches

When installing lighting in a large open-plan space, install multiple switches to cover the different areas. That way you can restrict your use of lighting to the area you want to use.

Install dimmers

Dimming reduces the amount of electricity a light uses and increases the life of low-voltage lighting such as halogen recessed lights. When you buy bulbs, check that they will work with a dimmer.

Use lamps

An electrical lamp will give you ample light at a lower cost than an overhead light. It can also enhance the ambience of a room or, if necessary, provide focused light for tasks such as sewing.

Install motion detectors

When installing security lighting outdoors, make sure the lights have built-in motion sensors or timers so they only operate when needed.

Go solar

Illuminate paths with lamps fitted with photocell batteries that store energy from the sun.

Keep lights clean

A dusty light bulb or a dirty lampshade can obstruct as much as half the light. Dust the bulb and wipe or wash the shade regularly.

Be natural

Install skylights in darker rooms or as natural recessed lights in work rooms such as kitchens. If you are buying or building a new house or apartment, or are undertaking a renovation, position the rooms and spaces where you spend most time during the day to the south or southeast so they capture the lion's share of daylight.

Turn the lights off

Unplug appliances as soon as you stop using them. This advice is as old as electric lighting itself, and still the key to saving on use and costs.

Lighting

The best lighting has four simple attributes: it is energy efficient, reliable, appropriate for the purpose and simple to manage.

▨ The natural look

You can simulate natural light by choosing bulbs according to their "color temperature," which is measured in degrees Kelvin (K). High-temperature bulbs (4000°K and above) contain a lot of blue light, which looks hard and cool. Lower-temperature bulbs (3000°K and below) contain more red light and are considered soft or warm. A 3500°K bulb will produce a neutral "white" light suited to most situations.

PROBLEMS WITH **FLUORESCENT LIGHTS**

★ Problem	★ Cause	★ Cure
Tube blinks on and off	Tube wearing out	Shut off power and rotate tube to clean terminals. If this doesn't work, replace tube.
Tube hard to start	Defective starter	Replace old-type starter with one of equal rating (see below). Replace ballast in rapid- or instant-starter.
Light flickers or swirls	New tube or very cold temperature	Leave new tube on for several hours to stabilize. Install low-temperature ballast.
Ends of tube blackened	Tube wearing out	Replace tube.
Fixture hums or vibrates	Loose parts or mounting screws; ballast short-circuiting	Tighten all screws. Replace defective ballast.

Replace a faulty fluorescent tube and starter

Some starters can be removed with the tubes in place

① **Remove the old tube**
Turn off the power, remove the light cover if one is fitted, and hand it to a helper standing below. Grasp the tube with both hands and rotate it with your fingers until the end pins are aligned vertically. Gently pull the tube down to disengage it.

② **Install the new tube**
Check that the new tube is the correct length and wattage. Align the end pins vertically and insert both ends simultaneously into their holder slots. Push the tube home, and then rotate it so that the pins engage and the tube is locked firmly into place.

③ **Replace the starter**
If a rapid- or instant-starter is faulty, replace the ballast. For fixtures with plug-type starters, grip and twist the starter to free the contacts. Withdraw the old unit and take it with you to buy a replacement. Reverse the procedure to install.

GREEN **LIGHTING**

Compact fluorescent lights (CFLs) are replacing incandescent bulbs as the standard household light in many parts of North America. Together with fluorescent tubes, light-emitting diodes (LEDs), low-voltage (LV) halogen lights and photocell battery lighting, they are reliable, economical and adaptable.

Compact fluorescents

Compact fluorescents (CFLs) give off the same amount of light as incandescent bulbs, but use 20 percent or less electricity and last about 10 times longer. They work by passing an electric current through a gas that emits ultraviolet light, causing a coating of phosphorous on the inside of the tube to glow.

CFLs are not all positive for the environment, however: they contain a small amount of mercury, so take care to dispose of old bulbs carefully by using a collection service or drop-off location, depending on your region. For advice and information, contact your local government.

Light-emitting diodes

Light-emitting diodes (LEDs) were once used solely for indicator and panel lights in cars and electronic equipment, but with the advent of ultra-bright versions, they are being used both individually and in groups as light sources in commercial, domestic and other settings where bright light is needed. A spotlight lamp made up of multiple LEDs has a life of up to 50,000 hours.

In addition to their longevity, LEDs have several important advantages. They don't emit heat. They consume very little electricity. And because they remain cool to the touch, they can be safely used in rooms where children play, and in floors as uplights without risk to sensitive surfaces, including bare feet.

LV halogen lamps

Low voltage (LV) halogen lamps are a type of incandescent light, but because of the way the tungsten filament interacts with certain chemicals, the bulb lasts longer than an incandescent bulb—although not as long as CFLs and LEDs, about 4000 to 5000 hours.

Halogen bulbs are made of quartz, or from glass with a high melting point. They emit a beautiful pure light suited to recessed lights, reading lamps and garden lights. Although you can achieve brilliant effects by featuring these lights in banks of three or more, it is not energy efficient and is best avoided.

Photocell battery lights

These lights don't use household electricity because they have photocell batteries that store energy from the sun. Best suited to the outdoors, they will also work in other areas with direct exposure to the sun.

Plumbing

Most plumbing tasks associated with water pipes require a plumbing permit, but you can fix the valves and faucets on your own.

▦ Turning off the water ▲

The supply valve for household water is usually at the front or side of a house or in the basement, beside the water meter. The valve is operated by a main shutoff. Turn the valve clockwise as far as it will go, using pliers if it is stiff.

Always know the LOCATION of your water main

▦ Valves in older houses ▲

In old houses the water shutoff valve valve may be somewhere at the front of the house, under a hinged inspection plate or even in the ground. If the water meter is not there, try tracing back the inlet pipes until you find the main shutoff valve.

▦ Independent valves

Some domestic appliances, such as hot-water systems, dishwashers and toilet tanks, are fitted with their own supply valves. If these valves are turned off, it's generally unnecessary to turn off the household water as well. ▼

▦ Valves in deep holes

Some supply valves are in deep holes and have T-bar shutoffs. To close, hire a plumber to fit a V-shaped slot sawn into one end of a piece of wood over the tap. The other end is turned with a handle, made by fastening another piece of wood crosswise.

SECRETS from the EXPERTS

As soon as you move to a new home, **locate the water meter and the main supply valve**. Work out how to operate the main shutoff and check that it is not jammed shut. Being able to shut off the water in an emergency could save you a fortune.

OBSERVE **THE PLUMBING CODE**

★ You must have a plumbing permit to alter, add to or install water and waste services. You can repair your own faucets, but make sure you know what you're doing— your insurance may cover mild leakage but not flooding or water damage caused by your plumbing efforts. So check with your local city hall or water authority before attempting a job. Even if you have your own well, all your alterations must comply with the local plumbing code. Ask a local plumber for advice.

Plumbing emergencies

Plumbing emergencies in the home usually involve flooding, freezing, foul smells—and potentially fatal electric shocks.

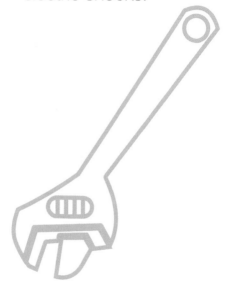

Knowing what to turn, pull or shut off can be a home saver and a life saver when an emergency strikes.

Cut the water supply
To stop water flooding out of a broken pipe, shut off the main water valve.

A deadly double act
Water and electricity are a deadly combination. Stay away from leaking or flooded water if there is any likelihood that it has come into contact with an electrical circuit. If you can reach the breakers without touching the water, turn off the power and disable the circuits.

Stop a leaking tank
There is usually a valve under the toilet tank. Turn it clockwise until the flow of water stops.

Think before you pump
If you need to pump out water, use an electrical pump plugged into a dry socket in another room. Don't use a gas- or diesel-driven pump inside, as it will build up hazardous fumes.

Protect yourself
Wear rubber boots and gloves if the leak is in a drain line or has been contaminated with sewage. Thoroughly disinfect an area after it has been cleaned and allowed to dry.

Make a dam
When a washing machine or dish-washer overflows, build a dam around the spill with beach towels or other large absorbent materials. This will confine the water, making it easier to mop up.

The nose knows
A strong smell of sewage from a fixture in a bathroom, kitchen or laundry may indicate that water in the trap in the waste pipe has dried up. Pour some water into the floor drain and wait to see if the smell goes away. If it doesn't, you may have more serious problems. Call in a licensed plumber.

Preventing frozen pipes
If very low temperatures threaten to freeze pipes, leave the faucets trickling a little bit until the weather warms up. Take the wind-chill factor into account when deciding if the temperature will fall below freezing.

Gently, gently ▲
Frozen pipes are best thawed gently. A hair dryer set on High will do the trick. Don't use a hot air gun or, worse, a propane torch. They will melt the ice quickly but, just as quickly, they will convert the water to steam and blow the pipe apart.

Work on the right side
Start thawing the ice in a frozen pipe from the side closest to a faucet, so the ice melt will have somewhere to drain. (Make sure you open the faucet first, of course.) Gradually work from the faucet side back into the frozen area.

Faucets

Flowing water with a simple turn of the wrist—clever plumbing, daily miracle.

▓ Choose faucets that last

To keep repair bills to a minimum, look beyond the styling of the faucet and consider the materials used to make it and the mechanism inside, to determine its reliability. Most top-quality faucets are made from cast brass, which is often plated—chromium plating is the most durable. Hard-wearing ceramic discs have now largely replaced rubber washers, which decay over time.

▓ Free a valve cover

Hold a hot air gun over a stuck valve cover. The warm air should make the metal expand and break the grip of the threads. If this doesn't work, squirt a little silicone lubricating fluid into the thread. You may need to repeat the process once or twice until the thread is freed. Don't try this on faucets fitted to an acrylic basin or bath, as the heat could damage it.

▓ Don't scratch

Wrap wrench jaws with thick duct tape or masking tape to prevent scratching a brass or plated faucet. Or use the cut-off fingertips of an old pair of leather gloves.

▓ Removing the handle

Some faucet handles can be pulled off, but most have a small screw. On a traditional faucet with a cross handle, the screw is on the side. On faucets with one piece cover handles, it is usually underneath the hot/cold indicator disc, and includes a small washer.

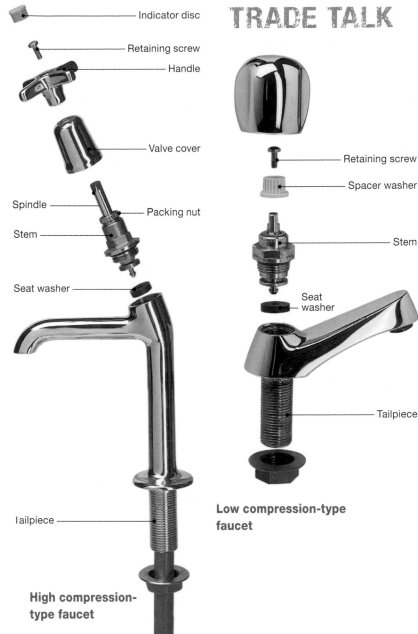

- Indicator disc
- Retaining screw
- Handle
- Valve cover
- Spindle
- Stem
- Packing nut
- Seat washer
- Tailpiece

High compression-type faucet

TRADE TALK

- Retaining screw
- Spacer washer
- Stem
- Seat washer
- Tailpiece

Low compression-type faucet

KNOW YOUR **FAUCET**

★ **Washer**
Most older faucets have washers—you can feel a gradual tightening as you close the faucet.

★ **Ceramic discs**
Many modern faucets have ceramic discs. Although a more reliable seal than washers, they can still leak, and cost more to replace. A ceramic disc faucet takes a quarter turn only to go from closed to fully open.

★ **Cartridge**
Lever-handled faucets mix flows in a single unit. They operate with ceramic cartridges, which are best replaced when they leak.

Replace the washer on a faucet

What you will need

- Screwdriver
- Wrench
- Pipe wrench (if required)
- New faucet washer

BEFORE YOU BEGIN

Replacing washers is worth the effort—a single dripping faucet can waste thousands of gallons of water in a year.

1 Turn off the water

Turn off the water supply and turn on the faucet to empty the pipes. Turn off the faucet, and plug the sink to stop faucet components falling down the drain. Unscrew or lever off the top plate or, if the faucet has a cross handle, remove the indicator disc and the retaining screw.

2 Expose the stem

Pull off the handle. If the faucet has a spacer washer, remove this also. If the faucet has a cross handle, it will have a spindle atop the stem, protected by a metal cover. Remove the cover.

▦ Form a line ◄

When removing faucet or fixture parts, line them up in the exact order of their removal. Put any replacements for faulty parts in the same position on the line. Then reassemble the faucet by picking up the parts in reverse order.

▦ Reverse the washer

If you don't have a replacement seat washer, remove the old one, turn it over and refit it. It will last a little longer, so you'll have a chance to get a new one.

▦ Saucer sense

Avoid losing lots of small parts down the drain when taking apart a faucet or sink fixture by using the plug. If it is missing, place a saucer upside down over the drain opening or plug up the hole with a thick dish cloth.

Apply penetrating oil if the nut is difficult to turn

seat washer

(3) Remove the stem

Loosen the stem nut with the wrench, then unscrew the stem from the body of the faucet. Don't use force if the stem is stiff. Brace the faucet body by hand or with a pipe wrench wrapped in cloth, to prevent the faucet from turning and fracturing pipes.

(4) Replace the washer

Unscrew or lever off the washer. Inspect the valve seat for wear or damage and restore if necessary (see "Re-seat a valve," below). Replace the seat washer and reassemble the faucet by following these steps in reverse order. Turn on the mains and then the faucet to check if the new washer is working.

If you have lever-handled mixer faucets with ceramic cartridges, call a plumber. Don't try to fix them yourself.

▓ Re-seat a valve

If a new washer will not stop a faucet from dripping, you may need to grind smooth the valve seat. The seat is the ring of metal that the washer presses against to close off the water supply. Over time, the seat can become corroded, allowing water to escape. Buy a seat wrench from a hardware store and remove the old seat ring. Install an exact replacement.

▓ Try a domed washer

A worn valve seat may still be workable, although the seal created by a standard washer may not be fully watertight. Try fitting a domed washer instead. This sits inside the seat, creating a seal at an unworn point. Warning! For a fast flow, you'll need to open the faucet fully by turning it further than usual.

▓ Check ceramic discs

Turn off the water supply. Remove the faucet handles and use a wrench to unscrew the stem. Remove the ceramic discs, keeping hot and cold separate. Check discs for dirt and wear. If they are worn, replace with identical ones. If they are dirty, clean them with a damp cloth. Replace the rubber seal, if it is worn. ▼

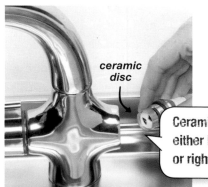

ceramic disc

Ceramic discs are either left-handed or right-handed

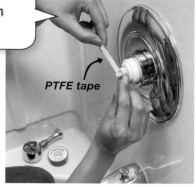

Always wind the PTFE tape on **CLOCKWISE**

PTFE tape

Don't use poorly fitting wrenches on a plumbing job—they will damage your fixtures, making them harder to grip next time.

Remove the handle and wrap the stem tightly with PTFE (Teflon) tape. A single wrap will usually create a snug fit. Then put the handle back on.

▓ Vinegar dip

If you cannot remove your faucet's aerator, you can still clean it. Pour white vinegar into a plastic sandwich bag and secure it around the spout with a rubber band. Make sure the aerator is completely immersed in the vinegar, and keep the bag in place overnight.

▓ The perfect shower

If you have an old single-lever valve in the shower, ensure the ideal water temperature every time by pressing a self-adhesive colored dot on the tiles to mark the position. You may prefer a slightly warmer setting in the colder months.

▓ Tighten a handle ▲

If the valve handle on a shower, bathroom or kitchen faucet is loose, pry off the metal button or indicator disc at the center of the handle and tighten the retaining screw underneath. Some handles have a setscrew near the base that may require a hex (or Allen) key. If tightening doesn't work, the stem inside the handle may be worn, especially if it's made of plastic.

Clean an aerator and faucet neck

What you will need

- Multi-grip pliers with padded jaws (if required)
- Old toothbrush
- Vinegar
- Replacement parts, as needed

BEFORE YOU BEGIN
Some modern faucets have water-saving devices that limit water pressure. Don't confuse one of these for a clogged aerator.

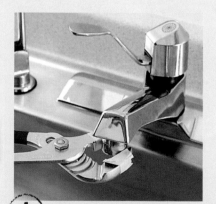

1 Remove, scour and flush
To remedy low water pressure at a kitchen faucet, try cleaning the faucet neck and aerator. Unscrew the aerator by hand. If it's more than finger tight, use a pair of multi-grip pliers with padded jaws. Scour the faucet neck with a toothbrush and then flush it with water.

2 Lay out the parts
Some newer aerators are not designed to be taken apart, so replace the entire assembly. Otherwise, disassemble carefully, laying out the parts in the proper sequence and orientation. There will be two or three screens, a perforated nylon disc and an O-ring.

Pipes

Pipes are out of sight and out of mind until they leak or groan, but there are various things you can try fixing yourself before calling the plumber.

Strap wrench

Make a strap wrench by wrapping a belt around a pipe, as shown, and pulling it tight. Hook the belt buckle on a nail driven into a 1 x 2 in. or a 2 x 3 in. block of wood, then exert leverage with the wood. ▼

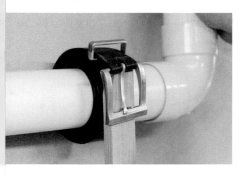

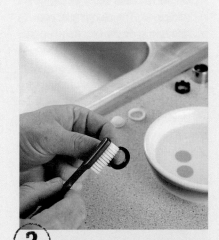

3 Clean and reinstall
Use a toothbrush to remove any sediment. Soak the screens in vinegar to remove minor corrosion. If a screen is too corroded or damaged, replace it or the entire aerator. To reinstall, reverse the same procedure.

Get out the threads

The threads or spiral ridges on a plastic pipe may stick while the pipe is being unscrewed, causing the pipe to break off. Use a propane torch to heat the jaws of a pair of long-nose pliers. Insert the pliers into the threaded section and slowly push the handles apart until the jaws make grooves in the plastic. Remove the pliers and let the plastic harden; insert the pliers and twist to unscrew the broken pipe. ▼

No more noise

"Water hammer" is the loud noise you sometimes hear throughout the house every time you turn off a faucet. It's usually caused by a valve closing very quickly, loose pipework or a combination of both. Trace the pipework and secure any loose sections with J-hooks.

Knock out water hammer

If water hammer is affecting pipe-lines concealed within walls, try turning down the water pressure slightly at the main shutoff. If the problem persists, have a plumber fit a water hammer arrestor in the line closest to the problem valve.

Firmness with foam

To stop a loose pipe inside a shower wall from moving around and banging, remove the decorative escutcheon from the wall and tape the pipe into position. Then spray aerosol foam insulation into the wall cavity. Once the foam is dry, it should be hard enough to hold the pipe firmly in position, and the banging noise should stop.

Sneaky leaks

If water seeps out from under your shower base, the water could be escaping from the shower valve body situated within the wall. To check, carefully remove the dress ring and check for leaks beneath. If there is a leak, ask a plumber to tighten the faucet body or replace the sealing ring. Make sure the decorative escutcheon is properly fitted afterward so that water cannot enter the wall.

Even sneakier leaks

If the problem cannot be traced to the shoer valve, check the grouting in the shower base and, if necessary, renew it. Alternatively, you can buy a silicone-based liquid that can be spread over the entire shower base to seal it against water seepage.

Toilets

Follow these tips for common problems with toilets, but be aware that some tanks can be complicated so you may need to call a plumber.

Quick Fix

MAKE YOUR OWN PLUNGER

If you don't have a toilet plunger to deal with a blockage, improvise by wrapping a plastic bag around a mop head. Tie the bag securely to the handle of the mop so it can't work free.

▓ Screaming tank

Does your tank make a blood-curdling wailing noise after each flush? The noise is generated as water rushes in to refill the tank. An excessively loud noise could be due to high water pressure. You can regulate the flow of water by adjusting the control valve, which you will find on the inlet pipe that carries water to the tank. First, turn the valve off. Flush the toilet, then slowly turn the valve back on until it makes the noise again. Turn the valve back a little bit until the sound stops. If this fails to correct the problem, ask a plumber to install a special low-noise inlet valve inside the tank.

▓ Raise the water level

If your toilet won't flush, check that the water level in the tank is up to the "full" mark. If it is too low, you can adjust the float arm. How you do this depends on the type of valve you have. With a plastic valve (below), you alter the angle of an arm by turning its adjustment screw with a screwdriver. With a brass valve, you can bend the float arm up a little, or loosen the securing nut on a moveable float and slide the clip up the arm slightly. ▼

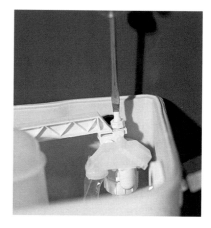

▓ Find the leak

Sometimes it can be difficult to know exactly where a leak is coming from. An easy way to find out is to pour enough food coloring into the tank to change the color of the water. If the water in the toilet bowl then changes color, you know the flush valve at the base of the tank is leaking. If colored water collects outside the toilet, the tank itself or the inlet seal is leaking.

▓ Non-performing seal

A major source of toilet leaks is the rubber inlet seal that connects the tank to the toilet bowl. Over the years the rubber degrades, allowing

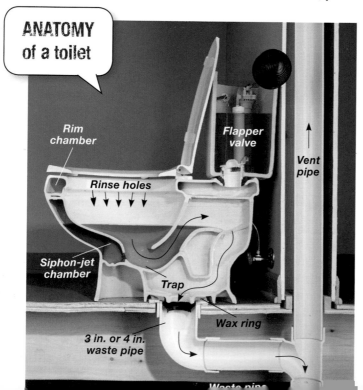

ANATOMY of a toilet

Rim chamber

Flapper valve

Vent pipe

Rinse holes

Siphon-jet chamber

Trap

Wax ring

3 in. or 4 in. waste pipe

Waste pipe

BEFORE YOU BEGIN

Replacing an old toilet seat can be tricky, as the metal bolts may be corroded and stuck.

Remove an old toilet seat

deep socket

1 **Try lubrication**

If the metal nuts on the toilet seat bolts are stiff and can't be loosened, apply some penetrating lubricant such as WD-40. Wait 15 minutes and try again. A socket wrench fitted with a deep socket is the best tool for the job.

2 **Drill it out**

If the lubricant doesn't free the nut, grab your drill and put on some safety goggles. Using a 5/64 in. (2 mm) bit, drill into the bolt where it meets the nut. Drill 1/4 in. (5 mm) into the bolt, then enlarge the hole with a slightly larger bit. Try the socket wrench again. Eventually the bolt will be so weakened it will break off.

---

water to escape through fine cracks. The deterioration is not always obvious, so examine the seal closely if damp patches appear on the floor. Replacement seals are readily available from home reno centers and hardware stores.

Heat treatment

Try clearing a blocked toilet by pouring a bucket of hot water down it. If it seems to be draining more quickly after one bucket, follow up immediately with two or three more.

Don't lose control

Toilet tanks are usually fitted with their own shutoff valve, which turns the incoming water on and off. Because these valves are rarely used, they can seize up altogether and become impossible to operate in an emergency. Prevent this from

happening by turning the valve on and off at least once a year. A squirt of penetrating oil will help to free up any stiffness.

Unblock it ▶

To unblock a clogged toilet, use a large plunger with a funnel cup. Place the tool so it seals completely over the drain opening, making sure the cup is covered with water. Then pump up and down as hard as you can several times. Remove the plunger. If the water has gone, fill a bucket with water and pour it into the bowl to clear the pipes.

Secure a toilet seat

Because they're slightly elastic, plastic bolts sometimes allow the toilet seat to slide from side to side. To prevent this, some manufacturers

add a plastic sleeve to the seat hinge. If your toilet seat doesn't have these, buy a roll of two-sided carpet tape and stick a small piece to the underside of each hinge.

House exterior

Bricks and mortar

Yes, it's true: you can do your own brickwork repairs! Just be sure to approach the work calmly and confidently. These tips will show you how.

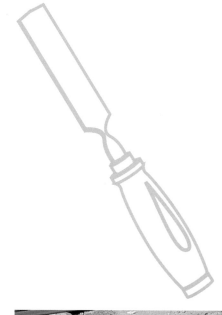

Give salt the brush-off

A white powdery deposit, called efflorescence, is common on new brick walls. It's produced when salts in the brick leach to the surface as the brick dries after rain. If you try to wash it off, the problem will only last longer. Instead, brush the affected area with a dry bristle brush until it stops recurring.

Avoid harsh measures

Think long and hard before you have the outside of your home sandblasted or cleaned with acidic chemicals, particularly if it's a home with some period character. In the process of cleaning the grime from the walls, both methods remove the surface layer of the bricks. Your brickwork may look fresh and new, but you stand to lose some of the charm of the old house's exterior. You may even damage the bricks to the point where they need to be coated with a sealant.

Water works

Remove years of grime from bricks with nothing more than a stiff-bristled brush and a running hose. Work in horizontal bands from the top to the bottom of each wall, checking the mortatr joints as you go. On really dirty areas use a solution of about ½ cup (120 mL) of household ammonia in one bucket of water. Wear goggles and rubber gloves for protection.

Take it all off

When removing clinging vines from brickwork, make sure you get it all off or the leftover vegetation will oxidize, leaving ugly marks. Pull off as much of the vine as you can, wait a week or two for the remainder to dry, then scrub the bricks with strong detergent and a stiff brush.

Draw out stubborn stains

Remove stubborn stains like tar and oil with a paste made from fuller's earth or ground chalk, mixed with paraffin or mineral spirits. First, wipe over the stain using a little of whichever solvent you used to make the paste. Next, spread the paste over the stain. Finally, tape a plastic bag or a piece of aluminum foil over the top to stop the paste drying out. Over a few days the paste will draw out the stain, and then you can wash the bricks clean. ◀

Make a move on mold

Mold and mildew thrive in shaded areas. In most cases they don't harm the brickwork, but they do cause discoloration. To remove mold, scrub clean with a solution of equal parts household bleach and water. Use a stiff-bristled brush and lots of elbow grease. After an hour, rinse with clean water.

Gather no moss

In damp, shady areas moss can become a recurrent problem on brickwork. If you want to be free of moss, try a dose of weed killer, applied according to the manufacturer's directions.

Be a softie

Mortar is softer and more porous than the bricks around it. If you're restoring period brickwork, get some advice from a heritage expert to find the right mortar for the job. Modern mortar mixes are very hard and can crumble the edges of softer period bricks.

Break a brick

Scrub specks of paint and mortar from brick surfaces with a fragment of broken brick that's the same color as the brick you're scrubbing. Always rub with the rough, broken interior (the smooth face of a brick is hard and can scratch).

Brick replacement

To replace a damaged brick, first remove the mortar around it with a cold chisel, being careful not to chip the surrounding bricks. Next, use the cold chisel to break up the brick. Pull out all the pieces. Dampen the opening. Spread mortar on the base of the cavity and on the topside and ends of a dampened new brick. Insert the new brick and tidy up the mortar as necessary. ▶

Keep brick fragments out of the cavity—they can form a bridge where damp can penetrate

Sandblasting can damage period brickwork—clean with a stiff bristled brush and water instead.

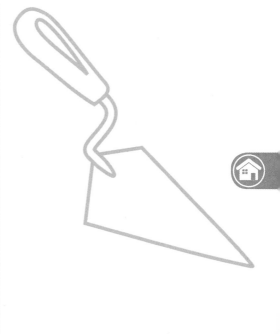

BRUSHING UP ON **BRICKWORK**

A guide to diagnosing and assessing brick troubles.

★ Symptom	★ What it means	★ Difficulty
Loose, crumbly and cracked mortar	Mortar has deteriorated and bricks need repointing.	Fairly easy but time-consuming.
Chipping or flaking bricks	Bricks are softer inside than outside and deteriorate as they weather. Badly weathered bricks should be replaced as soon as possible.	Fairly easy but time-consuming.
Cracks in walls	Hairline cracks are usually harmless. Zigzagging cracks along joints are more serious and may indicate that the foundations are gradually settling.	Easy to difficult, depending on the cause.

Repointing bricks

1 Scrape it out

Wearing safety glasses and gloves, remove loose, soft mortar to a depth of ¾ in. (2 cm), scraping it out with an old screwdriver. For more solid mortar, use a hammer and cold chisel, being careful not to chip brick edges. Carefully clear all chips and dust from the joints using a stiff-bristled brush.

2 Mix the mortar

To make the mortar, dry-mix four parts cement with one part sand then add water and a plasticizer to make a paste that is stiff, but not crumbly. Ask your cement supplier for advice on matching the color of the new mortar to the old, so the repair isn't noticeable.

Put the squeeze on

You can cut your work time substantially on big re-pointing jobs by using a grout bag instead of a pointing trowel to fill mortar joints. Just add a little more liquid than usual to the mortar to make it flow more easily, and control the flow by twisting the bag. ▼

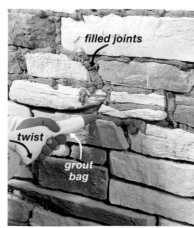

filled joints

twist

grout bag

Make an impression

To match the concave profile of a mortar joint, run a store-bought convex jointing tool across the stiffened mortar. Alternatively, make your own tool with a piece of metal tubing or the end of a spoon handle.

Strike a blow

Wiping off messy splashes of still-soft mortar will smear the surface of the brickwork. Instead, let the mortar splashes dry until they're completely hard, then strike them with a sharp blow from a trowel.

Carry that weight

A metal dustpan makes an excellent tool for carrying mortar around with you when you're re-pointing. It has sides to keep the mortar from spilling and a long, flat edge you can push up against the joints. You can also

For the easiest working angle, use the trowel upside down

③ Push it in

When the mortar is the right consistency, scoop some up on the trowel and push the mortar into the joints with your pointing tool, making sure they are completely filled. Avoid getting mortar onto the face of the bricks—this will save you having to clean them off later.

④ Rake the mortar

Once the mortar is thumbprint-hard, run a joint raker over the joints to smooth and shape them so they match the existing joints. Smooth out the areas where old jointing meets new jointing with a stiff whisk broom or hand brush.

⑤ Brush it down

Sweep the joints with a brush after the mortar begins to stiffen. This will help you match the texture of the old jointing and the new jointing. It will also remove any loose material and help to prevent shrinkage in the new mortar.

buy professional versions of this sort of equipment: they're usually called "mortar hawks."

▓ Nail it

A large-headed nail driven into a block of wood makes a useful mortar-raking tool. Work out what depth you're raking to, then fix the nail in the wood to match. Run the wood across the surface and let the nail do the raking. ▼

Dealing with dust

The fine dust generated when you're re-pointing mortar or replacing bricks can irritate the skin and the eyes. Protective goggles are essential, as are sturdy work gloves. It's also a good idea to dress in old clothes that you can just take off and throw away at the end of the job.

SAFETY FIRST

▓ Going gray

If the existing mortar is brown, yellow, black, red, gray or charcoal, use common gray cement in your mortar mix and color it with the appropriate pigment or oxide. The mix will lighten considerably as it dries so do a small test batch first. If the existing mortar is white or close to white, then use off-white, not gray, cement.

▓ Don't let mortar dry out

Mortar must be kept damp as it cures. Organize your job so that you're never working in direct sun. Keep it damp as it cures; spray it with water several times a day.

▓ Pretty harmful

Some vines are bad for mortar joints, causing them to crumble. Grow vines on trellises instead.

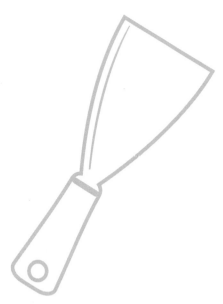

Wood siding

If you're comfortable using basic woodworking tools such as saws, hammers and nails, then you'll be able to make repairs to lap siding.

■ Looking for trouble

Stroll around the perimeter of your home periodically to look for pockets of rotten wood. If you find any, insert a screwdriver or awl to determine the depth of the decay, then make the necessary repairs quickly, before small problems turn into big ones.

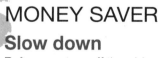

Treat every surface of a new board with preservative or wood primer before nailing it in place. This will delay the onset of rot in the future.

$ MONEY SAVER
Slow down

Before you tear off the old siding, check the price of its replacement. Wood can be very expensive so it may be worth your while to work slowly, saving as many of the old boards as possible.

■ Channel your efforts

Rotten siding near the base of a wall is often caused by rain running off the roof onto the ground and splashing back onto the siding. Before replacing the siding, fix blocked or leaky gutters so that water is caught and channeled away from vulnerable wood.

■ Make a match

Matching a particular siding profile can be difficult. One option is to replace all the boards on one side with a non-matching profile. Save any good boards you remove as they can be used to patch the other sides, if necessary.

■ Avoid rust stains

Always use galvanized nails to anchor the boards in place. They won't corrode and cause rust stains as ungalvanized steel nails do.

Punch the nail heads in slightly and fill the dimple with exterior filler for a neat and watertight finish.

■ Cut it out

If you discover areas of rot in your siding, don't waste time trying to patch the damage. Rot is a type of fungal attack that will ultimately destroy the wood. By the time the wood has gone soft, the rot is already well advanced. The best approach is to remove and replace the affected boards or sections of boards. It will save time and effort in the long run.

■ Space it out

Rainwater tends to cling to vegetation and brings moisture into contact with the wood siding. Keep plants and shrubs away from walls so that boards are less susceptible to rot. Trim back existing plants and position all new plants at least 20 in. (50 cm) away from the house. ▼

What you will need

- Hammer
- Small wedges of scrap wood and piece of scrap board
- Backsaw
- Keyhole saw
- Flat bar
- Hacksaw
- New siding
- Saw
- Drill
- Wood preservative
- Galvanized nails
- Sealant or putty
- Exterior-grade primer and paint
- Paintbrush

Replacing wood siding

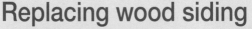

Make the cuts SQUARE so the new board will fit evenly

1 Expose the board

Drive small wedges of scrap wood beneath the damaged board. Wedge a piece of scrap board into the gap to protect the board below the saw. Use a backsaw to cut through the exposed portion of siding on each side of the damaged area. If repairing overlapping siding, work from the top of the wall down.

2 Complete the cut

Use two wedges to raise the siding that overlaps the damaged section. Reach up under the overlapping board with a keyhole saw to finish the cut (remember to hold the saw with the blade's teeth pointed out). Remove the wedges.

3 Take out exposed nails

Pry up the damaged board with a flat bar resting on a piece of scrap board. Next, remove the scrap board and use the bar to tap the siding gently back down, leaving the nailhead exposed. Pry out the nail.

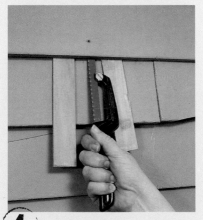

4 Remove hidden nails

Insert two wedges under the board overlapping the damaged board then slip a hacksaw blade between the boards and cut through any hidden nails. With nails out of the way, remove the damaged section of the siding. Now cut a replacement board, drilling the required nail holes and treating the sawn edges with preservative.

5 Replace the board

Drive the new board into place using a hammer and a scrap block of wood. Secure with galvanized nails to match the surrounding siding. Putty the nail holes and apply a gap sealant to the seams between new and old siding. Prime and paint. If replacing overlapping siding, work from the bottom of the wall upward.

What you will need

- Chisel
- Exterior wood glue
- Tape (if required)
- Wood block, screw and wedge (if required)
- Exterior-grade putty (if required)

BEFORE YOU BEGIN

Poor nailing often results in split boards. To avoid splits, attach boards with a single nail at each stud and always drill pilot holes.

Repair a split board

① Add the adhesive

To repair a split you'll need to glue the two segments of the board back together. Lever the split open with a chisel and squeeze in some exterior woodworking adhesive.

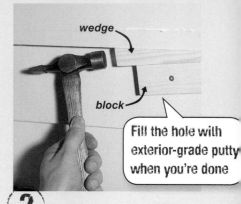

Fill the hole with exterior-grade putty when you're done

② Hold the repair

Hold the split closed while the adhesive dries. Duct tape may be strong enough. Otherwise, screw a block to the board below and drive a wedge between it and the bottom edge of the glued board.

SECRETS from the EXPERTS

To **stop splits** when nailing wood siding, blunt the sharp end of the nail with a hammer. This won't work at the ends of boards so always drill pilot holes first.

▦ Play the end game

The part of a board most likely to rot or decay is the end grain. As it dries, it acts like a sponge, soaking up moisture. When replacing boards, always be sure to give the end grains a generous extra coat of primer or oil stain before fixing in place. Do this and your walls will last much longer.

▦ Dig deeper

If a nail doesn't hold securely when hammered, it could be because the wood behind the clapboard is rotten or damaged by insects. Correct the underlying problem before repairing the siding.

▦ Go flat out

Flatten out warped boards by fixing them to the studs with long screws. Drill and countersink pilot holes to avoid splitting the boards. Use exterior-grade putty to conceal the screw heads. ▶

▦ Troubleshoot wood

Knots in wood siding can present a problem if not properly prepared before painting, as the resin they contain can bleed through to the surface, causing an unsightly patch of discoloration. To avoid this, seal all knots with a solution of shellac and denatured alcohol, or a commercial "stain sealer," before applying the final finish.

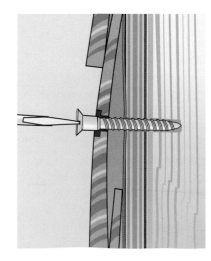

Vinyl and aluminum siding

If you want an exterior surface that's tough, attractive and affordable, go for vinyl or aluminum siding. It's also easy to repair and maintain.

Pick your battles
Shallow cracks in vinyl siding are easily repaired. Gently lever up one side of the crack with a toothpick, apply a special vinyl adhesive and then press the crack closed.

Patch the problem ▲
To fix cracked vinyl siding, remove the section and glue a piece of scrap siding to the rear. Prepare the area with PVC cleaner, apply PVC cement and press the patch in, finished side down.

Make a sneaky swap
For a subtle repair, replace damaged siding with a patch of weathered siding cut from an inconspicuous spot around the back of the house. Use brand-new siding to fill the gap.

Disguise with a dab
You can cover up small scratches on aluminum siding using a dab of acrylic paint. Sand the scratched area gently with fine steel wool first and prime with an oil-based metal primer before applying a finishing coat of paint.

Tips for tidy trims
For smooth edges when trimming vinyl with tin or aviation snips, cut with the first two-thirds of the blades only. Closing the snips fully will produce ragged edges.

Perk up with paint
It is possible to refresh vinyl siding with a coat of paint. Sand it lightly first to improve paint adhesion, and use an acrylic paint with a high solids content.

Have a light touch
When painting vinyl siding, choose a color that is at least as light as the original, if not lighter. Darker shades absorb more heat, which can cause the siding to overheat and warp.

Chase away chalk
The powdery white residue on aluminum siding, called "chalking," is caused by the natural self-cleaning action of the finish. Rain will wash it away eventually, but to get rid of it sooner rub with a soft rag and a solution of about 1/3 cup (80 mL) of household dishwashing detergent in 4 qt. (4 L) of water.

Wax up a shine
Use liquid car wax to give areas of dull aluminum a sheen (but only after the warranty has expired). First, wash the siding with a mild solution of dishwashing liquid and water, then rinse off. When it's completely dry, apply the wax with a damp sponge then buff it to a gloss with a very soft cloth.

A fresh coat of paint every couple of years will ensure that ageing aluminum siding stays in good condition.

Repairing dented aluminum siding

What you will need

- Drill
- Sheet-metal screws with flat washers
- Pliers
- Two-part car body filler and plastic spreading tool
- Fine sandpaper
- Oil-based metal primer
- Acrylic paint and paintbrush

① Drill into the dents

When repairing large dents, the first step is to make them as shallow as possible by pulling the siding back into place. Start by drilling ⅛ in. (3 mm) holes into the deepest parts of the dent.

② Raise the siding

Next, insert sheet-metal screws with into the drilled holes. Take some pliers and, gripping the heads, gently pull the screws outward. This will raise the dented areas. Remove the screws.

A flat-finish paint is best for hiding imperfections

③ Fill the dents

Patch the dent with two-part car body filler and level it off with the plastic spreader. Leave to harden. When set, sand the patch and apply an oil-based metal primer before finishing with two coats of good acrylic paint.

Fiber-cement

Modern fiber-cement siding is safe and easy to work with, but any jobs involving old-style asbestos cement should be left to the experts.

▓ Know your fiber-cement

It has been many years since some fiber-cement contained asbestos fibers. When concerns were raised about asbestos-related illnesses, the use of asbestos was discontinued. Do not cut, saw, sand or otherwise disturb fiber-cement if there is a chance it may contain asbestos. These days the product contains synthetic or cellulose fibers rather than asbestos. Fiber-cement poses

SAFETY FIRST

Leave asbestos alone

If you suspect an old roof or outbuilding might contain asbestos, do your research before attempting to dismantle and dispose of it. There are laws governing its safe disposal. If you can remove whole panels, it may be safe to do the job if you wear protective clothing and a dusk mask. But it is safer to arrange for a professional to remove it.

no health risks. Nonetheless, you should avoid inhaling the dust by wearing a dust mask and ensuring the work area is well ventilated.

For big jobs consider renting a fiber-cement cutter

▨ Score and snap ▲

The simplest way to cut fiber-cement is by the "score and snap" method. Repeatedly score the surface of the sheet to a depth of about one-third its total thickness using a stout blade and a straightedge. Press down on the straightedge and pull the outer edge of the sheet upward to snap it along the scored line. Fiber-cement manufacturers make a special tungsten-tipped tool for this job.

▨ Patching holes

Small holes in fiber-cement can be patched using an exterior-grade filler, fiberglass filler or car body filler. These commercial fillers are unlikely to shrink and, provided the original siding is sound and there are no crumbling edges to the hole, the patch should stick well. Don't bother filling the hole if it lies on a crack as the movement in the siding would most likely dislodge your patch. In that situation, the better solution would be to remove the siding entirely and replace it with a new siding.

Patch a hole in fiber-cement

What you will need

- Ruler and pencil
- Jigsaw
- Scrap fiber-cement
- Drill and drill bits
- String
- Adhesive
- Filler and putty knife
- Sandpaper
- Paint

BEFORE YOU BEGIN

Isolated holes and dents in fiber-cement are easily fixed. If they're part of a long crack, it's better to replace the section.

1 Cut clean edges

Start by removing a clean piece of the fiber-cement. Mark cutting lines around the damaged area with a pencil and a ruler, keeping the hole straight and square. Use a jigsaw or a narrow-bladed saw to cut out the square section.

2 Back up the hole

Cut a backing sheet to measure slightly larger than the hole you're patching. Drill two holes through its center and thread a loop of string through them. Apply adhesive to the edges of the backing, ease it through the hole, then pull it up tight against the back of the wall.

3 Set the patch

Allow the adhesive holding the backing sheet in place to set, then cut a patch to fit the hole exactly. Apply adhesive to the back of the patch and press it gently into place. Fill any gaps around the edges, sand smooth and repaint to match.

Stucco

Making repairs to stucco walls usually means filling and patching. Hairline cracks can often be left but anything else needs prompt attention.

Play detective

A close inspection with a magnifying glass can reveal the cause of cracked or flaking stucco. Salt crystals in the stucco are an indication that moisture on the inside of the house is migrating outward. If there are no crystals in the stucco, then the damage has come from outside.

Be flexible

Narrow cracks are best filled with pre-mixed mortar or a masonry sealant, both of which will maintain a flexible bond. Clean out the crack, chisel an undercut along the edges of the crack for good adhesion, then pack the gap with either mortar or sealant. If using mortar, smooth the repair with a clean putty knife for a neat finish.

Just say no

Hairline cracks in stucco may be unattractive but they are usually harmless and can be ignored. If you try to patch them you'll probably find that your repair is more unsightly than the original blemish.

Diagnose the damage

A long crack in the stucco can be an indication that the foundation supporting the wall is settling. To check, fix duct tape across the crack with epoxy adhesive and inspect it every two months. If the tape splits or twists, it means the masonry is moving and it's time to call in the experts.

Act now

To avoid serious damage, repair major cracks in stucco as soon as you notice them. Once a surface has started to break up, rain, insects and plants will get into the spaces and speed up the process of deterioration. If you're not careful, you'll end up having to refinish the entire exterior—and that's expensive.

What you will need

- Cold chisel
- Sledgehammer
- Brush
- Wet, flat sponge
- Stucco
- Steel float
- Pointed trowel or large nail
- Straight-edged length of wood (longer than the width of the patch)
- Wooden float

Patch a hole in stucco

1 Clear the area

Chisel out the loose stucco to give the patch a sound edge and clean out any crumbling joints in the brickwork or masonry to a depth of ½ in. (1 cm). Brush out all debris. Dampen the area with a wet sponge or cloth. This stops the stucco from losing moisture into the wall and drying too quickly, which could cause crumbling later.

2 Apply the first coat

Take some stucco onto a steel float. Spread it onto the wall, starting from the bottom of the patch and pressing the lower edge of the float hard against the wall as you sweep it smoothly upward. Continue until the stucco is smooth and the surface is sitting about ¼ in. (5 mm) below the level of the surrounding wall.

Fill hairline cracks in stucco with a coat of exterior masonry paint

▨ Tap and listen ◀

In cold climates, the bond between stucco and the wall can fail when moisture seeps between the two and freezes. To map the damage, tap the wall with the handle of a screwdriver. Wherever it sounds hollow you'll need to strip and replace the stucco.

▨ Build a better bond

New stucco will bond better if the underlying surface has a key. Before you begin, coat the wall with a mixture made up of one part cement to one part sharp sand mixed into PVA sealer, diluted with two parts water. Apply the mixture by "stabbing" it onto the masonry with a stiff brush. When it dries, the surface of the wall should feel like coarse sandpaper.

▨ Get the right recipe

For a good stucco, mix one part cement and one part hydrated lime, then blend in four parts plastering sand (also called "stucco sand" or "fine sharp sand"). Dilute with water to get the right consistency. A liquid plasticizer is an alternative to the lime; add it according to the manufacturer's directions.

▨ Be weather wise

Don't let the weather ruin your stucco job. If you're repairing in hot weather, add a drying retardant to extend your working time. If there's a risk of freezing, add a frost-proofing additive to the mix. The stucco has to dry slowly to be strong. In hot weather, regularly mist the patch with water for a couple of days after application.

③ Give it a key

After about 20 minutes the stucco will begin to harden. When that happens, scratch a crisscross of lines across the surface with a trowel or point of a large nail. This will make a key for the top coat. The first coat should be left to dry for at least 14 hours.

④ Apply the top coat

Take the same stucco mixture and apply it over the top of the first coat. This time, start at the upper left-hand corner of the patch. Sweep the float lightly across from left to right to spread the stucco over the area, leaving it standing slightly proud of the surrounding wall.

⑤ Level the patch

About 15 minutes after the top coat has been applied, just before it begins to set, draw a straight-edged piece of wood across the patch from bottom to top. If any hollows show after leveling off, fill them quickly and level again. As the stucco starts to set, smooth the surface gently with a damp sponge or a damp wooden float.

House painting

Painting the outside of a house is a huge task. Make a good job of it and it will be years before you have to paint again.

▓ Prepare for perfection

The secret to a successful house-painting job is proper preparation. First, check for peeling paint, cracked paint and mold, and treat as required, referring to the chart below. Next, wash the house with TSP and water. For a thorough job, rent a pressure washer to remove dirt and blast off any loose or flaking paint. If the walls are in good condition, or if the surface of your house consists of soft brickwork, then stick with a garden hose.

▓ How to wash wood

To avoid damaging wood siding when working with a pressure washer, keep the wand moving continuously and always keep the nozzle about 24 in. (60 cm) away from the wood's surface. Point the nozzle down so you don't force any water up between the boards.

▓ Seek the shade

When using a pressure washer, try to work on the shady side of the house. If you're washing in bright sunlight, the dirty suds can dry onto the siding before you've had a chance to rinse them away.

▓ Bottom up

Work from the bottom up when washing with a pressure washer. If you work from the top you'll streak the walls below. When rinsing, reverse directions.

COMMON **EXTERIOR PAINT PROBLEMS**

★ Problem	★ Cause	★ Cure
Peeling paint	Paint applied over dirty or moldy surface.	Wash exterior and remove mold with diluted bleach. Remove any loose paint. Prime all bare wood. Repaint with a high-quality acrylic paint that "breathes" and won't trap dampness.
	Moisture coming through substrate, plus poor flashing or sealing around windows and doors.	Install adequate flashing at roofs, chimneys and openings, or add sealant where needed.
	Defective vapor barrier in exterior walls.	Have a vapor barrier installed professionally.
Mold	Mold is a fungus. The growth of spores is supported by dirty, moist or warm surfaces.	Wash with a solution of three parts water to one part chlorine-based bleach—if it's mold, dirty spots will disappear. To prevent mold, regularly apply dish soap and hose off. Alternatively, apply a primer and paint containing fungicide.
	Too much shade encourages build-up of moisture.	Trim trees and shrubs to allow air and sunlight to reach affected area.
	Moist conditions produced by inadequate venting in eaves, porch ceilings or siding.	Install vents in areas where mold recurs. Make sure there are no water leaks in the area.
Cracked paint	Many coats of paint over an old surface.	Sand, scrape or strip off old paint, then repaint.
	Water-based paint applied over gloss oil paint.	Sand glossy surface to dull finish. Apply an appropriate primer, then repaint.
	Inferior siding material.	Replace siding.

What you will need

- Pressure washer or garden hose
- Dish soap and bleach
- Long-handled scraper
- Dust mask
- Electric sander
- Extra-coarse and medium sandpaper
- Awl
- Chisel (if required)
- Wood hardener (if required)
- Epoxy wood filler (if required)
- Brush
- Oil or acrylic primer
- Paintable sealant
- Wood preservative

Preparing wood siding

1 Wash the walls

If the exterior is in good condition, simply wash with a garden hose. If it's dirty and the paint is peeling, use a pressure washer, taking care not to let water shoot up between the boards. Spots of mildew should be removed with a solution of dish soap and bleach.

2 Smooth the surface

If areas of loose paint remain after washing, remove them with a long-handled scraper. Then, wearing a high-quality dust mask, use an electric sander to feather the edges or smooth any cracked or crazed paint. Start with an extra-coarse grade of sandpaper and move to a medium grade.

3 Stop the rot

Check for rotting wood, especially along the trim. If you find any soft wood, insert an awl to measure the depth. If the damage is shallow, simply sand it off. Deeper areas of rot need to be hollowed out with a chisel, treated with a wood hardener and left to dry, then patched with an epoxy wood filler.

4 Renew caulk joints

Remove crumbling sealant around doors and windows with the corner of the scraper. Sand the edges and then brush to clear out any dust or paint particles. Prime the wood then fill the exposed gaps with a paintable sealant.

The primer should be SIMILAR in color to the paint but not IDENTICAL

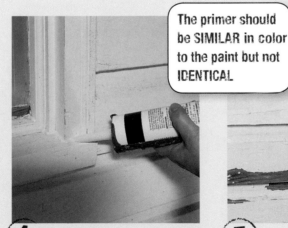

5 Prepare to paint

Work your way around the exterior, applying a wood preservative to any potential problem areas. Next, apply primer to all bare wood and all newly sanded areas. Make sure your primer is a good match for your selected paint. Paint within two weeks of priming.

What you will need

- Canvas drop cloths
- Sheets of plastic (if required)
- Garbage bags (if required)
- Ladder or scaffolding
- Paintbrush
- Paint pad
- Paint sprayer

Applying the paint

1 **Cover up**

Working on a dry, windless day, cover all surfaces below the work area with canvas drop cloths. Protect an air conditioner or mailbox with sheets of plastic. Tie back or trim overgrown shrubs. Cover them loosely with large plastic garbage bags, if necessary.

2 **Paint in stages**

Remove as many exterior fixtures as possible and paint them at your leisure. Paint wall siding first, then trim and windows, doors and railings, and finally entryways and steps. Always paint from the top of the house to the bottom, working in sections to avoid unsightly lap marks.

Spring and autumn, when air temperatures are neither too hot nor too cold, are the best times of year to paint your house.

▓ Prime chalky surfaces

Test the condition of existing paint on an outside wall by rubbing it down with a dry, dark-colored rag. If the rag collects a chalky deposit, scrub the wall with a stiff dry brush to remove the loose material, then apply a primer.

▓ Take care of siding

Scraping or sanding wet wood can leave tears and gouges. Instead, let the wood dry out before you proceed. Protruding rusty nails can either be knocked in or extracted. If extracting old nails, replace with new, galvanized nails driven in ½ in. (1 cm) away from the old holes.

▓ Listen as you work

A sharp paint scraper produces a mellow cutting sound during use, while a dull one gives a shrill screech. Carbide-tipped scrapers are the best choice: they stay sharper longer and you can buy replacement blades.

▓ Foiled again

Use heavy-duty aluminum foil to protect exterior hardware when painting. The foil will mold itself around irregular shapes, providing good cover, and will stay in place even when you accidentally knock it with a brush or roller. ▼

When using a paint sprayer, strive for a THIN, EVEN coat

3 Brush it on

First paint the underside of the boards. Apply the paint in short strokes, then spread it out using smooth, even strokes. Press brush bristles against cracks and rough surfaces to force paint in, checking periodically for drips. Once the undersides are coated, paint the faces of the boards.

4 Paint with a pad

If using a paint pad, load the pad and, as with the brush, paint the bottom edges first. Then pull the pad slowly but firmly along the length of each board. If the pad is narrower than the siding, overlap your strokes so you don't create a lap mark down the middle.

5 Spray smoothly

If using a paint sprayer, hold the gun horizontally about 10 in. (25 cm) from the siding and spray the bottom edge of each board. Then hold the nozzle in an upright position and paint each board in a series of parallel strokes, overlapping each strip of paint by about 1 in. (2.5 cm).

Hoe into it

A sharpened garden hoe will make short work of large areas of peeling paint and give you extended reach without having to grab a ladder. Remember to wear safety goggles while scraping.

Make a direct deposit

To clean and collect the sticky scrapings from a paint scraper, run the blade through a vertical slit cut in the side of an old coffee container. The scrapings will drop neatly into the can, and the blade will come out as clean as a whistle.

Think clearly

If the ornamental brick surrounds of doors, windows or chimney stacks have started to deteriorate and you want to protect them, coat them with a clear water-repellent silicone

sealer. Resist the temptation to paint them as the paint will be almost impossible to remove later.

Choose sides

Who says you have to paint an entire house all at the same time? The job will seem much more manageable if you plan to paint just one side every year.

Keep out of the sun

Structure your painting job so that you're always working in the shade. Direct sunlight makes the paint dry faster. Fast-drying paint is harder to work with and tends to blister, creating a soft paint surface that is easily damaged. You'll also find that sunlight reflects off the surface of the wet paint. If you work in the shade, you'll avoid the eyestrain caused by that glare.

Avoid the extremes

Spring and autumn, when air temperatures are neither too hot nor too cold, are the best times of year to paint the outside of your house. Not only will you be able to complete the job more comfortably, but the paint will stay wet longer, too. If you live in an area that has a defined wet season, then that time of year is definitely best avoided.

Time the task

Paint won't take to a damp surface, so the ideal time to paint is at the end of a dry spell. Avoid painting on windy days, as dust and grit will blow onto the new paint. You should never paint in frosty conditions or when it is raining. If it starts to rain, stop work and wait until the surface has completely dried out before resuming the work.

Choose the right tool

The best tools for applying a coat of masonry paint are a long-nap roller with a tough nylon pile, a large, synthetic-fiber brush or a medium-bristle dustpan brush with a comfortable handle. Apply the paint to the wall in vertical zigzags and fill in the gaps with vertical strokes.

Foolproof the frames

Paint windows and exterior doors early in the day so the paint is dry enough for them to be closed in the evening. The surfaces where openings and frames meet should be the first ones you paint. Wedge doors open so they can't blow shut or be closed by mistake. Smear a little petroleum jelly onto the stops before shutting up for the night; it will stop doors and windows from sticking and will wipe off easily in the morning.

Stay grit-free

When painting exterior masonry, work from a small paint container rather than directly from the can. It will help prevent transferring grit from the wall into your can.

Correct the color

No two cans of paint are exactly the same color, but there is a way to minimize the difference. When the open can starts to get low, top it up with paint from the new can and mix well. This "transition" paint will average out the color difference.

Dull the pipes

PVC gutters and downspouts can be left unpainted; just wash them down with diluted bleach. If you do want to paint them, don't feel you have to use an undercoat. PVC pipes that are brand new will need to be etch-primed to give the paint something to stick to. Otherwise,

let the pipes weather for a year to take the shine off the surface, and then paint.

▥ Getting behind pipes

If you want to paint the back of a downpipe without getting paint on the wall, you can use a special brush with an angled head. Alternatively, use an ordinary paintbrush and mask the masonry with a piece of cardboard. ▼

Sealing the exterior

Search for gaps and cracks around the house and seal them to stop drafts and water damage.

▥ Take a sneak peek

The gap between the foundations and the bottom edge of the wall siding is a significant source of drafts. Save your back when sealing the gap by using an old mirror so you can see what you're doing. ▼

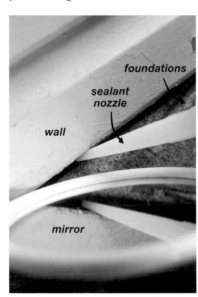

foundations
sealant nozzle
wall
mirror

▥ Renew when ready

Test old sealant by poking it with a screwdriver. If it cracks, scrape it out and squeeze in a fresh bead.

▥ Improve your metal

For a tight seal around aluminum, bronze or galvanized steel, wipe with a solvent such as acetone first to remove the coatings and oily deposits that could keep the sealant from adhering well.

▥ Climate control

In hot weather, refrigerate your sealant cartridge for 20 minutes before you start. On a cold day, wrap it in a hot pad for a while first.

Quick Fix

MAKE IT STICK

Sealant tends not to adhere well to very cold surfaces. For maximum adhesion on a cold day, prepare the surface by warming it up with hot air from a hair dryer before you apply the sealant.

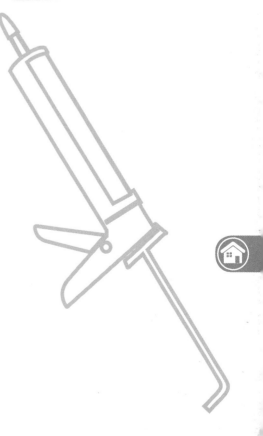

◾ Tighten up faucets ▲

To seal around an external faucet, first loosen any screws holding the faucet in place. Scrape out the old sealant with a putty knife. Squeeze a bead of silicone sealant behind the mounting plate, and screw the plate back in place. Smooth the sealant with a putty knife.

◾ Read the label

Always check the cartridge label to see if the sealant will accept paint. Some silicone sealants have exceptional adhesion and elasticity but will resist a coat of paint.

◾ Potato fingers

Pieces of potato cut to just the right shape are a smart way to smooth sealant around a joint. The juices will prevent the sealant from sticking to the potato. Keep the pieces moist in a plastic bag until you need them.

◾ Let it weep

When sealing the outside of a brick house, don't fill the small, regularly spaced holes or mortarless joints located above the foundations, doors and windows. These are "weep holes" that allow moisture to escape from the wall.

◾ Fill with foam

Use polyurethane foam instead of sealant for any cracks that are wider than ½ in. (1 cm). Foam expands by up to 30 percent so it's ideal for filling trouble-some gaps. Use it to silence squeaky stairs and cushion pipes that rattle against the house framing. Once dry, it can be trimmed to neaten it up.

◾ Bridge the gap

If the gap between the house's siding and foundation is more than ½ in. (1 cm) wide or ½ in. (1 cm) deep, insert a strip of open-cell polyethylene foam into the gap first. Top it with butyl rubber sealant. ▼

Working with ladders

Ladders make easy work of otherwise tricky jobs, but learn to use them safely and sensibly so you can avoid accidents.

◾ Get a grip

Hold the rungs, not the rails, when going up or down a ladder. If you slip while holding the rails of a metal ladder you'll get skin burns; from a wooden ladder you'll get splinters. If you're holding onto the rungs when you lose your footing, you won't slide at all. Make sure the ladder is properly set up and supported.

◾ Change to cordless

It's a safety hazard to have power cables hanging from a ladder as you work; use cordless power tools whenever you can.

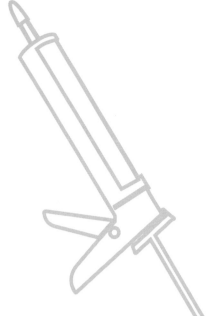

Polyurethane foam expands by up to 30 percent once it leaves the can so it's ideal for filling tricky gaps.

Setting up an extension ladder

① Walk it out

First place the ladder's feet against the base of the wall. Now lift the top rung and walk the ladder up, rung by rung, until vertical. Next, pull the feet out from the wall. Extend the ladder at least 3 ft. (1 m) above where you're working and lock it.

② Work the angles

Set the feet of the ladder on a solid, level surface at roughly a 75° angle to the ground. You should be able to stand with your toes touching the feet of the ladder, your arms and back straight, and your hands on the rungs at shoulder height.

③ Move on

When it comes time to move the ladder, unlock the extension and lower it, rung by rung, until it is all the way down. Carry the ladder parallel to the ground to the next location, and set it up as before.

▓ Don't climb too high

Use the top four rungs of a ladder as hand holds only. If you try to stand on those top rungs using something such as a gutter or windowsill for support, you're all too likely to have a nasty fall.

▓ Walk the boards

If the ground is soft, set the feet on a piece of plywood. The plywood should be ¾ in. (2 cm) thick and about 8 in. (20 cm) wider and deeper than the ladder's base. Stake the plywood on four sides so it doesn't shift.

▓ Keep off the glass ▶

When working on high windows, lash a length of wood measuring longer than the width of the window right across the top of your ladder. The wood will rest on the wall at either side of the window and hold the ladder away from the glass.

▓ Cushion the blow

After a few years of use, ladder-ends can get very rough and may even scar the paintwork or siding they're resting against. To prevent scratches, tie old socks, gloves or mittens around the tops of the rails.

▓ Don't be shocked

Working near power lines with a metal ladder or a damp wooden ladder is dangerous, since both can conduct an electrical current. If you must do it, use a ladder made from non-conductive fiberglass.

Wear shoes with thick rubber soles and a good grip

SAFETY ON THE ROOF

A roof is a dangerous place to be working. The surface is usually steep, often slippery and sometimes unstable. A mistake could result in a fall—easily enough to send you to the emergency ward. For safety's sake, buy or rent a roofer's harness kit before you start.

Watch the weather

Do not work in wet or windy conditions. Avoid going on the roof early in the morning when the surface may be covered with dew or even a thin layer of ice. Also avoid very hot conditions when you'll be at risk of sunburn, sunstroke or dehydration. The ideal time to work on the roof is on a sunny afternoon in the fall.

Work with a friend

Always have a helper on the ground. The helper should remain within hailing distance at all times in case there is an accident or emergency. If you're in a public place (for example, if your ladder is set up on a footpath), the helper can also keep passers-by at a safe distance.

Line up your ladder

Make sure your extension ladder is set firmly on the ground and angled. If your ladder rises 13 ft. (4 m) to the gutter, the base of the ladder should sit roughly 3 ft. (1 m) out from the wall. Extend the ladder so that it reaches at least 3 ft. (1 m) above the eaves.

Get a good footing

Wear shoes that have soft, rubber soles when you're working on the roof (running shoes will do the trick). And give the roof a quick sweep before you start work to ensure the area is clear of leaf debris that could become a slip hazard.

Tread lightly on tiles

Concrete and terracotta tiles can become brittle with age, so be careful where you step. As you walk across the roof, always try to place your feet near the front edge of each tile. This is where the tiles overlap, directly above the batten, so it's the best place to deposit your weight.

Don't tempt fate

Some roofing jobs are simply beyond the skills of the home handyperson. If the roof has a pitch greater than 30°, if it's permanently in the shade (and therefore likely to be covered in slippery moss) or if the idea of working at that height makes you feel uncomfortable in any way, call in the professionals.

Tiled roofs

The modular nature of a tiled roof means most repair jobs are quite manageable. The tricky part is working with tiles that are brittle with age.

Let it be

If your tile or slate roof is old, but sound and free of leaks, resist the temptation to mess with it. Old tiles and slates become brittle with age and are very easily cracked or broken, so even a simple spring cleaning can end up causing more problems than it solves.

Watch your step

Modern terracotta tiles can withstand a small amount of foot traffic, but older tiles can be extremely fragile. If you must walk across the roof, take care to walk on the strongest part, which is the front edge of each tile, where the tiles overlap. Wear soft-soled shoes. Do not wear thongs (flip-flops) as they can easily trip you up.

Move the moss

Lichens and mosses grow naturally on tiled roofs, particularly parts that are in permanent shade. Some homeowners like the look, but others prefer their roofs to be free of vegetation. Lichen is harmless but moss can trap moisture so is best removed. To remove it, wash the tiles with a solution of 4.5 lbs. (1 kg) of copper sulphate in 6 gal. (22 L) of water. The solution can damage gutters and downpipes, so rinse thoroughly when you are finished.

Stop the slide

Wrap rubber bands around the handles of tools to stop them from sliding down the roof as you work. The rubber will grip on roof pitches of up to 45°. ▶

Try some pressure

If you'd rather not use copper sulphate to get the lichen and moss off your tiles, consider using a pressure washer instead. Work from the top of the roof down, otherwise water will be forced up under the tiles. Walking on a wet roof is dangerous; don't do it unless you're wearing a safety harness.

Apply boot polish

New tiles can stand out among existing tiles. To tone them down and give them a more aged look, apply some boot polish. The polish will dull the tiles and make them a better match to the originals. Remember, this is not a permanent fix and the tiles may have to be touched up from time to time. After a while the new tiles will weather to match the older ones.

Track down tiles

The styles of terracotta tiles have varied enormously over the years and finding replacement tiles to patch up an existing roof can be a challenge. The best idea is to find a roof restoration specialist trading in second-hand tiles salvaged from demolition sites. (Most major cities will have one or two.) These businesses also tend to stock hard-to-find slates and concrete tiles.

Go salt-free

From time to time it is worth taking a look at the underside of your terracotta tiles to check for a sort of crumbling that occurs when salt from the atmosphere crystallizes under a tile's surface, gradually wearing off the top layer. The exposed side of the tile is rarely affected, probably because rain washes off any salt and keeps the tile's surface clean. This is most common near the ocean, but can also occur inland. Badly affected tiles must be replaced before they fail completely.

BEFORE YOU BEGIN
Broken roof tiles should be replaced promptly, but don't rush into the job without knowing how to work safely on the roof. See page 260 for advice.

Replace a damaged roof tile

1 Expose the tile
The first thing to do is gain access to the damaged tile. With one hand, raise the row of tiles immediately above the one that is to be replaced. Use the handle of a hammer or a couple of small softwood wedges to support the tiles while you work.

2 Snip the ties
Every second course of tiles is wired or nailed to the batten below. If the tile you're replacing is wired into place, try reaching in under the tile above with a pair of cutters to snip the ties. The alternative is to enter the attic and free the tile from below.

Don't let your tools scratch the sheet metal; if the protective surface is compromised, the roof will be vulnerable to rust.

Metal roofs

Sheet metal roofs are relatively easy to maintain. Just keep an eye on their weak points: the flashings and the edges where rain can penetrate.

Maintain order
If using more than one type of metal on the roof, put those that are more prone to oxidization (the less "noble" metals) above those that are less prone to oxidization (the more "noble" metals). The ideal order from the top down is zinc, aluminum, iron and steel, lead, copper, then stainless steel.

Follow the rafters
The light-gauge metal used on most domestic roofs can be permanently dented or crimped by your body weight. When walking across a metal roof, follow the line of the rafters, where the roof has maximum support. Sheets with a high profile don't dent as easily as those with a low profile, but still follow the rafters.

Soften the sound
The sound of light rain falling on a metal roof can be delightful, but a deluge is deafening. When putting on a new roof, install a fiberglass or similar material insulation blanket underneath. It will deaden the sound, reduce condensation in the attic and provide thermal insulation, too.

3 **Twist and remove**
Lift and twist the damaged tile to release it from the interlocking grooves of the adjacent tiles. Remember to take particular care when handling old tiles since they become very brittle with age and are easily damaged.

4 **Brush away grit**
Carefully brush dust and dirt from the interlocking grooves of the adjacent tiles. This area must be thoroughly cleaned as these grooves prevent water from entering the attic. Also ensure that the grooves on the replacement tile are clean and free from dirt.

> A single tile will rarely need to be wired or nailed in place

5 **Lock it in place**
Insert the new tile at an angle. Press down gently and rock the tile from side to side to ensure that it is firmly locked into the grooves of the adjacent tiles. Lower the row of tiles above the work area back into place, removing props if necessary.

▥ Repair or replace?
When a roof corrodes to the point where holes start to appear, it's time to replace it. If you need a temporary solution, try filling the holes with sealant or covering them with pop-rivetted patches—but make replacement a priority.

▥ Tighten the screws
Constant expansion and contraction of the sheet metal can cause roofing screws and nails to work loose. Check regularly, and tighten loose ones as soon as you spot them.

▥ Roof noises
Temperature changes cause sheet metal to expand and contract, resulting in creaks and groans. Aluminum and zinc expand twice as much as steel, so they tend to be the noisiest roofs.

▥ Defying gravity
Many metal sheet roofs are installed at a shallow angle, so there is always a danger that rainwater may flow back underneath by surface tension. Turning down the edge of the sheet where it discharges into the gutter can reduce the likelihood of leaks in your attic.

▥ Deal with drips
The lwashers sometimes used under galvanized roofing screws may become cup-shaped over time, allowing water to flow underneath them and into the roof. To solve the problem, apply a dab of sealant to the undersides of affected washers. Alternatively, replace the washers. ▼

washer with good seal

cupped washer

Asphalt shingle roofs

Asphalt shingles are the most common residential roofing material used in North America. Color and style choices are plentiful and some of the better, heavier grades are rated to last 40 to 50 years when properly installed. It's not uncommon, however, for these roofs to need spot repairs throughout their life span. Falling tree branches, roof-mounted hardware and uneven weathering can result in damage to individual shingles or small sections. Fortunately, such localized repairs are often easy to make, but before you haul out the ladder and tools, take a few minutes to assess the roof's overall condition.

Repair blemished shingles

1 Clean and caulk

For cosmetic blemishes, such as small gouges that don't require replacing the shingle, start the repair by cleaning the area thoroughly and applying a bead of clear silicone caulk.

2 Cover the scar

Rub the top surfaces of two shingle scraps firmly together above the blemished area. Granules will drop and become embedded in the caulk, disguising the scar.

Replace a shingle

1 Lift overlapping

Work on a warm but not hot day so shingles are flexible. Lift overlapping tab off the damaged shingle and pry out nails. Repeat with next row up, since those nails also penetrate the damaged shingle's top edge.

2 Insert new shingle

Place the new shingle underneath the row of tabs above. Nail it in place with galvanized roofing nails in approximately the same locations as those you removed.

3 Adhere new shingle

Apply a thin bead of roofing cement under the tabs of the new shingle and any existing tabs you folded back to make the repair. Press them flat to ensure adhesion.

Chimneys, vents and flashing

Chimneys and vents break the surface of the roof, so they're always potential trouble spots.

▨ Check ahead

Make regular inspections of the roof surface and chimney stacks so that faults can be fixed before any significant damage occurs. Only work on a roof if you feel competent; otherwise call in an expert.

▨ Start at the top

When inspecting chimney stacks, first check the flues and caps, then make sure the mortar holding them in place is intact. Next, inspect brickwork and pointing, making note of damaged bricks and missing mortar. Consider capping unused flues.

▨ Keep flashings flat

Galvanized steel or aluminum flashing makes the joint between the chimney stack and the roof surface waterproof. Make sure the upper edge is held securely in the mortar and the lower edges lie flat on the roof; otherwise rain can leak into the attic.

▨ Inspect the valleys

The internal angle where two roof slopes meet is usually lined with a special metal valley flashing. Keep it clear of wind-blown debris so it doesn't overflow. Check regularly for corrosion holes, too—any you find can be waterproofed temporarily with self-adhesive flashing tape.

Fit a vent flashing

What you will need

- Tape measure
- Utility knife
- New vent flashing
- Pencil
- Roofing sealant

BEFORE YOU BEGIN

First remove any old flashing that remains around the vent, scraping off as much of the old sealant as possible.

① Prepare the vent

Measure the diameter of the vent pipe and, using a sharp utility knife, cut a matching hole in the rubber of the new vent flashing.

② Slide it on

Slip the new flashing over the vent. If necessary, trim the neck of the rubber sleeve so that it fits the vent pipe snugly. Push the flashing down the vent pipe until it touches the roof, then carefully mold the base to fit the contours of the metal or tile roofing.

③ Seal it in

Mark the position of the flashing base on the roof and then pull the flashing back up the vent pipe. Lay a bed of sealant on the roof and then press the base of the flashing into it. Apply more sealant around the base and top of the flashing.

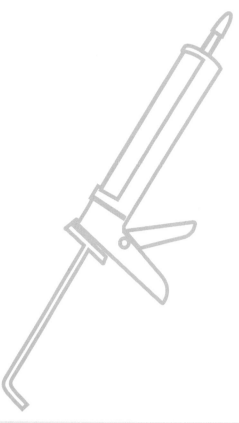

Cap the gap

If you live in a warmer climate, check that your roof vents are capped, otherwise pests and airborne debris could get in. Nylon screening secured with a hose clamp can be an effective substitute when a regular fitting is unavailable. ▼

TRACING A LEAK

★ Don't assume that a leak in the roof is located directly above a stain in the ceiling. Water may run along rafters for quite a distance before it finally drops.

You need to get up into the attic with a flashlight and look for the tell-tale signs: watermarks on siding and framing woods, and cone-shaped impressions left by drips on the surface of fiberglass insulation.

Follow the trail upward and mark the uppermost location with a waterproof marker. Next time it rains, go up into the attic and check the spot for dampness or dripping water.

Repair a leaking gutter

What you will need

- Wire brush or sandpaper
- Clean rags and a solvent (such as acetone)
- Fiberglass or metal patch
- Scissors or tin snips
- Fiberglass resin or gutter sealant
- Paintbrush or putty knife
- Work gloves (if required)
- Pop rivets and rivet gun (for metal patches)

(1) Ready the surface

Clean away dirt or rust with a wire brush or sandpaper, then wipe the area with solvent and allow to dry. For a fiberglass patch, cut a piece that will cover the area with an overlap of 2 in. (5 cm) on all sides; for a metal patch, you'll need to allow an overlap of 4 in. (10 cm).

(2) Make the bed

For a fiberglass patch (shown here), use a paintbrush to apply a thin coat of prepared fiberglass resin to the gutter. Wear gloves so the resin can't touch your hands. For a metal patch, use a putty knife to spread a ⅛ in. (3 mm) layer of sealant over the surface.

Gutters

Gutter maintenance is crucial to the health of the house. If water is leaking here, it can cause damage to the walls and foundations.

Think big
The gutter system must be able to cope with the volume of water coming off the roof. If you're ordering new materials, remember that a big roof area will need deep gutters and broad downspouts.

Go with the flow
When assembling sections of gutters, remember to overlap each joint by about 4 in. (10 cm) in the direction of the water flow. If the overlaps are set against the flow, water may leak through the joint.

Scoop the goop ▲
Make a gutter scoop by cutting the bottom out of a plastic motor-oil container and using the spout as a handle. Your scoop will hold much more than a garden trowel. Empty debris into a bucket hanging from the ladder.

Extend your reach
To avoid having to move the ladder frequently, make a gutter rake. Cut a small piece of plywood or solid wood to match the shape of the gutter. Screw this to the end of a length of broom handle about 4 ft. (1.2 m) long, then attach a loop of cord to the other end to secure it to your wrist. ▼

(3) Secure the patch
Press the patch into the resin or sealant with a rag. For fiberglass, apply a thin coat of resin over the patch, wait 24 hours, sand, and apply another coat. For metal, rivet the patch at both ends, then spread a layer of sealant over the edges and leave to dry.

Quick Fix

NO MORE LEAKS

For minor repairs to a leaking gutter, plug the trouble spot with a squirt of silicone. Clean the rusty area before applying the product. If the damage is more extensive, you should have the gutter replaced.

If there's bubbling paint or watermarks on the underside of the gutter, it's likely there's a leak that needs fixing.

Installing gutter screens or guards

What you will need

- Tape measure
- Gutter guards or screens
- Metal snips or household shears

BEFORE YOU BEGIN

Make sure that the gutters are clean and free of holes, and that the downspouts are clear and draining properly.

1 Clear the way

Measure the gutters and buy the lengths of guard or screen as appropriate. If the gutters have metal supports, measure the distance between them.

2 Cut to measure

Cut the screens or guards to match the length of the gutters. If there are metal supports, cut notches in the screens to accommodate them. If there are overhanging clips, cut screens into lengths that will fit in between them.

3 Install the screen

Position the screen or guard so that leaves will be washed straight over the top and onto the ground below. Eliminate any depression between the roof and the gutter, as leaves will build up there and prevent the roof from draining properly.

▦ Hang about

Turn an inexpensive plastic bucket into a handy gutter-cleaning aid. Snip the wire handle in half, bend the ends of the wires to form hooks, and hang the bucket on the gutter as you clean. Each time your gutter scoop fills up, just drop the debris into your bucket.

▦ Find the sag

To pinpoint a sag, pour a bucket of water into the high end of the gutter and watch where the puddle forms, then adjust the slope as necessary.

▦ Firm it up ▲

Correct a sagging gutter simply by adjusting the metal brackets. If the gutter is held on with suspension brackets, as in the picture above, use pliers to bend the metal. If it has support brackets, reattach those that are too low or too high to produce the right slope.

▦ Avoid blockages

When cleaning out your gutters, plug the top of the downpipe with a rag. This will prevent leaves and debris from falling into the drain and blocking it. (Remember to remove the rag later.) You can also buy mesh gutterguards that sit in the tops of downpipes to keep out windblown leaves and debris.

Decks

Outdoor living spaces such as decks are vulnerable to weather damage. Stay on top of little problems as they arise and you'll save time in the long run.

Double the grip

Tighten loose deck boards by driving in a new screw next to each old nail. First use a nail punch to drive existing nails deeper into the joists, then drive in coarse-threaded, galvanized or stainless-steel decking screws alongside. Stand, or kneel, on the boards so they're in tight contact with the joists as you drive in the new screws.

Stop the mudslide

Heavy rains seep through the spaces between deck boards and can wash away the soil beneath—especially on a slope. To minimize erosion, cover the soil with a thick layer of gravel.

New nails for old

A popped nail can be hammered back in, but it will soon work its way out again. Instead, remove the old nail and hammer in a new, longer nail at a slight angle so that it passes through fresh wood. Alternatively, replace the popped nail with a galvanized decking screw.

Take out the sway

Decks that rest on tall posts of 4 ft. (1.2 m) or more above the ground can sometimes sway as you walk across them. One way to stop the movement is to angle-brace the joists. Cut a length of 2 x 4 in. (5 x 10 cm) wood and fix it diagonally from corner to corner underneath the deck. At each joist, drive in two 3½ in. (100 mm) galvanized nails. These will secure the brace and stop the swaying. ▶

offset holes

carriage bolt

nut and washer

Firm up wobbly posts ▲

Wobbly railing posts can be strengthened with the addition of a couple of bolts. Measure the thickness of the post and framing assembly, then add ¾ in. (2 cm), and purchase ½ in. (1 cm) diameter galvanized carriage bolts in that length, plus a nut and washer for each. On each post, drill a couple of ½ in. (1 cm) holes roughly 1½ in. (4 cm) from the top of the framing, the other about 1½ in. (4 cm) from the bottom of the post. Tap in the bolts, slip on the washers and nuts, and then tighten until the bolt heads are set flush to the post.

Tighten loose deck boards by driving in a new screw to replace the old nail.

You'll need a helper to hold one end of the brace while you drive in the first nails

2 x 4 in. brace

What you will need

- Work gloves
- Flat bar or screwdriver
- Angle grinder or hacksaw blade (if required)
- Hammer and wood chisel
- Epoxy wood filler
- Preservative-treated joist
- Saw
- Carriage bolts
- Matching decking wood
- Water-repellent stain and sealer
- Galvanized nails or screws

Replace a deck board

① Remove the board

Take out the damaged deck board, using a flat bar to remove nails or a screwdriver to remove screws. If you can't get the nails or screws out, try cutting them from underneath the deck board using an angle grinder or hacksaw blade.

② Check the joist

Inspect the underlying joist. If you find rotten wood, remove it with a hammer and chisel, let the remaining wood dry, then patch with filler. Cut a preservative-treated reinforcing joist from hardwood and secure it to the damaged joist with carriage bolts.

Get into a regular maintenance routine with your deck and you'll save on costly repairs in the long run.

▓ The water test

Splash a glass of water onto the deck boards. If beads form, the wood is still water-repellent. If the water is absorbed, you'll need to apply a new coat of sealant.

▓ Keep it simple

For a low-maintenance deck, leave the wood untreated and simply clean it with a pressure washer each spring. If the wood is dirty, scrub it with dish soap.

▓ Cover up with color

If weathered decking wood isn't to your taste, give the surface some bold color with a coat of solid color deck stain.

▓ Don't overdress ▲

Moisture evaporates from the end grain of the wood, so never cover the ends of the boards with trim or nosing. If you do, you'll be encouraging rot and pests.

▓ Roll it on

Whether it's homemade or store-bought, a roller with an extension handle is the ideal tool for painting a deck. It's quick, and there are no drips or overspray.

Pre-drill pilot holes for deck screws

3 Fit the new piece

Cut the new deck board to the length and width of the existing deck boards. Treat it with a water-repellent stain and sealer. When it is dry, put the new board in place and attach it to the joists with galvanized nails or deck screws.

Scrub up for summer

Spring-clean paving and decking by scrubbing the surfaces with a pressure washer, or simply with a bucket of water and a stiff outdoor broom. From then until the end of summer, a daily sweep with a broom is all that's needed.

Stop the rot

If you find rot or pest infestation in a piece of wood, chances are that nearby wood is also affected. Before launching into repairs, inspect every support post, joist and board for damage.

Put a coat on

If you find some rot in a joist, dig it out, let the remaining wood dry off, then brush on two coats of deck preservative. If the hole is deep, you will need to fill it with a suitable external wood filler. You can buy fillers containing fungicides.

Keep moving on

Don't let pots and planters sit in one place for too long. Moisture is bound to persist under any permanent fixture, and the water will lead to rot in the deck boards below. Instead, move them around on a regular basis.

Finish on top

If you prefer to have a finish on a wood deck, choose a semi-transparent deck stain. Check the label to be sure the product is made to withstand foot traffic. One coat is usually enough; a second coat may create a film on the surface that will crack and wear.

Dry before you finish

New wood must be completely dry before the finish is applied; if it isn't, the finish won't take properly. To test, apply a small amount in an inconspicuous area. After about 15 to 20 minutes, most of the stain should be absorbed. If the stain beads up, wait and repeat the test a few days later.

SECRETS
from the EXPERTS

Always brush **an extra coat of deck sealer** onto the rough ends of deck boards, since they absorb more than the tops and bottoms.

Back-saver!

The regular recoating of an oiled deck is a back-breaking job. To simplify the task, pour the oil into a cheap bucket and apply it with a household sponge mop. Your back will be saved, the job will take less time and the sponge attachment can be thrown away afterward. ▼

Concrete and asphalt

The installation of concrete and asphalt is best left to the experts, but maintenance and repairs are easy to carry out yourself.

Soak away oil stains

If your concrete driveway is spoiled by unsightly oil stains, consider this unusual treatment. Pour a bottle of cola over the stain, leave it to soak in overnight, then rinse off the next morning using soapy water. The oil will have disappeared.

Wash down walkways

To keep asphalt driveways and pathways in good condition, wash them thoroughly once a year. First sweep away leaves and dirt with a broom. Next, mix one scoop of laundry detergent into a bucket containing 1 gal. (4 L) of water. For spot-cleaning, splash some onto the asphalt and scrub with a stiff broom. Then, working as quickly as possible so as not to waste water unnecessarily, give the whole surface a good rinse with the hose.

Scrub off tough stains

Use oven cleaner to lift tough stains off a concrete surface. Spray it on, let it settle for 5 to 10 minutes, scrub with a stiff brush, then rinse off with your hose running at full blast. Severe stains may require a second application.

Fill the cracks ◄

Concrete dust is an irritant, so make sure you wear goggles, dust mask and gloves. Shallow cracks can be filled with a cement-based sealant. To fill larger cracks, chip out loose edges with a narrow cold chisel, then trowel in some bonding agent and patching concrete, and smooth with a steel trowel or a wooden float.

Break it up

For areas of flaking concrete, first break up the surface with some light swings from a sledgehammer. (The weakened areas will sound hollow when tapped.) Scrub the exposed surface with a wire brush and rinse with water. When dry, apply a bonding agent and patching concrete, and smooth with a steel trowel or a wooden float. ▼

Strike a blow

Mortar or concrete that has set hard on your shovel can be difficult to remove. Don't risk damaging the blade by striking the edge of the shovel on a hard surface. Instead, give the back of the blade a sharp blow with a heavy hammer: the concrete should fall away cleanly.

New life for old slabs

Excavating an old concrete slab and installing a new one is expensive. A cheaper option is to cover the existing surface with a decorative layer of concrete. Search "concrete resurfacing" to find a professional who can liven up your old slab.

Repairing steps ▲
Use a cold chisel and sledge-hammer to break away loose concrete and square up rough edges. Set up some wood formwork to contain the patch. Dampen the area, then brush on a bonding agent. Fill with patching concrete and smooth. Run a stiff broom over the surface to roughen it before it sets.

Seal the slab
A concrete slab with a slightly powdery surface can be fixed with the application of a chemical sealer. First, clean the concrete using a wire brush, scrubbing brush, pressure washer or vacuum cleaner. Leave to dry. Next, apply a coat of chemical sealer with a large brush.

Fill when necessary
Hairline cracks in concrete can be ignored. They usually follow the lines of the contraction joints between sections. For bigger cracks use a concrete sealant or filler.

Hold back the rust
Metal railings and fasteners expand as they rust, causing the concrete surrounding them to chip or flake off. To reduce the problem, periodically seal the joint with a cement-based sealant where metal meets concrete.

Breaking-up made easy
Locate gas and water pipes before you start breaking up an old concrete slab. Rent a jackhammer to make the job easier—one with vibration damping will be less tiring to use. Wear ear and eye protection, work gloves and steel-toed footware.

Root cause
To prevent buckling and cracking of concrete slabs, sever tree and plant roots along the slab's edges each summer. Drive a spade 6 to 8 in. (15 to 20 cm) below the slab, withdraw it, then drive it in again, making sure to overlap the previous cut.

Use oven cleaner to shift tough stains off concrete. Severe stains may need more than one application.

Resetting a railing ▲
To secure a loose railing that's set into the concrete, first chip out the existing concrete to a depth of 2 in. (5 cm) and a radius of 1¼ in. (3 cm) around the post. Vacuum the hole, then dampen the surface. Fill the hole with a bonding agent and patching concrete, and smooth it with a steel trowel or wooden float.

In the garden

Garden hand tools

Although power tools are useful, most garden tasks rely on basic hand tools such as a spade, a hoe or a pair of bypass pruners.

▒ Tool finder
Tools with green, blue and wooden handles can be hard to find in garden greenery. Make them visible with red adhesive tape.

▒ Soft push
Heavy digging can be hard on the feet. To cushion your foot while you're pushing a spade or fork into heavy soil or tough grass, slip a pad made from a piece of old garden hose split lengthwise over the shoulder of the implement. If the pad falls off, stick it in place with epoxy resin adhesive. ▼

▒ No blisters ▲
To prevent your hands from blistering while you're raking up a big load of leaves, pad the rake handle with a length of slip-on foam pipe insulation used for copper pipe. Fix it in place with insulating tape if necessary.

▒ Blade care
Preserve bypass pruners and handsaw blades by cleaning off sap and dirt immediately after use, and sharpening after every 10 hours of use. After pruning one plant, and before moving on to the next, wipe the blades with a rag soaked in bleach. This helps to avoid spreading diseases.

▒ Weeding knife
A grapefruit knife makes a handy weeder. It's lightweight and comfortable to hold, allows you to work close to delicate plants, and its serrated edges will cut straight through gritty soil.

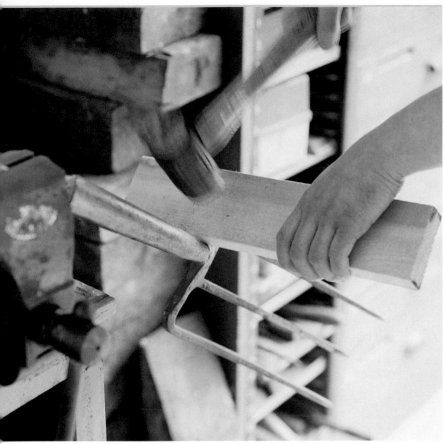

It's better to have a limited number of good-quality garden tools than a multitude of useless gadgets.

▦ Apply brute force ▲

If the wooden handle of a tool snaps off flush with the shaft, making it hard to extract, try some force. First, remove the rivets, drilling them out if necessary. Then drive a large wood screw into the broken piece of the handle. Grip the screw head in a vice, hold a scrap of wood against the shoulder of the tool, and strike it with a heavy hammer.

▦ Old rake, new tricks

If the handle of an old rake breaks, remove it, nail the rake head to a wall, and hang tools such as trowels on the outward facing tines.

▦ Preventing split ends

As the varnish wears away on wooden tool handles, the wood splits and splinters, absorbing moisture that will eventually rot the handle away. To seal the worn areas, rub them every so often with boiled linseed oil.

▦ A back-saving sled

Heaving a heavy weight into a wheelbarrow can strain your back badly. The next time you need to move a big rock, tree or shrub, make a simple sled out of a scrap piece of ¼ in. (5 mm) plywood. Drill a pair of holes in one end of the plywood and attach a loop of rope. Roll your load onto the sled and pull. It will slide easily across the lawn without damaging the grass—or your back.

▦ No-bend gardening

Be good to your back by standing up while weeding and planting bulbs. All you'll need are a few tools with long handles, which are available from most garden supply stores.

CHOOSING THE RIGHT **HAND TOOLS**

You don't need a complete range of garden tools, but what you do have should be sturdy, well-made and suited to your garden. Choose tools that are properly adapted to your build. In particular, take note of tool handles—they need to be solid yet light and a good fit for your hands. You'll get the most use out of your tools by keeping them clean, oiled, dry and sharp—and always putting them away after use.

1 Wheelbarrow

Wheelbarrows are vital for transporting plants, soil, compost, garden debris and tools. The most suitable wheelbarrow for heavy work is one with a single wheel and an inflatable tire to cushion the load. Wheelbarrows with two wheels are very stable and easy to load and unload, but are less maneuverable on uneven ground.

2 Bucket

A well-made bucket is useful for transporting small loads without having to fetch the wheelbarrow. Also use it for mixing fertilizer and as a receptacle for weeds.

3 Trowel

The trowel is an essential tool for planting and lifting small plants, especially in confined areas such as windowboxes and other containers. Choose a sturdy trowel with a long blade, but make sure it is not too broad.

4 Hand fork

Use the hand fork to till the soil (a garden claw is also good) and to loosen the soil when weeding around small plants.

5 Long-handled pruner

Use this tool to prune branches that are too high up or use the extra leverage to cut branches that are tough or thick for regular bypass pruners.

6 Shears

Shears are used for clipping and shaping hedges and trimming small patches of grass. It's important that shears be well-balanced or they will be tiring to use (see page 280).

7 Hose with trigger nozzle

A hose with a trigger nozzle saves water. When not in use, wind up your garden hose neatly and hang it on a large hook or bracket securely attached to a wall near your outdoor faucet.

8 Fork

A four-tined, strongly made fork is invaluable for aerating lawns, turning over a plot between crops, breaking up clumps of earth, lifting root crops and large plants. It is also useful for shifting garden garbage and compost.

9 Spade

A flat spade is an indispensable tool for breaking up or removing soil and for digging holes to plant for trees and shrubs.

10 Rake

A lawn rake (pictured) is designed for collecting fallen leaves and lawn clippings and for removing moss and dead grass. Garden rakes have short sturdy teeth and are used for seedbed preparation and soil leveling.

11 Hoe

Hoes are used for tilling, cultivating and weeding. There are several types, including the Dutch hoe which is used to cut through weeds at soil level, and the mattock which is used with a swinging action to break up areas of hard ground and to dig out deep-rooted weeds.

12 Watering can

Watering cans are ideal for irrigating small gardens and potted plants. A rose-type nozzle conserves water by dispersing it evenly.

13 Pruning saw

Use a pruning saw for cutting off branches too thick for bypass pruners.

14 Bypass pruners

Bypass pruners are used for pruning woody stems up to about ½ in. (1 cm) thick and soft shoots of any thickness. They must be kept clean, rust-free, oiled and sharp. Dull pruners will make ragged cuts and damage your plants.

Protect yourself from soil pathogens, thorns and poisons by always wearing gloves and proper footwear.

Good tines

It's easy to bend a tine in a fork accidentally. To fix, insert the tine in a 3 ft. (1 m) length of 1 in. (2.5 cm) diameter galvanized pipe and bend it until straight. Insert the pipe in the ground where you can access it easlly—but make sure it is sited where it won't be a trip hazard. ▼

Adjust your shears

Check the adjustment of garden shears by holding them by one handle and letting the other hang down. When the weight of the unsupported handle is just heavy enough for the jaws to open, it means the pivot adjusting screw is tightened correctly. ▼

Sand and steel ▲

To clean the steel component of tools such as trowels, forks, hoes and bypass pruners, first fill a box or bucket with sand, then add some oil until the sand is well soaked—any oil will do, including leftover car engine oil. Next, stab the tools several times into the sand and let them stand for a while. The sand will remove the dirt from the tools and the oil will protect them from rust.

One winter's day

Prepare for the growing season by devoting one day in winter to garden tool maintenance. Brush and wipe your tools with an oily cloth, sharpen blades, oil wooden handles, tighten screws, and inspect for missing parts and any major repair requirements. Come spring, you'll be ready to go.

Gardening wear

Protect yourself from the health hazards of gardening such as soil pathogens, thorns and poisons by wearing gloves and proper footwear. Avoid sunburn by wearing sunscreen, a hat and clothes that cover your arms and legs.

Lawn and garden power tools

A yard resplendent in grass, trees and shrubs will always draw the eye and move the soul—behind the scenes, a set of power tools.

Mowing slopes

Don't ever risk using a mower on a slope steeper than the maximum recommended by the mower manufacturer. Mow across the slope, not up and down—it's much easier on your arms and also safer, giving you greater control. Grip a mower extra firmly when mowing down the slope.

Leave to dry

Wait for the grass to dry before you mow it. Mowing wet grass results in an uneven cut, as well as clumps of clippings that smother the lawn and clog the mower. Wait for the soil to dry before using a ride-on or tractor-drawn mower to reduce the risk of bogging and ruts that are difficult to remove.

Gas or electric?

Petrol mowers are not the best choice for everyone: they are heavy and can be tricky to maintain. If you have a small yard, you might be better off with an electric mower. You can now buy them with rechargeable battery packs. As well as being cordless, the modern models are incredibly light.

Blunt warning

If your lawn develops a grayish brown coloring a day or two after mowing, it's a sign that your mower blade needs sharpening. Look closely at the grass and you'll see that the tips have been shredded rather than neatly sliced. The ragged ends not only look bad, they provide easy entry for grass diseases.

Don't spray while the mower is running

Cut the cake ▲

To stop grass cuttings from caking up the underside of your mower, clean the surface and spray it with a mixture of two parts kerosene to one part engine oil. The cuttings will stick to the coating as you mow and wipe off easily when you're finished. Make sure you clean them off every time you use the mower.

Ground check

Inspect the lawn before you mow for any sticks, stones, toys or metal items that could damage the blades or fly up and hit someone.

LAWNMOWER TROUBLE SHOOTING

★ Problem	★ Likely cause	★ Solution
Difficulty starting	Faulty ignition	Spray with WD-40 or a similar water-repellent aerosol.
	Damaged spark plug lead	If the lead is damaged, replace it.
	Dirty spark plug	Replace the spark plug or clean and reset the gap, taking care to remove any carbon lodged between the insulator nose and the outer shell.
Black smoke coming from the exhaust	Blocked air filter (gas mower)	If it's a paper filter, replace. If it's a sponge filter, wash it out with gasoline or kerosene.
Vibrations	Unbalanced blade (rotary mower)	Replace or sharpen the blade as soon as possible or the mounts will loosen and the bearings will wear out.

What you will need

- Work gloves
- Length of wood
- Wrench
- Hammer
- Vise
- Mill bastard file
- Screwdriver

Sharpen a mower blade

1 Remove the blade

Disconnect the spark-plug cable and wedge the blade into a stationary position using a piece of wood. Grasp the blade with your gloved hand and loosen the bolts with a wrench. If the bolts stick, tap the wrench with a hammer. Once the bolts are off, remove the blade.

2 Repair or replace blade

Inspect the blade (and the stiffener if the unit has one) for damage. Replace any damaged parts with new ones that are specified by the manufacturer. If the blade is bent, don't attempt to straighten it out; buy a new one and go straight to Step 5. Otherwise go to Step 3.

HOW TO TUNE A **LAWNMOWER**

Tune your mower at least once a year, or more often if you use it frequently. It's really worth the effort. A tuned engine lasts longer, increases fuel economy by up to a third, reduces repair costs and decreases emissions by up to half.

★ First you'll need to change the oil. Run the engine for a few minutes to warm up the oil so it will drain better. Stop the engine, remove the drain plug and empty the old oil. Tilt the mower back to get it all out. Replace the drain plug and fill the mower with oil, checking it is full by the oil fill hole or the dipstick.

★ A dirty air filter disrupts the fuel/air ratio, causing the mower to burn more fuel and emit overly noxious exhaust fumes. If your mower has a paper filter, remove and replace it, making sure the pleats face out. If it has a sponge filter, wash it clean with gasoline or kerosene.

★ Remove the old spark plug with a spark-plug wrench or deep socket. Remove any carbon that may have built up between the insulator nose and the outer shell. Hand-turn the new plug until the threads catch. Ratchet the plug down until it stops, then turn it another quarter turn—any more could break the plug or make it very difficult to remove.

▓ Chainsaw safety

Don't compromise on safety when handling a chainsaw—accidents can have horrific consequences. Dress protectively: gloves, earplugs, boots with a solid tread, safety glasses and helmet.

▓ Straight start

The starter cord on a chainsaw will fray if it is yanked repeatedly at an angle against the housing. Keep it in good condition by pulling it straight up from the housing.

▓ Reverse the bar

The guide bars of most chainsaws are reversible. This is a safety measure, to ensure that wear and tear is evenly spread. Keep a tally of the hours the saw is in use and make sure you reverse the bar every five hours.

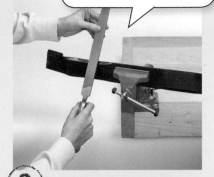

Don't aim for a razor-sharp blade—it will dull more quickly

An unbalanced blade can damage your mower's moving parts

3 Sharpen the blade

Using a mill bastard file, sharpen the blade along the original angle of each cutting edge, on opposing ends of the blade. File in one direction only—toward the cutting edge. Take equal amounts of metal off each edge.

4 Balance the blade

Check that the blade balances horizontally, using a screwdriver. Check the balance one way, then turn the blade over and check again. If the blade does not balance, file metal from the heavy end, taking care not to file the sharpened cutting edge. Keep filing until the blade balances.

5 Replace the blade

Once the blade is balanced, fix it back on to the mower, making sure that the lift wing on each end points toward the deck of the mower, not the ground. This will allow the blade to cut and discharge grass properly.

Sawdust warning

When your chainsaw starts to produce sawdust, it's a warning that the blade is dull. Stop work immediately and sharpen the teeth.

Chipper check

Keep a regular check of the fuel level of a chipper/shredder. If it runs out of gasoline while it's working, you'll have to unclog the hopper or the chipper chute and clean the discharge area before restarting the engine. Top it up before it runs dry.

Stay sharp

When the rate at which the chips discharge from the chipper starts to slow down, and/or the chips come out looking stringy, take it as a warning that the blades are becoming dull. Sharpen them without further delay.

Watch out for toxic plants

Never use a line trimmer (whipper) to prune oleander or other toxic plants. The trimmer reduces much of the pruned matter to minute particles, which, dispersed into the air, can cause damage through inhalation or contact with the skin.

SAFETY FIRST

Chip in the dry

Wait until leaves and branches that are green or wet have dried out before you put them through a shredder. Wet vegetation can clog or jam the machinery and yield a mulch that may turn moldy in time.

Saw blade cover

Before putting your chainsaw away, shield its teeth with a split piece of garden hose. It will protect the teeth from moisture and dust.

Keep your trimmer trim

What you will need

- Monofilament line or pre-wound spool

BEFORE YOU BEGIN

For performance and safety, regularly check the trimmer's locking ring, the automatic feed button and the line itself.

1 Remove locking ring

The locking ring stops the spool from falling out of the trimmer. To inspect, first press the locking tab on the side of the spool while rotating the ring counterclockwise. Pull off the ring and replace it if damaged.

2 Check feed button

The automatic-feed or "tap" button in the center of the spool monitors and adjusts the amount of line that the spool unfurls. Inspect and replace if cracked or damaged.

3 Replace the line

You will know the line is damaged if there is a drop in cutting quality. Act immediately. Unlock the spool, slide it from the hub, and either wind it with new line or install a new, pre-wound spool. If winding line onto a permanent spool, clip the end at a diagonal to make it easier to insert.

▓ Buy the right trimmer

Line trimmers are available in electric and gas-driven models. Electric models are ideal for average to small gardens, being lightweight and easy to start. But in a large garden the long extension cable is hard to drag around, and it will keep getting tangled in obstructions. When choosing a gas trimmer make sure that it is the right size and weight for your build. Check for excessive vibration, and that the starting cord is easy to pull.

> *Stop using your trimmer at least 4 in. (10 cm) from the trunks of trees and bushes to avoid damaging them.*

▓ No scalping

Always keep the cutting head of your line trimmer level. Tilting the head will give the grass an unsightly crew cut.

▓ Back off

Stop using your trimmer at least 4 in. (10 cm) from the trunks of trees and bushes or else protect the trunk with a heavy plastic collar, available at garden centers. The whirling line will cut even quite large plants, injuring or even killing them.

▓ Cable control

If using an electric trimmer, walk with the cable over your shoulder. This keeps it behind you, so you are less likely to slice through it.

Watering

Water is precious, but using it sensibly is really quite simple: be frugal with water-guzzling plants, and thoughtful about how and when you water.

When to water

To reduce evaporation, water your garden in the early morning or in the evening, and always in the evening in warm weather. This will give plants the whole night to benefit from a drenching and you won't have to water so often.

Deep water

Frequent light watering of young and mature plants encourages shallow root systems that are less able to withstand drought. Soaking or "deep watering"—watering less often but in greater quantities so that the water soaks deep into the soil—encourages hardy root systems and keeps the sub-surface soil damp for longer.

Water non-stop

Make a drip watering system with an empty soft drink bottle. Cut the bottom off and pierce some holes in the shoulder of the bottle. Leave the cap on and bury, cap down, next to the plant. Fill the bottle and the water will seep out slowly. ▼

A steady hose reel ▲

Hose reels are very convenient but tend to tip over when you're trying to wind them in or out. Keep your reel firmly upright and easy to use by screwing it to a piece of railroad tie or a chunk of treated pine.

Two cans

Keep two watering cans handy at all times, one for regular watering and one for applying water-soluble compounds, such as weedkiller, fertilizer or pesticides.

Big drip

Achieve consistent deep watering with a soaker hose—a porous or pierced tube that lets water seep gradually into the soil. Snake the hose around your plants close to their root zones and cover it with mulch to inhibit evaporation.

Quick drink

No matter what the time of day, if a plant is showing signs of stress due to a lack of water, give it a drink. Use a hose or a watering can.

MELT AND MEND

Repair pinpoint-sized leaks in a garden hose with a soldering iron. Heat up the iron for a few minutes then touch it carefully to the leaky spots until the surface melts and seals itself.

Laundry recyclables ▲

Instead of throwing away the plastic containers of laundry detergent, rinse them out thoroughly and recycle them as watering cans. Drill ⅛ in. (3 mm) holes in the top of the cap and a ½ in. (1 cm) hole just above the handle to let air in so the water flows freely.

Water crops not weeds

When growing vegetables, it saves time in the long run to use a watering can rather than a hose with a sprayer nozzle. With the watering can you can be precise with your watering, targeting your plants and not the weeds growing in between.

Lawncare

A grass lawn takes effort to establish and keeping it in top condition requires regular attention. A few simple tips will reduce the workload of lawncare.

Do you need a lawn?

A lawn is time-consuming and thirsty. So unless you really love your lawn or your children use it for play, consider replacing it or making it smaller by planting a mix of other ground-covering plants, shrubs and vegetables.

Needs-based watering

Don't over-water your lawn. To check if an established lawn needs watering, walk across it and see how long it takes for the grass to spring back in your footprints. Water if the spring-back rate is slow.

Fertilizing: the rules

Fertilize lawns four times a year after mowing at a cool time of day. Use a complete lawn food. When done, aerate the lawn with a garden fork and water deeply.

Flour power

It's often hard to tell which areas have been covered with fertilizer. Mix some kitchen flour with the fertilizer before you spread it to mark the areas you have covered without harming the lawn or the wildlife. The flour will disappear when you water the lawn or it rains.

What you will need

- Spade
- Cultivator
- Lawn fertilizer
- Soil rake
- Watering can
- Grass seed
- Straw
- Fine-mesh netting and pegs

Reseed a bare patch

1 Clear the site

Using a spade and cultivator, dislodge and remove grass, weeds and debris in a circular area about 6 in. (15 cm) bigger in diameter than the bare patch. Loosen the soil to a depth of 3 in. (7.5 cm). Avoid damaging the surrounding grass.

2 Fertilize, water and seed

Scatter fertilizer lightly and rake in well. Water until moist. Level the soil and cut seed furrows with a spade. Scatter with seed matching the variety in the lawn. Close furrows and press gently using the back of the rake.

Four-legged culprit

A patchy lawn may have several causes but by far the most common is dog urine. If you cannot train or dissuade your dog, keep a bucket of water handy and drench the lawn as soon as the dog has finished urinating. The water will dilute the highly nitrogenous liquid so that it doesn't cause harm.

Fertilize fast ▶

Here's a fast, simple way to fertilize your lawn. Find an old plastic plant pot, about 5 to 6 in. (12 to 15 cm) in diameter with plenty of rectangular drainage holes. Fill the pot with granular fertilizer and take a walk around the lawn, shaking the pot in a circular motion as you go. The fertilizer will cover a strip about 5 to 6½ ft. (1.5 to 2 m) wide. Cover the lawn in sections.

Keep your lawn adequately watered, mowed and fed, and the grass should be able to outgrow any weeds.

③ Mulch and nurture

Scatter a thin layer of straw over the seeds to insulate them as they germinate. Protect from birds and rodents by stretching netting over the patch and securing with pegs. Keep moist by watering lightly each day.

Rules for herbicides

Be cautious with herbicides. A single misdirected drop could kill a plant you love, while an excessive dose multiplied could affect a whole ecosystem:

SAFETY FIRST

• Consider every alternative to chemical weed control.

• Keep animals and children away from the area for the length of time recommended by the manufacturer.

• Keep herbicides away from watercourses.

• Do not spray when bees are foraging.

• Never buy and store more chemicals than you will need in a 12-month period.

• Spray first thing in the morning or in the evening, when it's cool and there is no wind.

• Spray at the manufacturer's recommended stage of weed development. Do not spray when rain is forecast.

• Never mix different herbicides unless recommended to do so on the label by the manufacturer.

• Adjust the nozzle to a medium to coarse spray. Keep the sprayer low to reduce drift.

• Wear eye protection and gloves. Wash hands and face after spraying.

• Do not make up more mixture than you will use.

What you will need

- Rented sod cutter
- Sod
- Straightedge
- Board to kneel on
- Soil rake or lawn roller
- Topdressing of sand and compost
- Watering can or hose

Laying the sod

Wait FOUR WEEKS before fertilizing a new lawn

1 Prepare and lay

Strip the site to bare soil using a sod cutter if possible. Prepare the soil and choose a suitable variety of sod. Lay the first strip against a straightedge. Butt the end of the next strip flush with the first. Set a board on the preceding row to kneel on. Stagger the horizontal joints.

2 Finish and nurture

Press the sod with the back of the rake or a light lawn roller. Then spread topdressing to fill gaps. Keep the lawn moist until it is firmly rooted. Leave the grass up to four weeks before cutting. Cut one quarter of the leaf length on the first mow, then gradually cut it shorter.

Tips for a flourishing garden

A beautiful garden is mostly the result of small tasks carried out regularly, from building a compost heap to timely pruning.

■ No frills composting ◄

Don't spend money needlessly on a compost container. You can make compost in an open pile covered with plastic tarpaulin to prevent leaching during rain, or in a closable container such as an old garbage can with holes cut in it for air circulation. An enclosure made with wire mesh supported by wooden posts will also do.

■ Keep it convenient

Locate the compost heap near the garden. Carrying garden debris to the heap and compost back for the garden will be that much easier.

■ Two's better than one

Instead of one deep compost heap, set up two shallower ones. Once the compost in the first is mature, use it while you build up the second. Then switch to the second while replenishing the first, and so on.

■ Green and brown

To help your compost "cook" nicely, mix one part of green material for nitrogen with three parts of brown material for carbon. Grass clippings, clover, manure and vegetable scraps make good greens. For browns use straw, dead leaves, strips of bark or even sawdust.

▦ Nice and hot ▶

Compost reaches a temperature of 130°F (55°C) as it decomposes—provided it's well aerated and has the right nitrogen and moisture content. If your compost is cold, turn the edges into the center every three to five days, mix in some manure. Add soil if it's too wet, or water if it's too dry.

▦ Compost don'ts

Don't compost oil, meat or dairy products—they'll smell, decompose slowly and attract pests. Put them in the garbage.

▦ Smaller the better

The smaller the ingredients in your compost, the quicker they'll decay. Cut up kitchen scraps or pulverize them in a blender. Shred leaves and garden debris with a shredder or mower, or place them in a garbage can and chop with a line trimmer. ▼

▦ Pests be gone

Deter mammalian pests by spraying your compost with a scent repellent or household ammonia. To repel flies and insects, soak up excess moisture with an occasional layer of soil or shredded newspaper; limit the amount of added manure; and keep the pile covered.

▦ Liquid refreshment

Keep the compost pile moist. Besides water, you can use leftover juice, coffee, tea or vegetable cooking broth.

▦ Pruning a tree branch ▶

Remove a mid-sized branch using the three-cut method. Make the first cut (the undercut) from below, about 12 in. (30 cm) from the trunk. Cut only about a third. Start the second cut not exactly above but about ¾ to 2 in. (2 to 5 cm) out from the undercut, so that the two cuts meet slightly apart. After the branch falls off, cut off the stump perpendicular to the trunk.

▦ Weed watch

Don't add weeds that have set seed to the compost pile. They may germinate and sprout once you spread the compost on the garden.

SECRETS
from the EXPERTS

To improve the air circulation of a compost pile, insert a **PVC pipe** drilled with holes into the center of the pile.

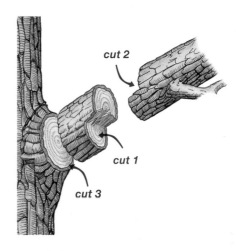

cut 2

cut 1

cut 3

What you will need

- Tape measure
- Stakes and string
- Spade
- Cultivator (claw hoe)
- Compost or other organic matter
- Untreated wood or old railroad ties cut to length
- Electric drill ⅜ in. rebar rods
- Galvanized nails and cleats
- Level
- Complete fertilizer
- Soil rake
- Garden hose

Make a raised bed

1 **Mark out the bed**

Select a location that gets at least six hours of direct sunlight daily, on a level site if possible. Outline a rectangular bed no more than 4 ft. (1.2 m) wide with stakes and string. If possible, orient the bed with the long sides running north–south. To check if the bed is straight, measure the diagonals; they should be equal.

2 **Prepare the soil**

Strip any sod from the bed with a spade and turn over the soil to a depth of 12 in. (30 cm), using a garden fork or cultivator. If the soil is poor, dig deeper. Incorporate compost, rotted manure, or other organic matter into the soil.

▦ Make your own mulch

Use a chipper-shredder to turn dry vegetation into mulch. Or lay 5 to 10 sheets of moistened newspaper and cover with soil—this will also inhibit weeds. Don't use colored newsprint as metals from the ink will leach into the soil.

▦ Waste not

Rather than burning autumn leaves after you've raked them up, make mulch for the coming spring. Put on a pair of safety goggles and run the leaves through a chipper.

▦ Healthy branches

A tree swing is fun for children but not so healthy for the branch. The sawing action of the rope cuts the cambium layer just under the bark, killing the branch. To prevent

damage, make a protective sleeve out of tough rubber, such as an old car tire. Staple it to the tree and tie the rope around the sleeve.

▦ Breathing room ▶

Mulch piled too closely to stems and trunks can shelter slugs, mice and other pests, and suffocate the roots or cause collar rot. Leave a ring of bare soil around each plant.

▦ Hold the plastic

Use plastic sheeting sparingly. It inhibits the circulation of water and air, heats the soil excessively in summer, and suffocates roots.

▦ Roll out the carpet

Use old pieces of wool or cotton carpet as a weed-suppressing mulch. Lay strips between the rows

in vegetable and flower gardens and in nursery beds. Camouflage the carpet with a thin layer of soil.

▦ Healthy bark

Bark protects trees from infection and disease so don't cut or bruise it by using tree trunks as posts on

Raised beds dry out quickly, so water as needed and spread mulch

③ Install a retaining wall

Create a 6–8 in. (15–20 cm) high wall with lengths of wood or ties set singly or in stacks. If the bed slopes, set the wall in a shallow perimeter trench. Butt single ends, nail them together and brace the corner with cleats. If a deeper bed is desired, stack wood so the ends overlap. Drill holes and drive rods 6 in. (15 cm) into the soil.

④ Enrich the soil

Fill the bed with topsoil liberally enriched with compost to a level 2 in. (5 cm) below the top of the wall to prevent the soil from being washed away. Work in some fertilizer. Make the soil as rich as possible as raised beds tend to be planted more intensively than traditional vegetable plots.

⑤ Plant and tend

Rake the soil until smooth and level. Water well, leave to settle, add more soil if needed and rake again. Plant with seeds or seedlings. Spread mulch to inhibit moisture loss and water as often as possible. Watch for pests. If you are troubled by mammals or birds, protect the beds with mesh or wire.

---

which to chain bicycles or nail signs. If there is nothing else handy on which to hang a sign, bind it on with cotton string.

▣ Foil it

Mulch mixed with a few strips of aluminum foil helps to deter slugs. And you can help a plant to grow straight by putting it in a foil-covered container, allowing the stem to grow through a hole in the foil. For several plants, pierce the foil with multiple holes.

▣ Tender staking

You can do your newly planted or transplanted tree a favor by letting the wind sway it around, thereby strengthening the trunk. Keep the stakes low and the support tie, which you can buy from garden

centers, just tight enough to keep the tree from toppling. Check the support as the tree grows to make sure it is not getting too tight. ▼

SECRETS
from the EXPERTS

To keep slugs and snails away from your vegetables or tender seedlings, try **spreading a mulch of cocoa shells**. Slugs and snails dislike the rough texture of the shells.

Pets in the garden

Making your beloved pets garden-friendly can be tough but you can always make your garden more resilient to them.

Keep cats out of your flowerbeds by burying pieces of orange, lemon and grapefruit peel in the soil.

Fresh repellent

Fed up with a dog repeatedly digging up the same spot in your garden? Keep the dog away by scattering a crumbled cake of toilet freshener over the area—the smell really puts them off.

Fruitful solution

Cats are repelled by the smell of citrus. To deter the local felines from digging up young plants, poke pieces of orange, grapefruit and lemon rind into the soil of flower and vegetable gardens, then dust lightly with soil. Stockpile peels in the freezer for when the fruit is out of season.

Ants can't swim

If your dog eats its meals in the yard, stop the ants from taking over by placing the food bowl in a dish filled with water.

No-tip dish

Put water for your dog in a ring-style cake-baking tin with a hole in the middle and place it in a shady spot in the garden. Then, to anchor the tin and prevent spills, drive a wooden stake through the hole.

Desirable doghouse

A good doghouse should be large enough for the dog to lie down and sit up comfortably, and small enough for the dog to keep warm with its body heat. Put hay inside for insulation and bedding but watch for allergic reactions. Shelter the entrance from wind and raise the floor to minimize dampness.

Paths and fences

Pathways, fences and other barriers can be used to good effect to break up the space within a garden, add interest and define boundaries.

Fake flagstones

Avoid hours of backbreaking stone-work by making a pathway or patio from poured concrete and carving "joints" into the smoothed surface with a brick jointing tool. Work quickly from a pattern so the concrete won't set before you're finished. Allow for expansion joints. Scatter the patio with pots and furniture and who would know?

What you will need

- Stepping stones about 2 in. (5 cm) thick
- Drywall saw or old bread knife
- Trowel
- Tarpaulin
- Sand (55 lbs./25 kg for every 10 stones)
- Rubber mallet

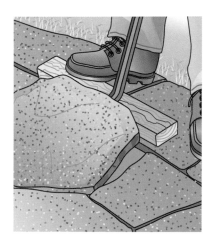

stain and work it in with a stiff scrubbing brush, then rinse with clean water. If this doesn't work, try mixing some household ammonia into the solution.

Trick for lifting pavers

Having problems lifting loose pavers? Try using a plumber's plunger. Wet the paver for maximum suction before applying the plunger.

Replacing a paver

If you need to remove a damaged paver from a path, first clear away any sand or soil surrounding the broken paver. Lever the paver out with a pointed trowel, taking care not to damage adjacent paving. Settle the replacement paver and press it down with a rubber mallet (or with a light sledge if the blows are softened with a stout piece of wood). Fill in any gaps between the pavers with fine sand. ▶

Lifting flagstones ▲

Ease the removal of flagstones laid on a sand paving bed by using a piece of wood as a fulcrum for the crowbar. It will reduce the pressure on your back and protect adjacent stones from damage.

Stained flagstones

Remove food stains on flagstones with a solution of dish soap and water. Swab the solution onto the

Make a stepping-stone path

① Cut sod

Space the stepping stones along the path to match the average stride of the most frequent users. Using the stones as patterns, cut through the sod around each stone with a drywall saw or bread knife.

② Make holes

Move the stones to the side and dig out the sod with a trowel. Dig about 2 in. (5 cm) deeper than the thickness of the stones to allow for the sand base. To make cleaning up easier, pile the sod and soil onto a tarpaulin as you work.

You'll need 55 lbs./25 kg of sand for 10 stones

③ Lay stones

Put sand into the hole to a depth of 2 in. (5 cm) and level it off. Set the stone on the sand and wiggle or tap it with a rubber mallet until it's flush with the grass. Add or remove sand as necessary. Repeat until you have positioned all the stones.

Enduring fences

For a rot-resistant wood fence, choose plantation-grown, pressure-treated pine. It will last a long time and require little or no maintenance.

Fencing the wind

Closed fences will block wind gusts but also create powerful downdrafts on the leeward side. Select a fence that will allow some air to filter through but at a much slower speed than wind gusts.

Post protection ◄

Fix wood, copper or plastic caps to the tops of wood posts to prevent rain soaking into and splitting the end grain. Alternatively, shape the post tops so they will shed rain.

Self-closing gates

A garden gate that closes automatically will help to prevent toddlers and pets from straying. The expensive option is an electrical remote-control device but there are more affordable options, too. A small gate will swing shut if you screw a spring or bar close to the hanging post. Position the hinges on a large gate slightly out of line and it will swing shut gently by means of gravity alone.

Gate maintenance

Gates should be treated with wood preservative or paint to prevent rotting. Small areas of rot on the gate can be cut back to sound

Repair uprooted pavers

What you will need

- Small crowbar or long screwdriver
- Steel float
- Chiel and hammer or pruning saw
- Paving sand
- Level
- Broom

1 Assess the problem

Identify the tree that is causing the problem—this might require some exploratory digging. Cutting a tree's roots can cause rot and instability, so you might want to consider moving the paving rather than risking a tree of which you are fond. Note that paving can also be disturbed as bedding sand is eroded.

2 Lift out the pavers

Use a small crowbar or long screwdriver to remove the uprooted pavers, tapping the surrounding pavers to loosen the grouting sand holding them in place. Clean the edges with a steel float.

wood and filled with a two-part epoxy-resin wood filler. Once set, smooth with medium grit sandpaper or a power sander. Rotting wood braces or pickets should be replaced. Keep an eye out for rust on gate latches and hinges. Scrub off with a wire brush (wear safety goggles) and cover the area with a rust-inhibiting paint.

▦ Fix a leaning fence post

Over time, a wood fence can begin to sag due to shifting in the ground, wood rot or wind damage. You can use a steel picket to brace the post as a temporary measure. For a permanent solution, you may have to dig out the post and reinforce its footing with packed stones or poured concrete, or replace it altogether. ▶

steel picket

tree root

chisel

③ Cut back the roots

Use a steel float to remove bedding sand and expose the roots to trim them back using a chisel and hammer or pruning saw. Replace the bedding sand, tamping it with the float.

④ Replace the pavers

Add paving sand so that the pavers will sit about ⅛ in. (3 mm) higher than the surrounding area, position the pavers then press them level with existing pavers. Use a level to check. Grout the pavers by using a broom to sweep dry sand into the joints.

Garden furniture

Half the pleasure of a beautiful garden is being able to sit out and enjoy it. Follow these tips to keep your garden furniture in good condition.

Freshen up wooden furniture

What you will need

- Masking tape
- Penetrating oil
- Open-end or socket wrench
- Hacksaw blade or nut splitter (if required)
- Scrubbing brush
- Dish soap
- Household bleach
- Pressure washer and sandpaper or wood restorer

1 Rusty bolts

Apply masking tape to the wood around the bolts to prevent staining. Soak the bolts for 24 hours in penetrating oil and remove with a wrench. If a bolt stays stuck, cut through it with a hacksaw or split with a nut splitter.

2 Mildew

Scrub the wood with dish soap diluted in warm water, then wipe with diluted household bleach and rinse. For stubborn mildew stains, use a stronger concentration of bleach.

3 Stains

Pressure washing is an easy, effective way to remove stains from wood and restore the original color. Sand wood lightly when dry. Alternatively, apply a wood-restoring chemical to the wood, following the manufacturer's directions.

Once a year

Outdoor furniture blends into the background so well that its need for maintenance tends to be overlooked. Set a few hours aside each year to check for worn finishes, rotting wood and rusting metal. A good set of furniture can be expensive to replace, and a regular coat of paint, preservative or oil can lengthen its life by several years.

Rust slow-down

Rust never sleeps but you can slow its grip on metal furniture by removing it down to the bare metal. If you can't, use a rust converter. This not only primes the metal but also neutralizes the rust and prevents it from spreading.

Rust brush

A wire brush operated by an electric drill whisks the rust off intricate metal furniture really quickly, including the twists and curves. The brushes come in fine, medium and coarse grades to match the size of the job. Always wear protective goggles when doing this job.

Cloth control

Wind can wreak havoc at a picnic—napkins and paper plates fly away and the tablecloth yearns to set sail. For a readymade anchor for your tablecloth, glue spring-type clothes pegs to the underside of your garden table with epoxy adhesive. Space them around the table, and tape them in place until the adhesive dries. Now you'll be able to secure your tablecloth quickly and firmly.

Barbecues

Open air. Relaxed atmosphere. Delicious aroma. Unique taste. Summer wouldn't be the same without friendly barbecues in the garden.

Let the dew clean it

The tedious part of using a barbecue is cleaning up afterward. Make it easier by leaving the cooled grill in a patch of grass overnight, with the cooking side facing down. In the morning, wipe the grill with damp paper towels. The grease will come away with the dew.

Tough grease

To remove baked-on grease from a grill, mix ½ cup (125 mL) of liquid dish soap with 1 gal. (4 L) of water. Put the grill in a heavy-duty plastic garbage bag and pour the cleaning mix over it. Seal the bag with a twist tie and leave it overnight. In the morning you'll be able to remove the residual grease using a stiff brush. Rinse the grill thoroughly.

Ceramic briquettes

If your gas barbecue features permanent ceramic briquettes (or "rocks") clean them regularly to avoid flare-ups and uneven heating. It's simple: turn the briquettes over, light the barbecue, set the temperature to high, close the cover, let it burn for 20 minutes, then turn off. Use the same technique for gas barbecue ceramic tiles.

Choice of fuel

Choose your fuel depending on how you want to use your barbecue. If speed and simplicity are paramount, opt for an electric or gas-fired barbecue. If you want the taste of food cooked over an open flame, and can spend a bit longer getting the barbecue going, use a solid fuel such as wood or charcoal. Many prefer using charcoal, but remember that a charcoal fire does create a lot of smoke, so it may be best to warn the neighbors first—or just invite them to the barbeque.

Light up safely

If you're in charge of a barbecue, don't wear flammable or loose clothes. Before lighting gas burners, open the lid to avoid blowing it off and causing serious injury. If the burners don't ignite in five seconds, shut them off to allow the gas to dissipate.

Avoid sticky racks

Brush wire racks with vegetable oil or spray them with cooking spray to prevent the food from sticking.

Taste test

No matter how much of a hurry you're in, don't be tempted to cook on a barbecue while the starter fluid is still burning—everything will smell and taste like lighter fluid.

Check supplies ▶

Save yourself the embarrassment of running out of fuel and disappointing hungry guests by weighing your propane tank before the big party. The empty weight of your bottle, called the "tare weight," is stamped beside the hand grip (the number is preceded by the word TARE). Simply subtract the tare weight from the actual weight to find out how much fuel remains.

Never be tempted to cook on a barbecue while the starter fluid is still burning.

Garage and toolshed

Car tips

No matter what its size, a well-planned garage will shelter your car and make it easy to do some regular maintenance, too.

Choosing and installing proper lighting in a garage is a must for completing tasks and preventing accidents.

▓ Park without pain ▲

Save your car and the garage wall from damage by installing a simple parking guide. A tennis ball hanging from the ceiling will do the trick. First, run a length of string through the tennis ball. Next, park the car in the ideal position. Now, hang the string so that the tennis ball is just touching the center of the windshield.

▓ Highlight the perfect spot

Centering a car in a narrow garage to allow for adequate door room on both sides can be a challenge. One way to make the task easier is to use a strip of reflective tape as a guide. Cut the tape to match the width of your car and fix it to the back wall of the garage in the perfect position. Line your car up with the strip as you drive in and you'll have a perfectly centered parking job every time.

▓ Soften the blow

If you're doing fine detailing work on your car, you'll want good lighting. A couple of portable halogen or fluorescent floodlights, either on stands or hooked onto the rafters, are a good option.

▓ Mount safety mirrors

For your safety you should be certain that your front and rear lights are always in good working order. Fix one mirror to one of the inside front corners of your garage and another to an inside back corner and set them so that you can see a pair of lights in each mirror. That way you can see at a glance whether your lights are working.

▓ Read the drips

To check for engine problems, line the garage floor with newspaper and park the car on top. Later, when you drive the car out, check the newspaper for drips and stains. Dark greasy droplets could mean an oil leak. Clear oily stains could be caused by leaking brake fluid. Red drips could indicate a loss of transmission fluid. Greenish puddles are likely to be escaped coolant.

▓ Trap the trickle

Until a leaking car can be fixed, protect the garage floor with a homemade drip pan. Lay a sheet of corrugated cardboard on a large baking tray and slide the tray under the site of the leak. ▼

Replace the cardboard when it becomes saturated

Garage doors

It only takes a few simple maintenance exercises to keep a garage door running smoothly, year-round for years to come.

▦ Roll up and stay up

To keep a manual roller-door from crashing down while you're working, wedge a stout piece of wood between the floor and the door's bottom corner, and then attach a C-clamp to the door track just in front of the top roller.

▦ Do the balancing act

A garage door that isn't properly balanced will strain an automatic opener. Check the door regularly and you could avoid expensive repairs down the track. Close the door then disengage it from the automatic opener by pulling down on the emergency release handle. Manually open the door halfway and let go. A balanced door will stay in the halfway position or creep down slowly. An unbalanced door will close quickly or need some hard tugs to bring it down. If the door is out of balance, call a garage door professional to correct the spring tension. ▶

More often than not, all a tricky garage door needs is a good cleaning and oiling of its moving parts.

Breathe easy

Toxic fumes can build up in a garage, whether from stored household chemicals and fertilizers, or from the exhaust vapors produced by cars and lawnmowers. For that reason, a garage must be well ventilated. Use weather stripping to keep out dust and debris, but stop short of making the garage an airtight space. And never run a car or mower in the garage unless the garage door is open.

Reverse gear

An automatic reversing function will trigger the garage door to retract when it comes into contact with an object (like a car or a misplaced bicycle). Check the function regularly by placing a roll of paper towels on the ground under the door. If the door doesn't retract when it hits the roll, call in a professional to service the mechanism. ▼

BEFORE YOU BEGIN

Grease and grit can build up in the moving parts of a garage door to form an abrasive sludge that slowly eats away at the rollers. To keep it in good condition, give your door an annual clean and oil.

A door that stops but does not reverse can trap a person

Steer clear of springs

Some garage doors have a spring directly above the door that acts as a counterbalance and determines how much effort it takes you to raise and lower the door. These springs, called torsion springs, have dangerously high tension and can cause serious injury. Call a professional to fix a faulty torsion spring.

SAFETY FIRST

Garage door maintenance

1 Clean the tracks

For a garage door to run smoothly, the tracks have to be clean and clear. All you need to do is dissolve the grease and dirt inside the tracks with a spray solvent then wipe the grime away with a cloth.

2 Lubricate the parts

Next, lubricate all moving parts with light machine oil or powdered graphite. The lubricant should be applied to metal axles, door-roller bearings and the pivot points and seams of all hinges and pulleys. If sticking or squeaks persist, replace the parts.

3 Oil the springs

Finally, oil the extension or torsion springs to prevent rust and squeaks. First close the door to stretch the springs then spray each one with an even coat of petroleum-based lubricant. To finish, open and close the door a few times to help distribute the lubricant.

▦ Hands-on maintenance

Once or twice a year, switch your garage door into manual mode and open and close it slowly by hand. If there are any emerging problems—if the springs are losing their tension or the rollers aren't running smoothly in their tracks—you'll feel it then.

▦ Off on vacation?

In order to burglar-proof your garage, go back to basics. Unplug the door opener and reactivate the manual lock. Also fit bolts with padlocks on the inside as an additional disincentive for thieves who enter through the house.

WHEN A DOOR GETS DENTED

Metal doors can dent very easily. If the dents are shallow, try tapping them out with a wood block and hammer. If they're deeper, consider calling the manufacturer and having the whole panel replaced.

SMOOTH OPERATION:
FIXING A SLUGGISH GARAGE DOOR

When the door won't open smoothly it usually means one of these four factors is at fault.

★ **Hardware**
Have the bolts or screws on the rollers worked loose? This could cause the door to get stuck or to wobble in its track.

★ **Rollers**
Have the rollers left the overhead track? The track may be bent.

★ **Lubrication**
Are the hinges, rollers or other moving parts corroded? Try oiling them lightly.

★ **Springs**
Have the springs lost tension? If so, get the doors professionally serviced.

Garage organization

Even the smallest of garages can serve as both storeroom and workspace, as long as it's well looked after.

Seal the floor

An unfinished concrete floor is a porous surface and any ignored oil spills will quickly turn into stains. Sealing the floor provides a permanent solution. First, sweep the floor, and then seal it with a paintable concrete sealer. To finish, apply one or two coats of garage floor paint (non-slip if possible). The heavy-duty gloss paint is impervious to liquids so you'll always be able to wipe up drips and spills.

Cleaning up concrete

A sealed concrete floor in the garage generally requires minimal maintenance. An annual wash down and a new coat of sealer should do the job. If you're painting the floor, use an acrylic paint rather than an oil-based masonry paint.

Between-stud storage ▲

If you have open studs in your shed or garage, make the most of them. To keep clamps sorted, drill holes in the studs and install lengths of threaded steel rod, tensioned with washers and nuts. Screw shelf brackets to the studs and then install as many shelves as you need. You can cut the shelves from scraps of wood.

Park the clutter

Organize the garage so that all the key items such as lawnmowers and bicycles fit neatly and easily. Then grab a can of bright yellow spray paint and mark out the "parking spaces" for each item. The outlines will remind you—and the rest of the household—where everything goes.

Free up the floor

An old hammock strung over the car in a garage bay can be a clever storage place for sports balls, empty bags and other bulky lightweight items. Attach the hammock with stout screw eyes that are secured to the joists.

THE **WELL-DESIGNED GARAGE**

When planning how to organize the garage, examine all your options. Here are some practical points to consider.

★ **Minimum clearance**

There should be a minimum of 3 ft. (1 m) between cars in a two-car garage, 3 ft. (1 m) between a car and the side walls, 24 in. (60 cm) between the car and the door, and 12 in. (30 cm) between the car and the front wall.

★ **Maximum storage**

Build shelves or wall-mounted cabinets around the contour of your car's hood and roof. To ensure safe parking, fasten a soft ball to a cord, and hang the ball so that it will bounce against your windshield when the car is in its correct place.

★ **An open-and-shut case**

When space is at a minimum in a garage, think about tilt-out bins, roll-down window blinds (installed on the front of cabinets or other furniture), or sliding doors instead of conventional doors.

▦ Banking a bike ▲

Store a lightweight bike off the garage floor with a couple of screw hooks attached to studs or joists. This is especially important if the bike is not in regular use. Tires eventually deflate and will rapidly deteriorate if a bicycle is left standing in one spot for too long.

▦ Laundry logistics

The garage can be a good spot for a washing machine, but the little odds and ends that come loose during washing can be lost and forgotten in the large, often dimly lit room. Buy a magnetic key box (available from car accessory suppliers and some variety stores) and stick it on the washing machine. It can be used to store loose buttons and lost coins.

▦ Velcro rescue

Many hand tools and even some lightweight power tools and pieces of gardening equipment can be attached to the wall using broad strips of hook-and-loop Velcro. Fix a long length of the hook side to the wall and shorter lengths of the loop side to each of the items you wish to hang. The gripping power of the Velcro will ensure that the items attach securely to the wall for storage. Remember that the hook side is the catching side: if you mistakenly fix that to your hand tool you'll find it sticks to everything from rags to your own clothes.

▦ Divide and conquer ▲

One clever way to maintain order in your garage is to group the clutter into activity-specific zones. Organize a section for gardening tools and products, another for sports gear, another for car maintenance tools and so on. You'll find it easier to locate an item when you need it.

Do not allow a garage to become a dumping ground—tidy things up immediately.

▦ Folding workbench

If there is no extra room anywhere for a workshop, install a fold-down workbench in the garage. The bench top can be made from a plain-surface solid-core door. Fasten it to the wall with a piano hinge about 35 in. (90 cm) above the floor. For legs, attach 2 x 4 in. (5 x 10 cm) lengths of wood to the outside corners with door hinges and tuck them underneath the bench when it folds down.

Toolshed

Whether your workspace is a stand-alone room or just a corner of the garage, the same rules apply: keep it tidy, and keep it safe.

Keep work surfaces clean and clear and ready for work— use shelves and other spaces for storage.

Save your outlets

If the electrical outlets around your workbench become clogged with sawdust, they can pose a fire hazard. A simple solution is to purchase some plastic childproof outlet covers and use them to plug up the outlets whenever they're not in use.

Manage messy cords

A workbench is easier and safer to use if all the power cords are hooked up and out of the way. For a hanger that lets a cord slide through without chafing it, cut a short length of old garden hose, slit it diagonally and tack it to the wall. Open the slit to insert or remove your cord as necessary. If you want to hold the cord in a fixed position, screw or glue some clothes pegs to overhead joists (or some other strategic positions) and drape the cord over them.

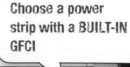

Choose a power strip with a BUILT-IN GFCI

Power from above ▲

For easy access to electricity, hang a retractable (reel-type) extension cord from a hook screwed into an overhead joist. Or mount a multi-outlet power strip on the wall above your workbench or on a drop-down board bolted to a joist. Plug your new overhead power source into an existing outlet. If you have to run an extension cord to it, secure the cord loosely with slit-hose hangers (refer to previous tip). Permanently attaching an extension may violate electrical codes.

Cold workshop?

Give it a quick warm-up by installing an infra-red heat lamp over your workbench. It will warm your hands and tools so that you can work comfortably on cold days. Heat lamps typically draw 250 watts, so use sparingly and check that the wiring can handle the lamp plus whatever other equipment you use on that circuit.

Peg it into place

Perforated hardboard, otherwise known as pegboard, is a simple and attractive way to hang up hand tools—but don't limit its use to workshop walls. Mount it on the inside of cabinet doors or on the sides of your workbench and cabinets and you'll substantially increase your storage potential.

Magnetic bagger

Keep a bar magnet and a box of plastic sandwich bags on hand and you'll always be able to pick up spilled metal washers, nuts or nails with ease. Drop the magnet into the bag and run it across the area of the spill. The spilled items will stick to the magnet. When you've collected all the loose items, turn the bag inside out, remove the magnet and pour the contents of the bag into a container.

Blow it away

If you have a spare hair dryer lying around the house, give it a new home at your workbench. It can be used to blow away dust, dirt and shavings, to dry sweaty hands before handling new wood and to speed the drying of paint touch-ups.

Toolbelt

Tack an old leather or strong canvas belt along the edge of a shelf to hold tools. As you nail it, leave small loops in the belt for tools to slip into.

TOOLSHED **SAFETY**

★ Ground Fault Circuit Interrupters (GFCIs)

A GFCI will monitor the flow of electricity and turn the power off in less than a second if it detects a problem. You can buy individual outlets with GFCIs, as well as portable GFCIs for use with extension cords, but sometimes an electrician will install surge protectors in the main electrical panel to protect outlets on a circuit.

★ Cords and plugs

Frayed or cracked electrical cords and plugs are dangerous and should be replaced immediately.

Keep cords free of tangles, off the ground and clear of the work surface, taking particular care when saws, grinders and other powered cutting tools are in use. And always use heavy-duty cords rated to handle more electrical current than your tools will draw.

★ Grounding

Have your metal workbench grounded to reduce the chances of a shock from shorted equipment. An electrician can ground it by running a wire from the bench to an electrical sub-board, or to a metallic electrical conduit.

Make a tool board

Wrap tools in plastic wrap and lay on a board. Fix nails where they are to hang. Spray the tools and board with paint and leave to dry. Unwrap the tools, then hang them in the marked places.

Stronger pull

Does the handle on a tool-laden drawer keep pulling off? Replace it with a garage door handle, or a similar item, secured with bolts going through the drawer front. Put flat and lock washers onto each bolt before screwing on the nut.

Soften your stance

Standing on a concrete floor in front of your workbench for hours on end can strain your legs and give you a chill. Be good to yourself and lay a scrap of carpet down on the floor, or go all the way and install a rubber mat. The softer surface will be more soothing for your joints and will prevent heat loss between your feet and the cold concrete floor.

Index

Trade Secrets

Writers Peter Harris, Jane Hyde, Julia Richardson
Project Editors Robert Ronald, Lachlan McLaine
Editors Sarah Baker, Jesse Corbeil, Jess Cox, Celia Coyne, Samantha Kent
U.S. Editorial Consultant Duane Johnson
Designers Chris A. Cant, Clare Forte
Photographic consultant Ed Frondo
Photography Stuart Scott, Chris Jones
Illustrator Stephen Pollitt
Proofreaders Matthew Brown, Kevin Diletti
Indexer Diane Harriman
Production Coordinator Gillian Sylvain
Vice President, Editorial, Canada Robert Goyette
Manager, English Book Editorial, Canada Pamela Johnson

THE READER'S DIGEST ASSOCIATION, INC.
President & Chief Executive Officer Robert H. Guth
**Executive Vice President, RDA &
  President, North America** Dan Lagani
**Executive Vice President, RDA &
  President, Allrecipes.com** Lisa Sharples
**Executive Vice President, RDA &
  President, Europe** Dawn Zier

Picture Credits Front cover Shutterstock; 2–3 Shutterstock; 5 Shutterstock; 6 Getty Images; 7 Shutterstock; 8–9 Photolibrary; 12 t Klein Tools; 15 t iStockphoto; 23 b iStockphoto; 28 l Shutterstock; 30 Shutterstock; 32–3 Photolibrary; 34 b Shutterstock; 35 tr Shutterstock; 40 l Shutterstock; 41 br Shutterstock; 46 b Shutterstock; 52 t LUXAFLEX® Window Fashions, ct LUXAFLEX® Window Fashions, c Shutterstock, cb Shutterstock, b iStockphoto; 53 b iStockphoto; 57 Shutterstock; 60–1 Getty Images; 62 tl Shutterstock; 67 Shutterstock; 76 tr Bona; 77 tl Bona, r Bona; 81 iStockphoto; 89 t Dreamstime; 98 iStockphoto; 104 t Shutterstock; 105 b Shutterstock; 106 l iStockphoto; 109 Shutterstock; 110–11 Shutterstock; 112 l Dulux Australia; 113 iStockphoto; 114 iStockphoto; 118 Shutterstock; 129 Shutterstock; 140 Shutterstock; 144–5 Getty Images; 156 Shutterstock; 160 Getty Images; 163 br iStockphoto; 168 Getty Images; 178–9 Shutterstock; 189 Shutterstock; 191 Shutterstock; 199 iStockphoto; 201 Shutterstock; 207 Shutterstock; 212–13 Getty Images; 218 Shutterstock; 222 Shutterstock; 229 Getty Images; 237 Shutterstock; 238–9 Photolibrary; 244 Shutterstock; 256 Getty Images; 260 Shutterstock; 274–5 iStockphoto; 289 br Shutterstock; 292 bl Shutterstock; 297 tr Shutterstock; 298–9 Shutterstock; 301 tl iStockphoto, bl Dreamstime, br Dreamstime, cr Shutterstock; 306 br Shutterstock.

All other images are the copyright of Reader's Digest.

Library of Congress Cataloging in Publication data available upon request

ISBN 978-1-60652-486-2

Address any comments on the content of this book to:

The Reader's Digest Association, Inc.
Adult Trade Publishing
44 South Broadway
White Plains, NY 10601

To order additional copies of Trade Secrets, call 1-800-788-6262.

Visit us on the Web, in the United States at **rd.com**
and in Canada at **readersdigest.ca**

Printed in China

Note to readers

The information in this book is general in nature and should not be substituted for expert advice. All do-it-yourself activities involve a degree of risk. Skills, materials, tools and site conditions vary widely. Although the editors have made every effort to ensure accuracy, the reader remains responsible for the selection and use of tools, materials and methods. Always observe local codes and laws, follow manufacturer's operating instructions and observe safety precautions. When in doubt, seek professional help.